Macroeconomics

FOR

DUMMIES

A Wiley Brand

UK Edition

Macroeconomics
FOR DUMMIES®
A Wiley Brand

UK Edition

by Manzur Rashid and
Peter Antonioni

FOR DUMMIES®
A Wiley Brand

Macroeconomics For Dummies®, UK Edition

Published by: **John Wiley & Sons, Ltd.,** The Atrium, Southern Gate, Chichester, www.wiley.com

This edition first published 2015

© 2016 John Wiley & Sons, Ltd, Chichester, West Sussex.

Registered office

John Wiley & Sons Ltd, The Atrium, Southern Gate, Chichester, West Sussex, PO19 8SQ, United Kingdom

For details of our global editorial offices, for customer services and for information about how to apply for permission to reuse the copyright material in this book please see our website at www.wiley.com.

All rights reserved. No part of this publication may be reproduced, stored in a retrieval system, or transmitted, in any form or by any means, electronic, mechanical, photocopying, recording or otherwise, except as permitted by the UK Copyright, Designs and Patents Act 1988, without the prior permission of the publisher.

Wiley publishes in a variety of print and electronic formats and by print-on-demand. Some material included with standard print versions of this book may not be included in e-books or in print-on-demand. If this book refers to media such as a CD or DVD that is not included in the version you purchased, you may download this material at http://booksupport.wiley.com. For more information about Wiley products, visit www.wiley.com.

Designations used by companies to distinguish their products are often claimed as trademarks. All brand names and product names used in this book are trade names, service marks, trademarks or registered trademarks of their respective owners. The publisher is not associated with any product or vendor mentioned in this book.

LIMIT OF LIABILITY/DISCLAIMER OF WARRANTY: WHILE THE PUBLISHER AND AUTHOR HAVE USED THEIR BEST EFFORTS IN PREPARING THIS BOOK, THEY MAKE NO REPRESENTATIONS OR WARRANTIES WITH THE RESPECT TO THE ACCURACY OR COMPLETENESS OF THE CONTENTS OF THIS BOOK AND SPECIFICALLY DISCLAIM ANY IMPLIED WARRANTIES OF MERCHANTABILITY OR FITNESS FOR A PARTICULAR PURPOSE. IT IS SOLD ON THE UNDERSTANDING THAT THE PUBLISHER IS NOT ENGAGED IN RENDERING PROFESSIONAL SERVICES AND NEITHER THE PUBLISHER NOR THE AUTHOR SHALL BE LIABLE FOR DAMAGES ARISING HEREFROM. IF PROFESSIONAL ADVICE OR OTHER EXPERT ASSISTANCE IS REQUIRED, THE SERVICES OF A COMPETENT PROFESSIONAL SHOULD BE SOUGHT.

For general information on our other products and services, please contact our Customer Care Department within the U.S. at 877-762-2974, outside the U.S. at (001) 317-572-3993, or fax 317-572-4002. For technical support, please visit www.wiley.com/techsupport.

Library of Congress Control Number: 2015950120

ISBN 978-1-119-02662-4 (paperback); ISBN 978-1-119-02667-9 (ebk); ISBN 978-1-119-02668-6 (ebk)

Printed and bound in Great Britain by TJ International Ltd, Padstow, Cornwall, UK

10 9 8 7 6 5 4 3 2 1

A Wiley Brand

Contents at a Glance

Table of Contents

Introduction

. . . .

Macroeconomics is the study of the economy as a whole. So if you want to understand key concepts that you come across every day in the news, such as inflation, unemployment and economic growth, this is the book for you!

This book helps you to tackle some of the biggest questions people ask about macroeconomics, such as

- ✔ Why are some countries rich and others poor? And what can poor countries do to become richer?
- ✔ What causes the prices of things to rise and fall?
- ✔ Why are some people unable to find work? And what can be done to reduce unemployment?
- ✔ Why is there so much inequality in the world and what can we do about it?

We don't pretend to have answers to all the questions, but we do think that macroeconomics provides some good answers to many questions about how the economy works.

Fortunately, some of the world's greatest minds have worked on macroeconomics and created a substantial body of work. Sadly, economists (and we're just as guilty) haven't done a great job at communicating the key ideas of macroeconomics to the public. As a result, all too often politicians and commentators are able to bamboozle people with nice-sounding but ultimately bad economics.

The point of this book is to introduce you to the fascinating world of macroeconomics so you can see how the economy works in reality, how you fit into it and, perhaps, ultimately how the world can be made a better place.

About This Book

Macroeconomics affects almost every part of your life. Whether you have a job or are unemployed, whether you earn millions or the minimum wage, whether you want to borrow money or earn income from your savings, macroeconomics matters to you.

In this book you find the core macroeconomic concepts presented in a way that's easy to digest. We skip as much unnecessary complexity as possible while still taking a rigorous approach to the issues.

You can use this book for reference, flicking straight to any chapter that interests you: reading the book from cover to cover isn't necessary. That said, if you're studying a macroeconomics course at school or university you may prefer to read it systematically, in which case taking the chapters in order makes sense.

Throughout the book you find sidebars that provide additional detail about different topics of interest. We hope that you find these useful, but you don't need them to understand the main text. Feel free to skip them without worrying too much.

Like it or not, mathematics is widely used in economics. Whenever we use mathematics we also explain the process in words so you're not lost in a sea of equations! Sometimes – in a sidebar – we derive some of the results explicitly for interested readers. Again, you can skip these without getting lost.

Foolish Assumptions

We make some assumptions about you and why you want to read this book:

- ✔ You're smart and interested in finding out how the economy works.

- ✔ You're considering taking a school, university or professional course that involves macroeconomics and you want an easy-to-read resource that explains modern macroeconomics clearly.

- ✔ You understand that having a good knowledge of macroeconomics is essential in the modern world so no one can pull the wool over your eyes!

- ✔ You're not scared about working through simple mathematical equations every now and again so long as they're clearly explained and allow you to gain a deeper understanding of the material.

- ✔ You're reading this book alongside our companion title *Microeconomics For Dummies* in order to master economics from a micro- (the study of individuals and firms) and macro- (the economy as a whole) perspective.

Icons Used in This Book

For Dummies books use icons, partly because they're pretty but also because they draw your attention to some important things. Here are the icons we use in this book.

Tips are small morsels of useful information to help you understand something.

This icon draws your attention to something quite important.

We use Warning icons to highlight confusing concepts. Whenever you see one of these, make sure you don't make the common error related to that topic.

This icon makes clear a word or an idea that's used in economics in a specific way, often not the way in which it's commonly understood.

Theory is all well and good but sometimes ideas are made clearer using a real-world example.

Beyond the Book

You'll have no difficulty applying your new knowledge of macroeconomics beyond this book. Just turn on the TV or read a newspaper and you inevitably find stories about the economy. You can consider whether the claims made or analysis provided make sense given what you discover about how the economy works. Often you find that they don't. When that happens (and trust us, it will), you're reaping the benefits of what you read in this book.

In addition to the material in this book plus the wealth of macroeconomic stories in the media, we also provide online content that specifically complements these sources:

✔ **Cheat Sheet:** At www.dummies.com/cheatsheet/macroeconomicsuk we summarise some key information about how the economy works, including:

   • The basics of fiscal and monetary policy.

- The key summary statistics that macroeconomists examine in order to assess the health of an economy: real GDP, unemployment, and inflation.

- How the economy behaves in the short run when prices are sticky and in the long run when prices are flexible.

The Cheat Sheet comes into its own when you find yourself without a copy of *Macroeconomics For Dummies* to hand (of course, this will only happen very rarely!) and you need quick and easy access to the key facts about the economy.

✔ **Extras articles:** At www.dummies.com/extras/macroeconomicsuk you can find some exclusive articles written especially for this book. The articles include

- The lowdown on the Solow model – the simplest but most widely used model of economic growth.

- The basics of the IS–LM mode, which tells you how the economy behaves in the very short run when prices are fixed.

- A quantitative easing quandary: why doesn't the Bank of England just write off the huge debts the government owes on the bonds bought during quantitative easing?

Where to Go from Here

We recommend that you dive straight into the juicy meat of this book. You don't need to start at the beginning, although clearly you're most welcome to. Here are a few pointers to get you started:

✔ If you want to know about financial crises, what causes them, and how they may be stopped, take a look at the chapters in Part V.

✔ If you have a burning desire to understand fiscal and monetary policy, flip to Chapters 10 and 11, respectively.

✔ If you want to know how to reduce unemployment, Chapter 6 describes the options.

✔ If you're clueless about why the prices of things tend to rise, check out Chapter 5.

✔ If you want to know what determines a country's living standards, head straight to Chapter 4.

Soon you'll be leafing through the broadsheets and wanting to apply your macroeconomic knowledge to putting the world to rights!

Part I

Getting Started with Macroeconomics

Visit www.dummies.com for free access to great Dummies content online.

In this part . . .

✔ Discover why macroeconomics is important and get an overview of the many concepts and policies it covers.

✔ Take a look at the key questions macroeconomists ask about the economy and gain an understanding of why they use models to arrive at answers.

✔ Understand the four factors that can cause the downfall of an economy.

Chapter 1

Discovering Why Macroeconomics Is a Big Deal

*M*acroeconomics is the study of the economy as a whole – in contrast to microeconomics, which is the study of individuals and firms. Or as the comedian PJ O'Rourke quipped: 'Microeconomics concerns things that economists are specifically wrong about, while macroeconomics concerns things economists are wrong about generally!'

Not only does O'Rourke's quote make even economists laugh, but also it touches on something important: since the global financial crisis of 2007–8, people have become increasingly sceptical of economists and economics. We think that's a shame (well, we would, wouldn't we!). But although economists certainly don't know everything about how the economy works – it's a hugely complex system that's difficult to analyse – they do know a lot.

This knowledge is important, because macroeconomics affects almost every part of your life. From whether you're employed or unemployed to how much you earn, how much tax you pay, what services the government provides and how easy or difficult you find borrowing money, macroeconomics really matters.

In addition, politicians frequently make promises about the economy and their different policies. You need to understand macroeconomics in order to make sense of these claims and, importantly, to tell the difference between a good policy and a bad policy that merely sounds good!

In short, without some macroeconomics knowledge, you're missing out on a big part of how the world works.

In this chapter we introduce you to macroeconomics and set the scene for the rest of the book. We include what it covers, its tools, how policy makers use it and how things can sometimes go horribly wrong.

The Big Picture: Checking Out the Economy as a Whole

Macroeconomists try to understand the economy as a whole, which means thinking about the aggregate behaviour of large numbers of individuals and firms. It entails working out what determines the level of output in an economy, the rate of inflation, the number of people unemployed and so on. Crucially, it also means considering how policy makers can influence the economy by using the different tools at their disposal.

As you can see, macroeconomics is a wide-ranging discipline. Therefore, it requires people with exceptional skills (ahem). Here we discuss just two: how macroeconomists are like detectives and doctors (just don't ask us to take a close look at that unsightly mole – please).

Investigating why macroeconomists are like detectives

Being a good macroeconomist is in many ways like being a detective at a crime scene. Good detectives carefully collect evidence and form theories about what may have happened. They then test these theories to see to what extent the available evidence supports them.

Similarly, macroeconomists gather evidence about economies in the form of data. They then form a hypothesis about how the data came to be and test it to see whether the data supports it or not.

Unfortunately, unlike the hypotheses of scientists, macroeconomists can't run experiments to test them. If they want to work out the impact on the economy of cutting government spending by half, they can't just do it and see what happens! They can, however, look at the data (across countries and across time) and try to infer the likely relationship between government spending and other macroeconomic *variables* (like inflation, unemployment and real GDP).

Practising macroeconomics isn't for the fainthearted, though, and is fraught with problems. For example, imagine that you notice two facts: that countries with higher levels of education tend to be richer and that as the people of a country become more educated, the country becomes richer. On the basis of these facts you reach the conclusion that more education *causes* people to become richer.

But wait a minute! How do you know that it isn't the other way around: When a country is richer, it spends more on education? In which case, people becoming richer is *causing* them to have more education. Or a third variable may be causing high levels of education and wealth (such as a well-functioning political and legal system), in which case a country being well-off and well-educated is *correlated* but not causally linked.

Macroeconomists and their questions

Macroeconomists are quite an ambitious bunch. They want to understand why the world is the way it is, and they ask some of the biggest questions around:

- ✔ Why are some countries rich and others poor (and relatedly, why are some people rich and others poor)?
- ✔ What causes the prices of things to rise or fall?
- ✔ What determines unemployment and can anything be done to reduce it? (Chapter 6 discusses unemployment in loads of detail.)

Thanks to macroeconomics a lot is now known about the answers to these and many other questions. But being an economist is much more than just 'knowing stuff' – good economists are able to look at a problem they've never seen before and use their analytical tools to see something that others may have overlooked.

Chapter 2 contains plenty more on the questions that macroeconomists like to ask.

Macroeconomists and their models

Economists love building *models* – simplified versions of reality – in order to think through complex problems (see the later section 'Modelling the Economy' for more on models).

The advantage of doing so is that it forces you to think about what ingredients in a problem are the ones that really matter and which factors you can safely ignore.

For example, a macroeconomist trying to explain why average wages in the UK are much higher than average wages in Bangladesh can build a model that completely ignores the fact that both countries contain a lot of variability across people – some people have low wages, others have high wages, some people have low ability, others have high ability – and instead she can just assume that everyone's labour within each country is identical.

This approach is probably a useful simplification, because the economist isn't trying to explain why *different* people in the UK have *different* wages, but why the *average* wage in the UK is higher than the *average* wage in Bangladesh. If she were trying to explain why some people in the UK are paid more than others, this simplification probably wouldn't be appropriate.

We talk more about modelling in Chapter 2. Plus, you can turn to Chapters 7, 8 and 9 to read about some of the popular macroeconomic models (the ones that always get invited to parties).

Diagnosing why macroeconomists are like doctors

If you get sick, you're likely to visit a medical doctor. The physician checks out your symptoms and makes a diagnosis about the likely cause of your illness. Based on this diagnosis, she recommends a course of treatment to cure you in no time – you hope.

Just like people, economies can also get sick with things such as recessions, high inflation and high unemployment. Much like a doctor, macroeconomists have to observe the economy and try to work out the underlying cause of these problems. After working out the likely cause, they can think about policies that those in charge can implement to return the economy to health.

For example, an economy is in recession if its *Gross Domestic Product* (GDP) falls: that is, the amount of stuff it produces falls, as we discuss in Chapter 4. Often recessions are caused by insufficient demand in the economy for goods and services. Knowing this, macroeconomists can prescribe some medicine: perhaps temporarily stimulating demand in the economy.

Policy makers can do so in two basic ways (we talk more about them in this chapter's later 'Plotting Economic Policy' section):

- ✔ **Use monetary policy:** Basically pumping new money into the economy in the hope that this reduces interest rates throughout the economy and thereby encourages households to consume and firms to invest. Chapter 10 has loads more on monetary policy.

✔ **Use fiscal policy:** Increasing government spending – which increases the demand for goods and services directly – or decreasing taxes – which policy makers hope encourages households to consume and firms to invest. Flip to Chapter 11 for the lowdown on fiscal policy.

Economies can also suffer from high levels of inflation. Macroeconomists have worked out that the cause of high inflation is an excessive growth in the money supply, which leads to people having high inflation expectations (they expect inflation to be high); this expectation and the behaviour it creates cause actual high inflation (check out Chapter 12).

Accordingly, if policy makers are to reduce inflation, they need to reduce inflation expectations. In order to do that, they need to convince people that they aren't going to print as much money in the future as they did in the past!

Looking at the Key Macroeconomic Variables

In order to work out what's going on in an economy, macroeconomists need to see cold hard facts. They need to know how much stuff is being produced in the economy, at what rate prices are going up and how easy or difficult it is for people to get jobs.

Fortunately, in many countries (and all developed ones) statistics on output (GDP), inflation and unemployment (as well as lots of other variables of interest) are today measured relatively accurately and on a regular basis.

Considering all this GDP malarkey

When macroeconomists look at an economy, one of the first things they want to know is how much economic activity is taking place. They ask questions such as:

✔ How much are people trading with each other?

✔ How good is the economy at producing goods and services that people want?

✔ What are people's average living standards?

Luckily, a basic indicator tells them a lot about all these things – *Gross Domestic Product* (GDP), the subject of Chapter 4. A country's GDP tells you the value of all goods and services produced in one year.

In the UK, for example, in 2015 the combined value of everything produced is estimated to equal around $3 trillion (yes, we know, people use the pound in the UK, but lots of economic statistics are quoted in US dollars for easy comparison).

This figure means that goods and services worth about $3 trillion will be traded in the economy. It also means that if you were to add up everyone's income, it should equal around $3 trillion, because your income gives you the right to consume some share of the nation's GDP. Therefore, everyone's share (their income) better add up to equal the total amount of goods and services available. That is, the sum of everyone's slice of cake better be equal to the cake as a whole!

The US's GDP in 2015 is estimated to be around $18 trillion, which straight-away shows you something interesting about the economies of the UK and the US: in one year, the US produces goods and services worth six times more than those produced in one year in the UK. You can say that the US economy is six times the size of the UK economy.

Often you want to know how much on average each person in a country gets, instead of its total GDP. No problem. By dividing GDP by the number of people in a country you get *GDP per capita* (average income per person). This figure allows you to compare living standards between the two countries. In 2013, the UK had GDP per capita of around $42,000 while in the US it was around $53,000. Therefore, the average American earned around $11,000 more than the average Brit.

Questioning whether inflation really makes people poorer

If you ask people how they feel about inflation, they probably tell you that they dislike it. Ask them why, and they probably say that it makes them poorer. But although that may be true in the short run, economists think that in the long run inflation shouldn't impact the things that really matter, such as *real wages* (how much stuff you can buy with your wage).

In the short run

Consider this example, which shows that inflation in the short term can indeed make you worse off.

Imagine that you're negotiating your wage with your employer for next year. Both you and your employer expect inflation to be 2 per cent. You go into the negotiation high and ask for a 5 per cent pay increase. You argue that as a highly skilled and experienced professional, you deserve a pay rise. Plus, if inflation is going to be 2 per cent, you're only really asking for an increase in your *real wage* of 3 per cent.

Your employer is having none of it. Business is tough and the firm is being squeezed from all sides: she can't possibly offer you any pay rise at all. You think about this answer for a moment and realise that if your pay doesn't go up at all, your real wage will fall by 2 per cent because of inflation. That's not on! You threaten to leave for your employer's deadliest competitor. After some discussion, you both compromise and agree on a 2 per cent pay rise so that in real terms your expected pay is unchanged.

The contract is written up and signed. Next year comes along and low-and-behold inflation isn't 2 per cent as expected; it's 4 per cent. How are you feeling? Probably not great, and for good reason: your real wage fell, because your 2 per cent pay rise is insufficient to cover inflation. In fact, you're getting paid 2 per cent less in real terms than you were last year (2 per cent minus 4 per cent = –2 per cent). You're one unhappy bunny.

In the long run

In the short run, if inflation isn't equal to expected inflation people can be worse off. But in the long run, after prices have had time to adjust and contracts have had time to be rewritten, inflation shouldn't have any impact on your real wage. This is because macroeconomists think (and the data supports) that in the long run people care about real things. You care about your real wage, your boss cares about how much she's paying you in real terms and so on. Therefore, any impact of inflation on your real wage or your real wealth should disappear.

We're not saying that whether an economy has low or high inflation doesn't matter. Not at all. High inflation has all sorts of other costs, which can be substantial and which you can read about in Chapter 5.

Finding a job – and a spouse

Economists call searching for a job a *matching problem*: two groups (in this case, employers and workers) want to join up with each other.

Marriage is a good example of a matching problem. The 'marriage market' contains a bunch of men and women. Each man is looking to match with a woman, and each woman is looking to match with a man. Where things get interesting is that the men differ from each other in their characteristics. Some are short and some are tall, some are academic and some are sporty, some are handsome and others less so, and so on. Likewise for women (are women handsome? Anyway you know what we mean!). Each man has preferences about which women he'd prefer to be matched with and so do the women about the men.

Now, the marriage market would be a relatively easy problem to solve if everyone had perfect information about each other, so everyone's characteristics and preferences were common knowledge. People would just match up according to their preferences: 'I like you, you like me, let's match!' People in particularly high demand would be able to take their pick from their admirers. But real life is much more interesting: people have *imperfect* information about the other side of the market – two people could be an amazing match and yet never get to meet.

The labour market shares many characteristics with the marriage market. It has two sides, firms and workers, and each firm is different in some ways to the others and each worker has different skills and other attributes. Each side has preferences about the other side but they're imperfectly informed – this means that the resultant matching isn't always ideal: people get matched to jobs they don't want, firms hire workers who aren't a good fit and people have difficulty getting a job in which they could've succeeded if given the chance. These labour market *frictions* (which loosely means 'imperfections') are part of the reason for unemployment.

Modelling the Economy

Economists love modelling – no, not prancing down the catwalk, though they're an attractive bunch, obviously. The sort of modelling economists engage in uses simplified versions of the world to think through complex problems. We introduce you to this concept here.

In the chapters in Part III, we build a simple model of the economy, which can be used to analyse how the economy works and how different macroeconomic variables affect one another.

Unearthing why economists model

The big question is: why do macroeconomists bother modelling (apart from the chance to wear all those delightful clothes, of course)? Why not just tackle the complete problem in all its warts-and-all complexity first time round? Here are a few answers to this question:

✔ **Macroeconomic problems are complex:** So complex that trying to tackle them head-on is almost bound to fail. Just too many diverse agents (consumers, firms, the government) are doing their own thing, each with their own objectives, that you're bound to get lost.

Economists prefer to work with a very simple model to begin with and assume, for example, that all households are the same, or that the government is a completely benevolent social planner, or that people want to buy only one good called the *consumption good*. Economists then try to understand how this simple world works. When they've achieved that aim, they can relax the assumptions one at a time to see whether things change: for example, 'I wonder what would happen if households were different to one another, or if politicians were mainly interested in winning the next election?'

✔ **Modelling forces you to make your assumptions explicit:** Results in economics papers often read along the following lines: 'If we assume X and Y, then Z must be true.' For example:

- 'If prices are "sticky" in the short run and policy makers increase the money supply, then the real interest rate will fall and output increase in the short run.'

- 'If prices are fully flexible and policy makers increase the money supply, then the real interest rate and output will remain unchanged, and only inflation will increase.'

- 'If the government doesn't default on its debt and reduce taxes today, then it will either have to increase taxes or reduce spending (or both) in the future.'

This is good practice because it means economists can't easily pull the wool over people's eyes. In other words, it keeps economists honest!

✔ **Intuition can lead you astray:** You can spend a lot of time thinking about an economic problem and come to a conclusion that modelling subsequently proves is wrong.

For example, your intuition may tell you that firms rather than workers should pay payroll taxes (the mandatory taxes due when someone works) so that ordinary people get to keep more of their income. But by modelling this problem, economists worked out that it doesn't matter who officially pays the tax (the worker or the firm), the outcome is the same regardless. That is, if the firm officially pays the tax, then it passes some of the tax onto the worker by lowering wages, and if the worker officially pays the tax, then she passes on some of the tax to the firm by only being willing to work for a higher wage.

✔ **Comparative statics:** Don't let the jargon scare you; the term simply means comparing the outcome before and after some change. Modelling allows you to see what would happen if certain things within the model change. For example, after you've written down your model, you may want to see what would happen to the economy if government spending increased. The model allows you to see the impact without having to change government spending in the real world!

Meeting the agents that participate in the models

Economic models feature three types of *agents* (or decision-makers) who interact with each other.

Here, we introduce briefly the different decision-makers represented in an economic model and what they do:

- ✔ **Consumers/households:** Individuals like you who have to make choices, such as how much should I buy? What should I buy? How much should I work? and so on.

    Economists sometimes use consumers and households interchangeably, because often decisions about what choices to make are made at the level of the household. The working assumption for how consumers behave is that they're *rational* and that they try to *maximise their utility* subject to any constraints they face.

    Economists are often criticised for assuming that people are rational, but much of this criticism stems from a misunderstanding about what economic rationality means. Individuals are considered rational in an economic sense if they're able to rank options according to their preferences. So, for example, if presented with three options – watch TV, eat chocolate and go to the gym – a rational person can rank the options and decide: first, eat chocolate; second, watch TV; third, go to the gym. That's all rationality means. Similarly, *maximise their utility* simply means that people choose the thing that they prefer most.

- ✔ **Firms:** Organisations that turn *inputs* (such as raw materials and labour) into *outputs* (goods and services people want to buy). Economists assume that firms *maximise their profits*, which sort of makes sense because in a market economy the owners of any business are likely to want as much profit as possible. That's not to say that some businesses don't have other objectives, such as revenue maximisation or certain social objectives. But for most businesses, these objectives are secondary to profit maximisation.

- ✔ **Government/policy makers:** People who can change economic policy. For example, they can decide what tax rates or interest rates to set, or how much the government should spend. In some economic models, policy makers are assumed to be *benevolent social planners*, which means that they're just trying to do what's best for society. In other models, they're *rent-seeking* or *strategic*, meaning that they may want to win the next election or increase the size of the departments. The correct assumption depends on the problem at hand.

Plotting Economic Policy

Policy makers are potentially some seriously powerful people. They can take actions that can influence the economy not only today but also for years to come. Here's a brief overview of economic policy.

Monetary policy: Controlling the economy's money supply

Monetary policy refers to policy directed towards changing the amount of money in circulation and thereby influencing the interest rates in an economy.

In the UK, the Bank of England manages monetary policy, whereas in the US the job falls to the Federal Reserve. Although the government sets the objectives of monetary policy, central banks have a large amount of autonomy regarding how exactly they use the tools at their disposal to meet those objectives. For example, in the UK the government has set an inflation target of 2 per cent, but control over monetary policy is delegated to the central bank, which can set interest rates as it pleases in order to achieve the 2 per cent target.

Here are the two types of monetary policy:

- **Expansionary monetary policy:** Involves increasing the supply of money in order to reduce the interest rate and stimulate the economy. In the short run, it usually results in higher output but also higher inflation.

- **Contractionary monetary policy:** Involves reducing the supply of money in order to increase the interest rate and slow down the economy. In the short run, it usually results in lower output but also lower inflation.

Conventional monetary policy involves changes in the official interest rate in the hope that this action filters throughout the economy. In recent times, however, many central banks (including those of the UK, US and EU) have engaged in *quantitative easing*: increasing the money supply in the hope of stimulating the economy by increasing *liquidity* (making it easier to borrow money by making sure there is enough cash around) and also inflation.

Check out Chapter 10 for loads more on monetary policy.

Fiscal policy: Spending or taxing more

Fiscal policy refers to any changes in government spending or taxation. Unlike monetary policy, fiscal policy isn't usually delegated to some independent authority, such as the central bank. Instead, politicians decide it and civil servants implement it 'in-house'.

Like monetary policy, fiscal policy can have a large impact on the economy (at least in the short run), and it also comes in two sweet or bitter flavours:

- ✔ **Expansionary fiscal policy:** Involves increasing government spending, reducing taxation or both. It's designed to stimulate the economy and in the short run is likely to lead to higher output but also higher inflation.

- ✔ **Contractionary fiscal policy:** Involves decreasing government spending, increasing taxation or both. It's designed to slow down the economy and in the short run is likely to lead to lower output but also lower inflation.

We discuss fiscal policy at length in Chapter 11.

Playing policy games

Both fiscal and monetary policy have the potential to be misused by politicians acting in their own self-interest.

For example, stimulating the economy shortly before an election in order to reduce unemployment and increase output is perfectly possible (perish the thought). In the long run, however, output and unemployment return to their original levels – only inflation is permanently higher. The government may even need to engineer a recession to get inflation back down again after the election, leading to *boom and bust* (a period of rising prosperity and falling unemployment followed by a sharp fall in living standards and a rise in unemployment).

For this reason, economists have been arguing for some time that policy makers need to be constrained in some way by *rules*, so they can't just use their *discretion* to game the system to their advantage. In the past few decades, macroeconomists have been winning the debate. In many countries, monetary policy is now *operationally independent* of government: that is, central banks are allowed to operate with little government interference. This change has led to a period of low and stable inflation in those countries.

Similar proposals have been made for fiscal policy, for example, requiring that the government balances its books on average. This change, however, hasn't happened. Most governments are quite happy to run persistent deficits, which future generations will have to pay back.

We discuss strategic policy makers and the rules versus discretion debate in detail in Chapters 12 and 13.

Financial Crises! Going Wrong on a Global Scale

Financial crises are scary things. People's assets such as their houses and their pensions lose large amounts of their value. Banks and other businesses go bankrupt. Banks suffer bank runs as people worry about the ability of banks to stay afloat, which in turn makes them more likely to go under. Borrowing money becomes almost impossible.

In short, these crises are super stressful times for the economy and the people within the economy, plus things can go really, badly wrong if policy makers aren't quick to respond (Chapter 3 has more on identifying financial crises).

Lots of interesting and complicated issues are involved in this important subject. Luckily we dedicate the chapters in Part V to understanding financial crises. So, at least that's one thing you don't have to worry about!

Looking at two scary facts about banks

We don't want to freak you out (this isn't a Stephen King novel), but we're obliged to share a couple of scary facts with you about the economy.

Any bank can fail if people believe that it may fail

This thought is pretty scary: all that's needed is for people to believe that a bank is in trouble for it actually to be in trouble!

Banks keep only a small proportion of deposits in reserve: if you deposit £100, perhaps only £5 is kept in reserve in order to facilitate withdrawals – the bank lends out the other £95. The idea is that on any given day, not many depositors are likely to withdraw money, so no need exists to keep much in reserve. This system is known as *fractional reserve banking* (see Chapter 14).

The problem with fractional reserve banking is that if people get worried about their bank's ability to facilitate withdrawals, they may all rush to try to withdraw all their savings – a classic bank run. Of course, no bank (no matter how healthy) has sufficient reserves to be able to pay up if all depositors come knocking simultaneously. In the absence of some kind of emergency funding, the bank is likely to go under.

If one large bank fails, many others can also fail

Banks and financial institutions are all connected in a complex web of transactions. Therefore, if one bank fails, the event has widespread repercussions for all other banks and can easily lead to their failure.

Like the domino effect (it takes only one domino to fall to trigger the fall of many, many dominoes), the failure of one bank can cause a cascading failure of many other banks and financial institutions. This effect is true even if those other financial institutions weren't experiencing any difficulties and were well-run beforehand.

Recognising the dangers of moral hazard

The widespread failure of large numbers of banks and other financial institutions is such a catastrophic outcome that governments will do almost anything to stop it happening. Indeed, you saw this response during the global financial crisis of 2007–8: governments around the world pumped huge amounts of taxpayer funds into the banking sector to keep it afloat.

But bankers aren't a silly bunch. They're quite aware that their industry is vital to the well-functioning of the wider economy. They also know that because of this importance, if they do find themselves in difficulty, a very good chance exists that the government will bail them out.

This knowledge leads to what economists call *moral hazard*. Basically, banks and other financial institutions have incentives to take on excessive risk, safe in the knowledge that if things turn out badly the government will ride to the rescue. But if the risks turn out well, the banks' employees and shareholders earn bumper profits. Flip to Chapter 15 for more on moral hazard.

One of the big challenges following the 2007–08 global financial crisis is: how can governments ensure that taxpayers are never left in the position where they're on the hook for the losses incurred by the financial sector? We discuss what can be done (if anything) in Chapter 16.

Chapter 2

Looking at Key Questions and Concepts

Macroeconomists are a pretty ambitious bunch. They try to explain and predict the behaviour of the economy as a whole. As a result, macro-economics attempts to answer some of the biggest questions around: why are some countries rich and others poor? What causes inflation? How can nations reduce unemployment? Why do countries experience recessions?

As you can imagine, sorting out these and other questions is no easy task. Unsurprisingly, macroeconomists disagree about many of these issues. Nevertheless, a common body of knowledge has developed on which most macroeconomists agree.

In this chapter, we present the central questions that fascinate macroecono-mists. You also see how economists look at the world and how this helps them to answer difficult questions. Finally, we introduce some concepts in economics that frequently confuse newcomers. By nipping them in the bud now, you will be well on your way to understanding the economy!

Seeing the Questions that Intrigue Macroeconomists

If you want to understand something, the obvious starting point is to ask pertinent questions: why does the phone ring as soon as you step into the shower? Why is it almost impossible to find a matching pair of socks? What's the point of celebrity chefs?

This section introduces the key questions of interest to macroeconomists and gives you an idea about why these questions are important. The ideas introduced here come up over and over again in this book, so don't worry if you still have questions the first time around – we'll do our best to answer them!

In this section we take a look at some of the core questions that keep macroeconomists up at night (fortunately none involve Gordon Ramsey!).

Why are some countries rich and others poor?

Of all the questions in economics, this is the big-un. Why are living standards in rich countries such as the US so much higher than in poor countries like Bangladesh? (To give you an idea: average annual income in the US is over $50,000, while in Bangladesh it's around $1,000.) Can Bangladesh take any actions to make its people richer? If so, what are they?

These kinds of question are so pressing and so important that the Nobel Prize–winning economist Robert Lucas said that, 'once one starts to think about them, it is hard to think about anything else'.

Macroeconomists aren't obsessed with this question because they're obsessed with money and riches in and of themselves. Instead, countries with high incomes tend to have other things that people care about: lower infant mortality, longer life expectancy, better healthcare and education, and so on. In surveys, people in richer countries also tend to report higher levels of life satisfaction. So although being richer isn't the be-all and end-all, it certainly matters. In many poor countries – where large numbers of people live without basic needs such as enough food to eat, a roof over their heads or basic sanitation – increasing people's incomes is a necessary step towards improving their lives.

In order to become richer, countries need *economic growth*. An economy is said to *grow* when the total amount of goods and services that it can produce increases. Economic growth is usually expressed as a percentage change over a year: if the UK economy grows by 2 per cent this year, that means it can produce 2 per cent more 'stuff' this year than the year before.

Small differences in growth rates can make a big difference over long periods of time. For example, if an economy grows at 2 per cent a year, it takes about 35 years to double in size. If, however, it's able to increase its growth rate to 4 per cent a year, the economy doubles in only 18 years. If it grows at 10 per cent a year, it doubles in just 7 years!

So you can see why finding ways of boosting economic growth (especially in poor countries) is high on the agenda for macroeconomists.

What causes the price of things to rise?

Think back to when you were a kid (or if you're one, ask your parents or grandparents). No doubt you remember that things were much cheaper in the past. After school you could walk into a newsagent and buy a chocolate bar, fizzy drink and a magazine and still have change from a pound (or even less, depending on how old you are. . .); oh, those were the days!

When prices rise on average in an economy, it's called *inflation*. In the recent past in developed economies, inflation has only been a few per cent per year, but some decades ago double-digit inflation, even in developed economies, wasn't unusual. One of the reasons that inflation has come under control is that economists now have quite a good understanding of what causes it and how countries can go about reducing it.

Although inflation (increasing prices) is the norm, some countries (such as Japan) have experienced prolonged *deflation*, that is, falling prices, which mean that people and firms often put off spending in order to wait for a lower price. This behaviour puts more downward pressure on prices. (We discuss the case of Japan in more detail in Chapter 5.)

Other countries (at times) have experienced such extremely high inflation that economists have a special name for it: *hyperinflation*. Germany after the First World War is the classic example of hyperinflation, but it also occurred more recently in Zimbabwe where – at the peak – prices doubled every day!

The reason why inflation occurs is quite straightforward: an increase in the amount of money in the economy. But many nuances apply, which we go into in Chapter 5.

What causes unemployment?

Economists really dislike unemployment. Seeing people sitting at home who want to work and have nothing to do makes them sad. But most important, the unemployed could be working and thereby helping to produce goods or services that people value.

When large numbers of people are unemployed, the economy isn't producing as much 'stuff' as it could, and therefore living standards are lower than they could be.

Some countries have succeeded in keeping unemployment relatively low. In Figure 2-1, you can see that in the US, before the 2008 crisis, unemployment hovered around the 5 per cent mark. After the crisis it increased to around 10 per cent but has been falling since then to the pre-crisis level of 5 per cent.

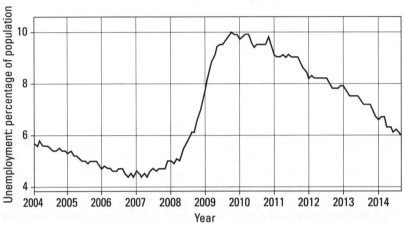

Figure 2-1:
US unemployment.

© John Wiley & Sons

Spain, on the other hand, had a 'reasonable' unemployment rate of 10 per cent before the crisis only for it to balloon to around 25 per cent post-crisis – and over 50 per cent for under-25s. Clearly, if over half of all young people who want to work can't find jobs, something is going deeply wrong in the Spanish economy.

Economists have come up with a number of answers to explain the marked difference between the unemployment rates in different countries (we look at these aspects in more detail in Chapter 6):

- ✔ **Labour market flexibility:** This phrase refers to how able the labour market is to respond to 'shocks'; for example, if the economy isn't doing so well, are wages able to easily adjust downwards to ensure that unemployment doesn't rise too much?

  Economists also think that making it too hard for firms to fire workers isn't a good idea. This may seem harsh, but if getting rid of someone is difficult, firms become reluctant to hire new people and this increases unemployment.

- ✔ **Level of out-of-work benefits:** In many developed countries, the government provides money and other benefits (for example, housing subsidies) to the unemployed to ensure that people don't experience undue hardship. Economists start to worry if unemployment benefits look overly generous compared to the wages from working. They expect that the higher out-of-work benefits are, the higher the rate of unemployment will be, because high benefits reduce people's incentives to search for work.

✔ **Trade union power:** These organisations exist to support their members and negotiate on their behalf with their employers. They serve an important function, for example by ensuring that people are treated fairly at work. Trade unions are typically allowed to organise strikes (subject to certain legal requirements) in order to improve their members' pay and conditions.

Economists worry when trade unions lobby for much higher wages than the going market wage. Many people would be willing to work for those high wages but are unable to because firms aren't willing to hire as many workers at the higher wage. In these circumstances economists say that trade unions benefit *insiders* (those currently employed) to the detriment of *outsiders* (those not employed in the industry but who'd like to be). By effectively restricting the number of jobs in an industry, powerful trade unions can mean higher unemployment.

Thinking Like an Economist: Learning to Love Modelling

Economists look like normal people, walk like normal people and (usually) talk like normal people. You can pass one in the street or sit opposite one on the train and be none the wiser. But they have one secret: they often think very differently to non-economists.

In this section we discuss what makes economics a distinctive way of thinking about the world. Central to this approach is the use of models (attractive though all economists undoubtedly are, we're talking economic models here rather than the catwalk variety!). Although it may not be the only way of thinking about the world, we hope to convince you that 'thinking like an economist' has its advantages!

Modelling to understand the world

Many economic questions and problems are complex: for example, trying to work out the best way of reducing unemployment or analysing the likely impact of boosting government spending on the economy or even understanding how geopolitical events in the Middle East will impact global economic growth. These issues are so complex in fact that economists believe that trying to think about these problems head-on in all their complexity is almost bound to fail.

Instead, economists create models. An *economic model* is a simplified representation of the real world. A good model is one that focuses on the particular variables of interest while moving irrelevant (or less relevant) details to one side.

An example of a model is a street map. A good street map includes useful details such as roads along with their names; it probably also indicates a number of places of interest and perhaps train stations. You don't expect the map to tell you where every tree is on your route or the location of each and every traffic light. In fact, you'd be positively annoyed if it did, because it would clutter up the map and make it much less useful.

The same idea applies with economic models: cut the irrelevant stuff in order to focus on the things that matter. We use many different models in this book to help you understand different aspects of the economy.

Sometimes economists are criticised for making too many assumptions about people or the economy in their models – they're told that their models are too simple and that the real world is more complex. That may be true, but economists prefer to have a simple model they can fully understand rather than a complicated one that they can't make head or tail of. Moreover, when they understand the simple model, they can slowly complicate it to see what happens. In macroeconomics, as in life, you need to learn to walk before you can run.

Ensuring that intuition doesn't fail you

Another reason economists like working with models is that often human intuition alone can lead people astray.

Here's a classic example: the government is going to increase payroll taxes by 10 per cent (these taxes are paid by either the employee or the employer when someone works). A fierce political debate rages between two rival camps:

- **Camp A thinks that employers should pay the extra tax:** Their slogan is 'Why should hardworking people have to pay more tax?'.

- **Camp B thinks that employees should pay the extra tax:** Their slogan is 'Taxing employers is a tax on jobs'.

Who's right? Both camps have attractive arguments and are arguing for them passionately. Intuition says that employees should prefer employers to pay the tax and vice versa. But intuition is wrong! It makes no difference whether the tax is formally levied on the employer or the employee – the take-home pay of the employee is the same in both cases.

Macro meets micro

Economics is often split into microeconomics and macroeconomics. Microeconomics is the study of individual and firm behavior, and macroeconomics is the study of the economy as a whole. Decades ago they were very different fields with different ways of doing things:

✔ Microeconomics stressed the importance of modelling individuals and firms as *optimising agents*. This means that when people and companies make choices, they consider all possible options and then choose the one they prefer most. Economists say that individuals maximise their *utility* and firms maximise their *profits*.

✔ Macroeconomics used a number of basically ad hoc models in order to explain different aspects of the economy, which was fine for a while until some serious problems soon became apparent. For one, it was just too easy for macroeconomists to 'explain' any macroeconomic event

by coming up with a new model every time something happened that existing models were unable to explain. So, if they wanted to 'explain' why unemployment and inflation rose together in the 1970s all they needed to do was create a model where unemployment and inflation rise together. Want to 'explain' why countries go into recession when oil prices rise? No problem, just write down a model where an increase in oil prices leads to a recession. Essentially, it looked like they were cooking the books.

Not happy with this situation, many economists felt that because the economy is made up of millions of interactions between individuals and firms, macroeconomic models should have as their building blocks microeconomic foundations – so macroeconomic models (explicitly or implicitly) should have optimising agents within them. In short, most economists now feel that good macroeconomics should be based on sound so-called microfoundations.

If the employer 'pays' the tax, it will pass some of it on to its workers by reducing wages. If employees 'pay' the tax, they'll only be willing to work for a higher wage – which means some of the tax is actually paid by the employer. The eventual outcome is identical in both cases!

This result is counterintuitive – you'd be unlikely to come to this conclusion by sitting down and just thinking really hard. Nonetheless, it's true and the empirical evidence (the data) supports this conclusion.

The beauty of modelling is that it allows economists to find results that would be almost impossible to find otherwise.

Clarifying Important Macroeconomic Concepts

Switch on the news or read a newspaper and inevitably you're confronted with a number of stories about the economy: perhaps the latest interest rate move by the Bank of England, the most recent GDP figures or what's happened to the budget deficit.

In this section we present some of the central concepts and terms of macroeconomics.

Many of the terms used by economists can be confusing to non-economists, partly because, like all disciplines, economics has developed its own jargon for describing different things. Plus, some common words take on a different meaning when economists use them! We make every effort to cut through the jargon of macroeconomics.

Knowing that what's real counts

Economists make a crucial distinction between real variables and nominal variables:

- **Nominal:** Variables quoted in terms of *money*. For example, the price of something or your hourly wage in pounds.
- **Real:** Variables that are quoted in terms of *quantities*. For example, the number of people unemployed or how much you are paid in terms of goods.

Imagine you're offered a job in the exotic location of Econland. Before deciding whether to accept, you want to ask some questions. One is, 'What's the salary?'. The firm tells you that the salary is 1 million ecos (the currency of Econland). You get very excited and picture buying a yacht. But wait a minute – before you accept and go on a spending spree, one important piece of information is missing. How much do things cost in Econland? Or equivalently, how much can you actually buy with 1 million Ecos?

Economists call the answer to the first question the *nominal* wage: it tells you how much you're going to be paid in terms of *money*. The answer to the second question is the *real* wage: it tells you how much you're paid in terms of *goods*. Economists think that the real wage is what matters. After all, it determines your standard of living. The nominal wage is just a name, and economists think that the names of things shouldn't really matter.

You encounter this distinction between real variables and nominal variables throughout the book. In almost every case, economists think that the real variable is what really counts.

Stocking up and going with the flow

What makes someone rich: earning a high salary; having a big house; having a lot of money in the bank; or something completely different such as having a loving family?

Because of the ambiguity, economists don't really like using the word 'rich'. Instead, if someone has a large salary, they say that they have a high *income*. If they have a lot of money in the bank or own a number of properties, they say that they're *wealthy*.

Income and wealth are related but different concepts. Economists call income a *flow* variable. A bit like how a shower sprays a certain amount of water every minute, income pays a certain amount of money over a certain period of time. You see income quoted as an hourly, daily, weekly, monthly or yearly rate.

Wealth, on the other hand, is a *stock* variable. A bit like how a bath has a certain amount of water in it at a point in time, your wealth is the total value of your assets at any given point in time.

Unlike income, when you're describing someone's wealth, you don't need to say over what period of time. So John may say that his income is £25,000 *per year*, but for his wealth he'd just say £100,000.

Of course, an intimate relationship exists between someone's income and his wealth. Wealth is the accumulation of a lifetime of income less expenditure. Other examples of stocks and flows are:

- ✔ A person's level of debt is a stock, whereas his borrowing from year to year is a flow.
- ✔ The total number of unemployed workers is a stock, whereas the weekly number of people finding (and losing their) jobs is a flow.
- ✔ The total number of houses in the UK is a stock, whereas the new houses that are built (and destroyed) every year is a flow.

Differentiating investment and capital

Investment and capital are perhaps the most easily misunderstood terms that economists use. The reason is because what an economist and non-economist mean by them is very different!

Investment

To the non-economist, an investment is buying something in the hope that it will increase in value over time and/or yield some kind of income. For example, buying a Victorian terraced house can be considered an investment: you hope that it rises in value and earns you a decent rental income. Similarly, buying shares is an investment: you hope that they go up in price and that you get some healthy dividends along the way.

To economists, however, neither of these counts as investment. Instead, an *investment* is buying something new that can be used to produce something in the future. Examples of investment include a firm building a new factory, buying a new machine or even buying some new computers. All these things help it to produce goods and services, which it can then sell to consumers.

An individual buying a house isn't considered a form of investment by economists, except in the case of buying a newly built house. This is because you can think about a new house as 'providing housing services' in the future. This approach may sound like a strange way of thinking about this situation, but it makes clear why buying an already existing house from someone doesn't count as investment: it doesn't create any new 'housing services'. Instead you've just transferred the right to existing housing services from someone else to yourself.

Similarly, a firm buying a machine second-hand from another firm doesn't count as investment, because the total number of machines hasn't increased.

Capital

If you hear an entrepreneur complaining that he doesn't have enough capital, he probably means that he needs more money to get his business off the ground.

When economists talk about *capital,* they (usually) mean *capital stock.* This is all the machines, offices, computers and so on that are used to produce goods and services.

Investment and capital stock are closely linked. Investment is the purchase of new capital goods (goods that can be used to produce other goods and services). Thus, the capital stock, as its name suggests, is a stock variable, and investment is the yearly addition to the capital stock, so it's a flow variable (see the preceding section).

Does this mean that the capital stock in a country can only ever rise? Well, no. Every year machines and other capital goods get worn down (they *depreciate*). In order for the capital stock to rise, investment that year has to be more than the depreciation of the existing capital stock.

Economists often use mathematical equations in order to express ideas concisely, and you can express the relationship between investment and capital as follows:

$$K_{t+1} = (1-\delta)K_t + I_t$$

In words, this equation says that the capital stock tomorrow (K_{t+1}) is equal to the capital stock today (K_t), less depreciation (δK_t, proportion δ of the capital stock depreciates) plus investment today (I_t, which is just the new capital purchased today).

Sorting levels from growth rates

Another source of confusion is the level of a variable versus its growth rate:

- **Level:** The value that a variable takes at a particular time.

- **Growth rate:** The percentage change in a variable over a period of time (usually a year).

Here's an example: one of the economic success stories of the recent past is China. Over the last decade or more, the Chinese economy has grown by around 10 per cent per year. At the same time, growth in the West has been a paltry few percentage points a year (if at all). No doubt China has made huge strides and the living standards of its people have improved substantially. But does this mean that the Chinese economy is now 'better' than the economies of the West?

Well, to an economist probably not. Although China has experienced substantial economic *growth,* it started off from a very low *level:* average income in 2000 was around $1,000 per person, whereas at that time in the US average income per person was around $40,000. So, even though the Chinese economy has grown a lot since then, living standards in China are still far below living standards in the US. The average American today still earns over 7 times more than the average Chinese.

The lesson is: although growth rates of variables are important, don't lose sight of the overall level of the variable.

Here are some other examples of variables that are levels: the amount of unemployment, the overall price level, the value of a stock index and the average house price in London. The percentage change of these variables is a growth rate; for example, the percentage change in the price level over a year is called the *rate of inflation*: it's the growth rate of the price level.

Investigating interest rates: The price of money

Economists say that the price of money is the *interest rate*: It tells you the cost of borrowing money and how much return you can expect if you lend out your money. (As anyone who's tried to borrow money knows, these two rates are rarely the same! Ignore this complication for the moment.)

The interest rate is an important variable in macroeconomics – it can have a big impact on the behaviour of individuals and firms:

- **Individuals:** Imagine that the interest rate is very high, so you get a large return on your savings. How would that affect your choices? Well, probably you'd think twice before spending your money. After all, if you spend it now, you give up the opportunity to save it and earn a high return. In this situation, economists say that the *opportunity cost* of consuming is high. Similarly, if you want to buy a car or a house and you need to borrow money, you're much less likely to do so if the interest rate is high.

  These two effects mean that, when the interest rate is high, consumption is relatively low, and when the interest rate is low, consumption is relatively high.

- **Firms:** Large firms, especially, often have surplus cash lying around. What should they do with their excess cash? One option is to save it and earn the interest rate. Another option is to buy some more capital (stuff such as machines – check out the earlier section 'Differentiating investment and capital'). If the interest rate is high, buying a new machine had better give the firm a really good return – otherwise it should have just saved the cash and earned the interest rate. In this situation, economists say that the *opportunity cost* of investment (buying capital) is the return the firm would've earned if it had just saved the money.

  If the interest rate is high, not many firms want to engage in investment. Conversely, a low interest rate makes investment very attractive.

The interest rate is such a powerful tool that setting it is the responsibility of the central bank. This is known as *monetary policy*, something we look at closely in Chapter 10.

Discovering five important terms (though knowing one is enough)

Like all practices, economics has its own terminology. We aim to keep the jargon in this book to an absolute minimum, but here are five essential terms that you hear economists using.

When calculated for the economy as a whole, all these measures are equal!

- ✔ **Gross Domestic Product (GDP):** Value of final goods and services an economy produces in one year (a *final* good or service is one directly provided to the end user). Specifying that it's only the value of final goods and services is important to avoid double counting. So if you own a coffee shop, every time you sell a coffee for £3 that adds exactly £3 to GDP. The cost of coffee beans and milk and so on is already included in that £3, so it can't be added again to GDP.

- ✔ **Output:** Aggregate output of an economy is also a measure of the value of the goods and services produced by an economy in a year. So output is really just GDP by another name!

- ✔ **Production:** The aggregate production of an economy is just the total value of everything produced by firms in one year. Of course, firms produce the goods and services in the economy, so production is really just GDP or output by another name! (Perhaps you're wondering whether it really is just firms that produce goods and services. What about if you set up a market stall selling handbags or even do some babysitting for a neighbour? Economists bypass these questions by just calling anyone or anything that provides a good or a service a 'firm'.)

- ✔ **Income:** Aggregate income is the sum of everyone's income in an economy. And where does income come from? Well, it comes from selling the output/production/GDP of the economy. No surprise, then, that income must also be equal to the others.

- ✔ **Expenditure:** Aggregate *expenditure* is just the sum of everyone's expenditure, that is, their spending on goods and services. Because every £1 of income must have been spent by somebody, aggregate expenditure must also be equal to aggregate income.

So now you know: next time some smart-alec economist or politician tries to bamboozle you with any of these terms, they're all equivalent!

Chapter 3

Curing a Sick Economy of Four Afflictions

In This Chapter

▶ Understanding recessions and how to get out of one

▶ Looking at the causes of and solutions to hyperinflation

▶ Seeing why financial crises can be so devastating

▶ Investigating unemployment

A market economy is a wonderfully dynamic way of organising the production and distribution of goods and services, though if you've grown up in one, you can take it for granted. As the following funny but profound anecdote makes clear, that's not the case for everyone. Shortly after the collapse of the Soviet Union, a Russian official asked the economist Paul Seabright: 'Who's in charge of the supply of bread to the population of London?' Seabright replied, 'Nobody. . .'!

When you think about it, the fact that no one is directing all the people involved in getting bread to consumers (the flour producer, the baker, the delivery driver, the shopkeeper and so on) is quite amazing! No one needs to tell them to trade, they just do it! They're just trying to do the best for themselves, and in doing so, you get your fresh, tasty wholemeal loaf!

Similarly, we bet very few individuals have the knowledge and ability to create a single pencil from scratch, and yet you can easily go into a shop and buy one. Again, the market economy succeeds in co-ordinating the activities of many different individuals to a productive end.

Economists love markets, where individuals meet to trade for their *mutual* benefit. But however much you love something, you have to admit that occasionally it can misfire. For example, even a committed Robbie Williams fan may see the so-called swing period as just plain wrong! Similarly, even economists realise that market economies can sometimes get sick.

In this chapter, you get to play physician as we introduce four important illnesses that can afflict economies: recessions, hyperinflation, financial crises and high unemployment. Fortunately, macroeconomists have also worked out some ways to 'treat' these health threats and get an economy moving again, so we can discuss answers as well. We don't worry too much about the finer details here but just lay out the basics. We cover all these topics in much more detail throughout the book: how to deal with recessions (in Chapters 10–11), hyperinflation (Chapter 5), unemployment (Chapter 6) and financial crises (Part V).

Reading about Recessions

In case you hadn't realised, recessions aren't good: they reduce people's living standards and usually lead to an increase in unemployment (a problem we discuss in the later 'Uncovering Unemployment: Causes and Responses' section).

Identifying a recession

A *recession* refers to a fall in *real Gross Domestic Product* (GDP), which basically measures the value of all the goods and services an economy produces in one year (check out Chapter 2 for more on GDP). The norm is for real GDP to increase over time, which is why living standards now are much higher than those of a few generations ago. Economies are just better at producing things now than they used to be. In Figure 3-1, you can see that, on average, real GDP has increased over time. This increase is a persistent phenomenon – since the Industrial Revolution of the late eighteenth and early nineteenth centuries! You can also see, however, that real GDP fell quite significantly during 2008 – the fallout from the global financial crisis – and it took several years to recover its previous peak.

People's incomes must ultimately come from the production of goods and services (where else could they come from?), so a recession reduces average income in a country or *real GDP per capita*. Indeed, as of 2015, real GDP per capita in the UK still hasn't recovered its pre-crisis peak.

Recessions occur for two main reasons:

- ✔ **A fall in aggregate demand for goods and services:** For whatever reason, if consumers, firms or the government demand fewer goods and services, this behaviour can cause a recession.

- ✔ **An adverse supply shock:** If something happens that makes it more difficult for firms to produce goods and services – for example, a large increase in energy prices – the result is likely to be a recession.

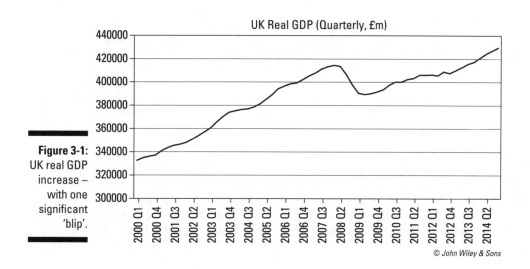

UK Real GDP (Quarterly, £m)

© John Wiley & Sons

Figure 3-1: UK real GDP increase – with one significant 'blip'.

Recessions also tend to increase unemployment, because when fewer goods and services are being produced, firms no longer need as many workers as before. Unsurprisingly, therefore, recessions are big deals politically as well as economically. Voters often attribute a recession to bad economic policy making, which can hurt the incumbent in the next election.

Addressing recessions with fiscal or monetary policies

Policy makers have a few tools they can use to combat a recession. Here we introduce a couple of policies that affect the demand side of the economy (see Chapters 10–11), although we also discuss many ways of stimulating the supply-side of the economy (check out Chapter 6):

- ✔ **Expansionary fiscal policy:** Increasing government spending on goods and services and/or reducing taxes for consumers and firms. Both these actions increase the aggregate demand for goods and services, the former directly and the latter indirectly: households have greater disposable income to use to increase consumption, and investment looks attractive to firms because they get to keep more of the profits.

- ✔ **Expansionary monetary policy:** Cutting the official interest rate – the rate at which commercial banks can borrow from the central bank. The hope is that this action reduces interest rates throughout the economy and encourages consumers to spend and firms to invest.

Here's a small catch, though: when the official interest rate is at (or close to) zero, not much more can be achieved by conventional monetary policy. You may have noticed that, for many years now, interest rates in many developed countries – including the UK and US – have been close to zero. This situation led to some unconventional monetary policies, including most prominently *quantitative easing*: the flooding of the financial system with liquidity, or in other words, creating lots of new money (ease over to Chapter 10 for more).

Macroeconomists tend to favour expansionary monetary policy over fiscal policy for stimulating the economy. The reason is that the latter usually results in a *fiscal deficit* (the government spending more money than it earns in taxation), which requires it to borrow. This borrowing has to be paid back at some point and adds to the nation's indebtedness. Expansionary monetary policy, on the other hand, has a similar impact but without increasing government debt.

Getting Hyper about High Inflation

No one likes inflation (well, actually that's not true; economists like a little bit of inflation, but more on that in Chapter 5). Inflation means that on average the prices of things in an economy are rising. Whereas small amounts of inflation can be a mild inconvenience, very high inflation or *hyperinflation* is seriously bad news and threatens the very fabric of society.

When inflation goes wild

Historical examples of hyperinflation include Germany in 1923, which experienced inflation so high that prices in shops were doubling around every four days. Following World War I, Germany was required to make very large reparation payments to the Allies. The British economist John Keynes had warned that the terms were so punitive that Germany would never be able to afford them. The Germans were expected to make the payments either in gold or foreign currency, neither of which Germany had. Instead, they decided to print domestic currency (the mark) on an industrial scale and then use these to purchase foreign currency. Inevitably, the mark became almost worthless, hence hyperinflation. Germany's hyperinflation (and consequent economic collapse) is seen as one of the main factors that contributed to the rise of fascism in Germany.

Much more recently, in the late 2000s, Zimbabwe experienced hyperinflation that caused prices to double almost every day. On a monthly basis, inflation was around 80,000,000,000 per cent (yikes!). We daren't even try to work out the equivalent annual inflation rate! Zimbabwe, under the leadership of Robert Mugabe – following unsuccessful land reforms and international sanctions – was experiencing severe fiscal problems. Unable to borrow from international capital markets, they too turned to the printing press in order to fund the government. Hyperinflation was the inevitable result.

Soaring to an understanding of hyperinflation

Although no agreed precise definition exists of what counts as hyperinflation, it's essentially very high inflation – so high that you can notice on a day-to-day or even hour-to-hour basis that the prices of things are going up. The nearby sidebar 'When inflation goes wild' contains a couple of examples.

Hyperinflation almost completely devastates an economy:

- ✔ People's savings and pensions are completely wiped out.

- ✔ People need to spend any income they earn almost immediately; otherwise, it loses value and quickly becomes worthless. As a result, people waste large amounts of their time (literally) running to and from the bank and shops.

- ✔ Prices stop functioning as a reliable indicator of the relative scarcity of different goods.

- ✔ Ultimately, if hyperinflation isn't contained, people stop using local currency and use more reliable stores of value such as US dollars, gold or even cigarettes!

Hyperinflation is always caused by one thing: excessive growth in the money supply – basically the central bank is creating too much new money. Clearly this approach makes money less scarce and worth less: that is, the prices of things go up because the rate at which you can convert money into goods has become worse (because so much money is around).

The underlying cause of the excessive growth in the money supply is almost always because the government is short of money (it's spending more than it earns in taxes) and instead of borrowing the difference by issuing bonds (perhaps no one is willing to lend to it), it decides to run the printing presses.

Tackling hyperinflation: Stop printing money!

Sometimes people talk about inflation as if it's a force of nature, something that was bound to happen and outside anyone's control. The truth, however, is that whether (and indeed how much) a country experiences inflation is very much in the control of policy makers.

For example, since 2003, the UK has targeted an inflation rate of 2 per cent: politicians have told the central bank that this is the rate of inflation that they want to see in the UK. They could just as well have chosen no inflation or 10 per cent inflation or even 2 per cent deflation (a fall in prices). Although achieving the target exactly all the time is impossible, hitting it on average is quite possible.

Very high levels of inflation are a direct consequence of policy makers creating far too much money. So the simple solution to ending hyperinflation is to tell them to stop printing so much! But things aren't that simple. In order to allow the authorities to stop printing so much money, policy makers have to address the underlying cause of their fiscal problems first (that is, the fact that the government isn't raising enough taxes to cover its spending).

For this reason, economists advising countries experiencing hyperinflation almost always prescribe tax increases and cuts in government spending. The medicine hurts, but it's the only way the government can end its addiction to the printing press.

Finding Out about Financial Crises

Financial crises are never fun: they often involve massive falls in asset prices, an increase in unemployment, a fall in living standards, loan defaults, bank runs and bailouts. If policy makers could find some way of stopping them from happening, that would be great. Unfortunately, a financial crisis happens somewhere in the world quite regularly. Here are just a few recent ones: 2014 Russian crisis, 2010 European sovereign debt crisis, 2001 dot-com bubble, 1998 Russian crisis (yes, again), 1997 Asian crisis and so on. Not forgetting of course the 2007–08 global financial crisis, which we cover fully in Chapters 14, 15 and 16.

Diagnosing a financial crisis

The defining feature of a *financial crisis* is that financial assets such as stocks suddenly lose a large amount of their value. In essence, people pull their money out of anything that they perceive as remotely risky and put it somewhere where they think it'll be safe – which is why gold and central London property do so well during crises.

As part of this 'flight from risk', financial institutions become very reluctant to lend money to people (or even each other) – sometimes called a *credit crunch*. This reluctance causes problems for lots of good, well-run businesses, which are profitable but need some short-term cash for liquidity reasons. Without funding, many such businesses go under.

Your local butcher or baker going bankrupt is one thing – it's certainly sad for them and their employees, but any wider fallout is unlikely (except perhaps for your stomach). But a large financial institution going under is another thing altogether – it has the potential to create widespread panic and chaos, because such a business is in the middle of a complex web of transactions with other financial institutions.

The failure of just one large bank can easily reverberate throughout the economy and lead to multiple bank failures and even the collapse of the financial system as a whole – this process is called *financial contagion*.

To avoid financial contagion, governments often feel obliged to bail out the financial sector during times of crisis. This response tends to be unpopular with the public, because previously private liabilities become the responsibility of the taxpayer. You may have heard the phrase 'heads I win, tails you lose', which refers to the idea that financial institutions and their employees do very well for themselves during the good times, but that during the bad times taxpayers are left with the bill.

Fighting financial crises: Lender of last resort

One of the main problems financial institutions (and indeed other businesses) face during a financial crisis is that they have extreme difficulty borrowing money.

Many of these institutions have lots of assets – in theory more than enough to cover their liabilities. But a lot of these assets are *illiquid* – that is, turning them into cash quickly is difficult. For example, a bank may own your mortgage, which is a valuable asset because it gives the bank the right to a stream of payments from you over a number of years. But what good is something that pays out in 10 or 20 years when the bank needs the cash now?

Furthermore, trying to sell these assets isn't going to help: the financial crisis means that no one wants to buy assets – and if they do, they'll pay only a fraction of their value during 'normal times' (called a *fire sale*). In 'normal times' a financial institution wouldn't even need to sell its assets to borrow money – it would use them as *collateral* to get a loan on the understanding that if it fails to repay, the lender seizes the collateral as compensation.

But during a financial crisis, asset prices have fallen so much that lenders are reticent to lend money *even if* collateral is offered to secure the loan. Here's where policy makers (typically the central bank) can step in and act as a *lender of last resort*. In practice, this term means being willing to lend to financial institutions that can't easily borrow elsewhere, and furthermore, accepting collateral from them based on the market value of that collateral in 'normal times' rather than the current (very low) market value.

The role of the lender of last resort isn't to stop *insolvent* businesses from going under – that is, businesses whose assets (even in normal times) are insufficient to cover their liabilities. No, the lender of last resort's job is to help businesses that – due to the crisis – are suffering from short-term *liquidity* (cash flow) problems. They have enough assets to cover their liabilities; the crisis is just making borrowing hard for them.

Uncovering Unemployment: Causes and Responses

An ideal world would have no unemployment: everyone who's able and willing to work would be able to find a job. Sadly, in real life unemployment does exist, and in some economies a large proportion of people are unable to find work.

Fortunately, macroeconomists have a good idea what causes unemployment and what policy makers can do to reduce it. For loads more on this subject, check out Chapter 6.

Recognising that unemployment is bad for society

Unemployment involves many costs:

- ✔ **Personal costs:** Unemployed people bear much of the impact, compared with employed people:
  - • Worse physical and mental health
  - • More likely to be divorced
  - • Lower life expectancy

- ✔ **Economic costs:** Unemployment reduces the amount of tax revenue the government is able to raise and at the same time increases expenditure on social assistance programmes.

Unemployment leads to what economists call a *deadweight-loss*: basically the time that people spend not working they could've spent working and doing something productive. Instead that time is lost and can never be recovered.

Working on unemployment: Labour market flexibility

Some level of unemployment is inevitable. In general terms it falls into the two categories we describe in this section.

Frictional unemployment

Frictional unemployment arises mostly from the natural flows of people in and out of employment. Technological advances and changes in consumer tastes mean that the skills that firms are looking for and the skills that workers possess sometimes differ.

For instance, the UK used to have a large coalmining industry, but technological advances (for example, cheap nuclear power) and competition from abroad meant that mining coal in the UK was no longer economical. Sadly, many people lost their jobs and had difficulty finding other work – their skills were no longer in demand.

Limited information is another cause of frictional unemployment. Firms have limited information about which workers would be a good fit for them and workers have limited information about which firms they'd enjoy working for. This problem makes it costly – in time and effort – for workers to find suitable jobs and firms to find workers they want to hire.

In short, a certain level of frictional unemployment is inevitable in a market economy and policy makers can do little about it. (Some economists point out that generous unemployment benefits may contribute to frictional unemployment by reducing the incentives to search for work.)

Structural unemployment

High levels of unemployment indicate that the labour market isn't working properly and that structural problems are stopping it from reaching *equilibrium*. The labour market is in equilibrium when the quantity of labour that firms want to hire is equal to the quantity of labour workers want to supply.

We illustrate this situation in Figure 3-2:

- ✔ **Demand curve (D):** How much labour firms are willing to hire at different wage rates; the lower the wage rate, the more labour firms want to hire.

- ✔ **Supply curve (S):** How much labour workers are willing to supply at different wage rates; the higher the wage, the more people want to work.

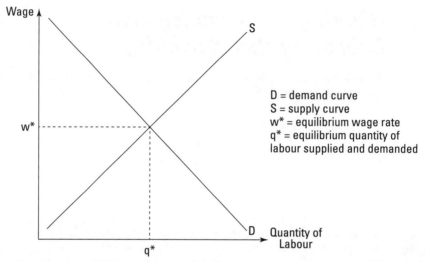

© John Wiley & Sons

Figure 3-2:
Labour
market
equilibrium.

Where supply and demand meet represents equilibrium in the labour market. Here, the amount of labour supplied (q^*) is exactly equal to the amount of labour demanded (also q^*). Notice also that the wage rate needs to equal w^* in equilibrium.

Several reasons can prevent the labour market from reaching equilibrium:

- ✔ **Minimum wage:** Sets a legal minimum that workers must be paid. For most workers it's *not binding* – they'd earn more than the minimum wage in any case – and so the minimum wage has no impact on them. But for some workers the minimum wage is *binding* – their equilibrium wage is lower than the minimum. For these workers the minimum wage has an impact, both positive and negative:

  - The positive impact is that low-paid workers who find work are paid better.

  - The negative impact is that unemployment increases (see Figure 3-3).

  Figure 3-3 shows that the minimum wage has been set at w_m, which is higher than the equilibrium wage rate. Now, more people want to work (q_s) than firms want to hire (q_d) leading to an increase in unemployment for this group of workers of ($q_s - q_d$).

Instead of having a minimum wage – which is likely to increase unemployment, especially for those with the lowest wages – many economists think that a better idea is to directly give poor people money. This is because trying to redistribute by having a minimum wage increases firms' labour costs and reduces the number of workers hired, increasing unemployment. Ideally, you want firms to pay the correct equilibrium wage (which reduces unemployment). If the government is worried that this figure is too low, it can directly redistribute to those people using the tax system.

✔ **Powerful unions:** Trade unions are important organisations that help to protect workers from unfair treatment at work. What worries economists is when a union is so powerful that – through industrial action (striking or threatening to strike) – it's able to raise significantly the wages paid to workers above the equilibrium level. Much like the binding minimum wage shown in Figure 3-3, this action increases unemployment.

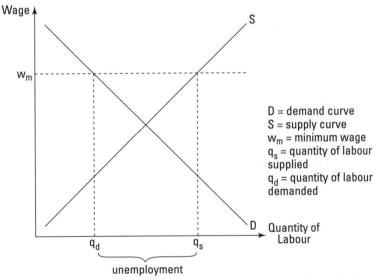

D = demand curve
S = supply curve
w_m = minimum wage
q_s = quantity of labour supplied
q_d = quantity of labour demanded

Figure 3-3: Minimum wage and unemployment.

unemployment

© John Wiley & Sons

Economists point out that unions that successfully increase wages above the equilibrium level benefit *insiders* (union members) to the detriment of *outsiders* (people who'd like to work in the industry but can't). Ideally, in a market economy, union industrial action isn't necessary to maintain workers' wages. Instead, firms competing with each other to hire workers ensures that workers are fairly paid (and unemployment is kept low). Any firm not paying the market rate soon finds itself in trouble because a large fraction of its workforce leaves.

✔ **Too much regulation:** Some regulation of the labour market is a good thing – for example, making sure that firms provide a safe working environment. Too much regulation, however, can significantly add to the cost of hiring workers. Some regulation can even hurt the people it intends to help. For example, making it very difficult to fire workers may be intended to keep unemployment low by making firings rare, but doing so is likely to make firms think twice before offering someone a job and may instead make hiring rare! Ironically, having less regulation and making it easier for firms to 'hire and fire' could reduce unemployment.

Part II
Measuring the Things that Matter

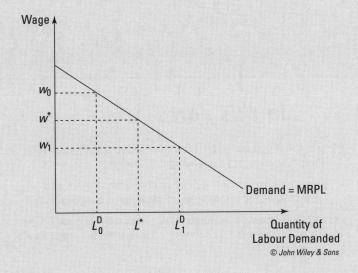

© John Wiley & Sons

web extras

The Solow model of economic growth is a benchmark model of macroeconomics taught throughout the world. Check out the free article about its lessons at www.dummies.com/extras/macroeconomicsuk.

In this part . . .

✔ Get a firm grip on Gross Domestic Product (GDP) and everything that goes into calculating it.

✔ Discover why so many people worry about inflation and understand why a little bit of inflation may be a good thing.

✔ See how unemployment affects an economy, understand how it's measured and find out what causes unemployment levels to change.

Chapter 4

Totting up a Country's Economic Activity: Gross Domestic Product

In This Chapter

▶ Understanding the importance of GDP

▶ Seeing what determines wages in an economy

▶ Discovering how to calculate GDP

▶ Using GDP to measure living standards

*M*acroeconomists love talking about Gross Domestic Product (GDP for short) – as much as sci-fi fans love discussing *Star Trek,* TV chefs the benefits of organic turnips and MPs how few expenses they can claim now and why it's soooo unfair! When economists examine a country's economy, GDP is probably the first thing they look at – and for good reason.

Gross Domestic Product provides a convenient snapshot of the total amount of economic activity taking place in a country. More precisely, it reveals the value of everything an economy produces in one year.

Here's a simple way to view GDP. Imagine that every year in the UK Mary Berry bakes a massive Victoria sponge, dripping with strawberry jam (no drooling!). It's delicious, of course, and everyone wants a piece. Now think of the entire cake as the UK's GDP and each person's slice as their personal income that year. Economists dream about two objectives for the cake, er, for GDP:

✔ **Efficiency:** They want the economy to be as big and tasty as possible.

✔ **Equity:** They'd like everyone to get a similarly sized slice.

In this chapter we look at GDP in some detail, why it's important, show how economists calculate it and how equally it's shared, and describe the light it can shed on people's living standards.

Grasping the Idea of GDP

As of 2015, the UK's GDP is more than £1.5 trillion (that's £1,500 billion or £1,500,000 million): basically, it's an awful lot of lolly.

In practice, if you add up the value of everything produced in the UK in one year it comes to more than £1.5 trillion. But note this important point: to avoid double counting, economists count only the value of *final goods* produced, not *intermediate goods*. So if a car manufacturer produces a car worth £20,000 but uses parts worth £8,000 to physically make the car, the total addition to GDP is just the final £20,000.

In this section we describe a few of the ways in which economists view GDP.

Adding up total value added

Sometimes you hear people calling GDP the *total value added*. They do so because you can think of the contribution of a good or service to GDP as the value that is added to it at each stage of production.

For example, the car manufacturer we mention has added value worth £12,000 (by buying the parts for £8,000 and then selling the car for £12,000 more). The same applies to the parts for which component manufacturers may have had to buy raw materials for £2,000 in order to produce the £8,000 worth of parts. They have then added value worth £6,000.

As Table 4-1 shows, the value of the car (the final good being produced) is £20,000. This is exactly equal to the total value added by the raw materials, the component manufacturer and the car manufacturer.

Table 4-1	Total Value Added		
	Cost of Inputs (£)	*Value of Output (£)*	*Value Added (£)*
Raw materials	–	2,000	2,000
Component manufacturers	2,000	8,000	6,000
Car manufacturer	8,000	20,000	12,000
Total value added	–	–	20,000

Determining a country's income – and not consuming it all at once!

GDP tells you the aggregate amount of income of an economy. In other words, if you add up everyone's individual income, that should be equal to GDP.

So, to continue the example from the preceding section, the car manufacturer has managed to turn £8,000 worth of parts into a £20,000 car, leaving it with a surplus of £12,000. Some of this surplus goes to pay the workers in the factory (say £5,000), leaving a profit of £7,000. Ultimately, people own all firms, so this profit also provides an income. Thus the manufacturer's value added is entirely distributed as income either to its workers or its owners.

The same is true for the component manufacturer and the owners of the raw materials: the value added must have been paid to someone as income; because the total value added equals GDP, so too must total income equal GDP.

Of course, when you have your share of the 'GDP cake' (and everyone gets a certain share), you have to decide what to do with it. You have a number of options:

✔ **You can consume it all:** This would mean spending all your income. Another way of thinking about this option is that your income gives you a claim to a certain share of national output (your slice of the cake). By spending it all now, you're choosing to use your entire claim on consumption today (you eat the entire slice).

✔ **You can consume some of it and save the rest:** This would mean you spend only part of your income. By saving some of your share, you give up some of your claim to consumption today. You do so because in return you get a claim to future consumption. Economists think of *saving* as a way of converting consumption today into consumption in the future.

✔ **You can consume more than your share.** How? By borrowing from someone who wants to save part of his share. The catch is that you'll have to pay that person back at some point by giving up some of your own future consumption. Thus economists think of *borrowing* as a way of converting consumption in the future into consumption today.

Watching a nation's GDP flow

GDP is the same thing as aggregate annual income; therefore, it must be a *flow variable*: one that's measured per unit of time – yearly, in this case (see Chapter 2 for more on flow (and stock) variables).

The great thing about the 'GDP cake', therefore, is that a new one is 'baked' every year and every year you get a slice: every year, you get a share of the UK's national output in the form of income. (Of course, different people get different sized slices – something we discuss later in the 'Getting Out What You (Marginally) Put In' section.) If (in the aggregate) people consume less than their income, this adds to a nation's wealth. So, although the UK's GDP is around £1.5 trillion, its total wealth is around £10 trillion.

Be wary when you hear people compare the size of a country's economy to the size of large corporations. You know the sort of thing: 'Company X is now so large that it's bigger than the entire Norwegian economy'. These statements are usually misleading, because they typically compare a country's GDP (a flow variable measured every year) to the total value (market capitalisation) of a firm (all its assets, basically its wealth, which is a *stock variable*). A more appropriate comparison would be to compare the wealth of a country to the value of a firm. In this case, the world's large economies dwarf even the largest corporations.

Distinguishing real and nominal GDP

In this section we distinguish between real and nominal GDP and go on to explain why real GDP is the focus of economists' attention.

Suppose that GDP in the UK last year was calculated to be £1 trillion. Suppose, further, that this year the economy experienced a lot of inflation – so much so that the price of everything doubled. Plus, imagine that the total quantity of goods and services produced this year is the same as last year. The question is: what's GDP this year?

Well, because the price of everything doubled and the quantity of goods remained the same, you could argue that GDP is now £2 trillion (that's the 'value' today of everything being produced). But that doesn't sound quite right, does it? The economy is producing just as much this year as last year and yet GDP appears to have doubled!

In such a situation economists say that, although nominal GDP has doubled, real GDP has remained unchanged. Here's the difference:

- **Nominal GDP:** Measured using *current prices* – that is, the prices that were current at the time.

- **Real GDP:** Measured using *constant prices* – which means that an arbitrary year is chosen to be the *base year* and GDP in all other years is calculated on the basis of prices in the base year.

Why real GDP is the real deal

Real GDP is what really interests economists – because it tells them how much stuff the economy is producing in a year. Similarly, if real GDP goes up by 2 per cent, they know that the quantity of goods and services produced in an economy has gone up by 2 per cent. Nominal GDP figures are less helpful: for example, a number of reasons may explain why nominal GDP rises by 5 per cent in a year:

- ✔ The price level was unchanged and the actual quantity of goods being produced increased by 5 per cent.

- ✔ The price level increased by 5 per cent and the actual quantity of goods being produced remained unchanged.

- ✔ The price level increased by 10 per cent and the actual quantity of goods being produced fell by 5 per cent.

Despite these very different scenarios, in all three cases nominal GDP has risen by 5 per cent. Real GDP, however, has increased by 5 per cent in the first case, remained unchanged in the second case and fallen by 5 per cent in the third case. Economists think that people should care about the amount of goods being produced rather than the nominal value of those goods, so the changes in real GDP are what really count!

Nominal GDP equals real GDP in the base year

As the preceding section explains, real GDP is calculated using the price level in the base year. Figure 4-1 shows the real and nominal GDP for the UK. Real GDP is calculated using 2011 as the base year, which means that real GDP in all other years is calculated using the price of things in 2011. This approach allows economists to compare output in a meaningful way across time. For example, the UK produced about twice as much output in the mid-2000s as it did in the late 1970s/early 1980s. Equally, you can see that total output fell in the late 2000s as a result of the global financial crisis.

Another thing to notice is that real GDP and nominal GDP are exactly equal in 2011. This isn't by accident: 2011 is the base year and real GDP that year has been calculated on the basis of prices in 2011. Nominal GDP is always calculated using the prices that were prevalent at the time. Thus real GDP and nominal GDP always coincide at the base year.

We chose the base year of 2011 arbitrarily and could equally have chosen another year. A different choice wouldn't affect the graph of nominal GDP but would change the graph of real GDP to ensure that it was equal to nominal GDP during the base year. For example, if the base year was 1980, the real GDP 'number' for all the years would be much lower than the numbers in Figure 4-1, not because a different base year affects total output or living standards, but because the real GDP figures would be based on what you could buy with £1 in 1980.

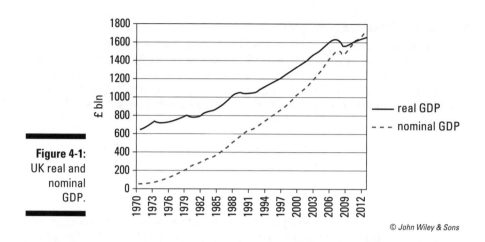

© John Wiley & Sons

Figure 4-1: UK real and nominal GDP.

Getting Out What You (Marginally) Put In

You don't have to be an economist to know that some people get a relatively large share of a nation's output while others get very little at all. Why is this? Can economics shine any light on this important question?

In this section we describe a simple model that provides some clues. You will see that 'factors of production' like labour and capital are compensated according to their *marginal product* – that is, what they contribute personally to the firm's output. However, to see this we need to build up the model slowly. First, we look at what firms do. Then, we show how a firm's output varies with the amount of labour or capital it uses. Finally, we show how this determines the demand for labour and capital and ultimately the wages that workers receive and the rental income that the owners of capital receive. After you know these, you know how much of the 'GDP cake' each person receives! Don't worry – we're gonna take you through this slowly!

Modelling what firms do

We take a look at what firms do here because firms' choices determine the demand for labour and capital – this is key in determining who gets what.

Firms use *inputs* such as workers, machines, factories and raw materials to produce outputs. Here are some examples:

✔ **A company making chocolate:**

- *Likely inputs*: Employees, raw materials such as cocoa beans and milk, machines and a factory to house its workers and machines.

- *Outputs*: Chocolate bars.

✔ **An airline:**

- *Likely inputs*: Staff (pilots, cabin crew, check-in staff), planes, fuel, the use of the airport.

- *Output*: Flights.

✔ **A hotel:**

- *Likely inputs*: Staff (cleaners, cooks, receptionist, the manager) and the hotel building.

- *Output*: A room for the night.

Instead of looking at every industry or firm in isolation, economists prefer to create general models that they can – in principle – apply to all industries and firms.

Here are the building blocks of the model:

✔ Firms use inputs to produce outputs.

✔ How they turn inputs into outputs depends on their *technology*.

✔ Economists represent a firm's technology with a *production function*, which tells them exactly how many units of output result from using a certain amount of inputs.

✔ Firms use two inputs:

- **Capital:** Things such as machines and factories

- **Labour:** People hired to work the machines and in the factories

Figure 4-2 shows a firm using its technology to transform K units of capital and L units of labour into $f(K,L)$ units of output. For example, if the firm can transform 2 units of capital and 3 units of labour into 4 units of output, we write $f(2,3) = 4$. The firm can then sell each unit of output for the price p, yielding it a total revenue of $p \times f(K,L)$.

The costs to the firm are those of hiring workers and renting capital. The firm can hire workers by paying them each a wage of w and it can rent each unit of capital at a cost of r. The total costs of the firm can then be expressed as $wL + rK$, that is, the cost of hiring the worker plus the cost of renting the capital.

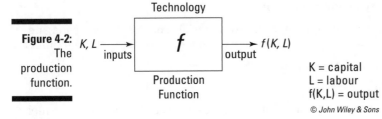

© John Wiley & Sons

Figure 4-2: The production function.

Technology

f

inputs K, L → Production Function → output $f(K, L)$

K = capital
L = labour
f(K,L) = output

Firms choose the quantity of capital (K) and labour (L) in order to maximise profits (π):

$$\pi = pf(K,L) - wL - rK$$

Perusing the properties of the production function

After you understand that firms are trying to choose the amount of labour and capital they want to hire in order to maximise their profits (see the preceding section), you need to understand how the production function $f(K, L)$ works. Firms' demand for labour and capital (and ultimately wages and the returns to capital) depends on the behaviour of the production function.

To work out how much capital and labour firms will hire, you first need to understand how the production function works:

✔ The production function is *increasing in labour* means that if a firm hires an additional worker, it's able to produce more output. The amount that output increases by if an additional worker is hired is called the *marginal product of labour* (*MPL*).

✔ The production function is *increasing in capital* means that an extra unit of capital is going to increase the firm's output. The amount that output increases by if a unit of capital is added is called the *marginal product of capital* (*MPK*).

Mathematically, we can write:

$$MPL = f(K, L+1) - f(K, L)$$
$$MPK = f(K+1, L) - f(K, L)$$

Clearly, *MPL* and *MPK* should always be positive: having more people or more/better machines can never reduce output. At this point precocious students usually put up their hands and ask, 'Yeah, but what if you have so many people in the factory that they literally can't move?' To which we reply, 'You can always ask people not to turn up to work if you really have too many!' Economists call this the assumption of *free disposal*.

The next question is: what happens to *MPL* as *L* rises? Here, a thought experiment helps. Imagine that a firm has 5 machines but no workers to work them. With no workers, it's unable to produce anything, that is, $f(5,0) = 0$. Now imagine adding a single worker (while keeping capital fixed at 5 machines). The first worker is likely to be able to add a lot to output, or in other words, his *MPL* is high. The next worker also adds to output, but probably a bit less than the first worker – his *MPL* is high but a bit lower. Adding a third worker increases output further – but probably less than the increase due to the first and second workers.

At some point, adding more workers isn't going to add much to output at all – imagine having 100 workers and still only 5 machines: you don't need an extra worker, you need more machines!

The idea that the *MPL* should fall as the quantity of labour increases (holding capital fixed) is called the *diminishing marginal product of labour*. A similar argument can be made for what happens when a firm increases its capital while holding its labour fixed. The first unit of capital adds a lot to output (high *MPK*), but subsequent units add less to output. In other words, you can also have *diminishing marginal product of capital*.

Figure 4-3 shows what happens to output as the quantity of labour varies (holding capital fixed). Looking closely, you can see that when there isn't much labour, adding an extra unit increases output by a lot. But when a lot of labour already exists, increasing it further doesn't increase output by much. This is precisely what diminishing *MPL* means. If we were to draw the equivalent diagram for capital, it would look much the same: output would increase a lot for the first few units of capital and then less for each additional unit of capital (holding labour fixed).

Working out the demand for labour and capital

Okay, almost there. You know how firms work and how the production function behaves. Now we tie it all together to derive firms' demand for labour and capital. This determines wages and the rental price of capital, which determines what share of GDP individuals receive.

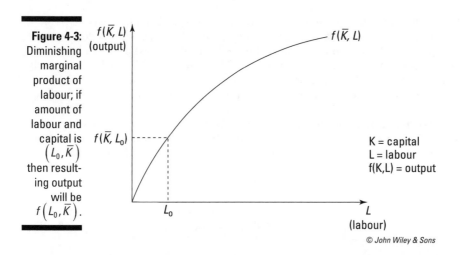

Figure 4-3:
Diminishing marginal product of labour; if amount of labour and capital is $\left(L_0, \bar{K}\right)$ then resulting output will be $f\left(L_0, \bar{K}\right)$.

© John Wiley & Sons

Imagine that you're the manager of a firm thinking about whether to hire an additional worker. You know that it will cost you £w, but what will you gain from the new worker? Well, by hiring him, your firm would produce more output. How much more output? Exactly the marginal product of labour from the preceding section! If you sell that extra output, you'd receive £p per unit of additional output, and so the additional revenue would equal $p \times MPL$.

So if $p \times MPL > w$, hiring the extra worker makes sense, whereas if $p \times MPL < w$, it doesn't make sense. In other words, you should only hire if the revenue gained from an extra worker is greater than the wage. Equally, the absolute most a firm would be willing to pay a worker for his services is $p \times MPL$ (the *marginal revenue product of labour* or *MRPL* for short). The firm would like to pay less, but this is the most that it would pay. For example, if employing Ahmed is going to mean that you can produce 5 more units of output that you can sell for £1,000 each, the most you'd be willing to pay Ahmed for his services (his *MRPL*) is £5,000.

Knowing that the most a firm would be willing to pay for a unit of labour is equal to the *MRPL* has certain implications for the *demand for labour*. After all, the first worker has a relatively high *MRPL*, the second worker a lower *MRPL* and the third worker lower still. Why? Because of the diminishing marginal product of labour! We can show this on a graph.

Figure 4-4 shows that when the wage rate that a firm has to pay is high, it doesn't hire many workers because only the first few workers have an *MRPL* higher than the wage w. As the wage falls, hiring more workers becomes profitable for the firm; even though their marginal productivity is less than the previous workers, hiring them still makes sense.

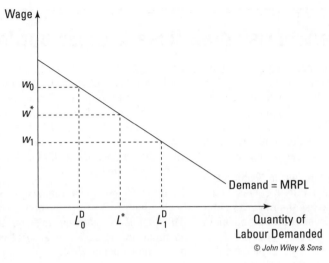

© John Wiley & Sons

Figure 4-4:
The demand for labour: At different wage rates w_0', w^*, w_1 firms wish to hire amount of labour L^D_0, L^*, L^D_1 respectively.

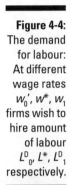

The first few workers are more productive than later workers not because they're intrinsically more skilled or talented, but because of the diminishing marginal product of labour.

The thing is, however, that the firm probably can't just choose the wage that it pays its workers. It has to pay the going wage in the labour market – the wage that all the other employers are paying. Calling this wage w^*, we can now say exactly how many workers the firm will hire:

The firm will continue to hire workers until the MRPL is exactly equal to the wage rate.

All the workers employed are paid w^* and they all (now) have *MRPL* equal to w^* whether they were hired first or not. The reason is: if any individual employee were to now leave, the firm would experience a loss of revenue exactly equal to that person's *MRPL*, which is equal to w^*.

Of course, the real world contains many different types of firms and different types of workers. Some people are good with their hands, others with numbers; some people are very productive, and others are less so. Whatever the case may be, the logic is still the same: economists expect that people's wages reflect their marginal productivity, so each person is paid a wage equal to his marginal revenue product.

If you want to know how to earn more money, you need to increase your (marginal) contribution, either by producing (or helping to produce) more or by producing something that's highly valued in the marketplace and can therefore demand a high price. Easier said than done!

Why do people risk their lives to cross borders?

Every year tens of thousands of people risk their lives trying to enter Europe illegally. They often pay people traffickers large sums to facilitate the dangerous journey. Those same traffickers typically send dangerously overcrowded and unsafe boats across the Mediterranean. Tragically, every year, thousands don't make it.

The simple model we present in 'Getting Out What You (Marginally) Put In' gives some idea about why people risk their lives to enter another country. A distinct pattern applies to the flow of people across the world, legally as well as illegally. Unsurprisingly, people want to move from countries with relatively low wages to countries with relatively high wages. After all, who wouldn't want a higher standard of living?

But we can also go a step deeper and say *why* one country has higher wages than another. We start with the equilibrium labour market condition:

$$w = p \cdot MPL$$

where *MPL* is marginal product of labour. This equation says that a person's wage *w* is equal to his marginal revenue product of labour (*MRPL*). Economists often call *w* the *nominal wage*, because it's the amount of *cash* that the worker is paid. Economists, however, think that people should really care about their *real wage*: the amount of goods they can actually buy with their wage. Conveniently, we can easily convert someone's nominal wage into his real wage. When we divide both sides of the equation above, we get:

$$\frac{w}{p} = MPL$$

w/p is the real wage (how much stuff you can actually buy with your cash wage of *w*). For example, if your nominal wage is *w* = £10, and you work for a chocolate factory selling chocolate at a price *p* = £2, your real wage is

w/*p* = 10/2 = 5: you're paid the equivalent of 5 chocolate bars. Obviously, you don't have to spend all your wage on chocolate – but you can if you want to! To earn the real wage of '5 chocolate bars' your *MPL* must be exactly 5 chocolate bars. That is, you working for the chocolate factory means that it can produce 5 more chocolate bars.

Therefore, to get a high real wage you need to have a high *MPL*. The question is: why is the *MPL* higher in relatively rich countries such as those in the EU? The answer lies in the production function *f(K,L)*:

✔ **Rich countries tend to have high levels of capital (*K*):** They have lots of high quality machines/factories/offices/computers. They also tend to have relatively few people – low levels of labour (*L*). When *K* is large and *L* is small, the *MPL* is large. Think about it: if you work for a firm with a lot of sophisticated equipment, your *MPL* is likely to be large. Furthermore, if not many people work for your company, your personal input is also likely to be particularly important – again increasing your *MPL*.

✔ **Poor countries tend to have low levels of capital (*K*):** They have few high quality machines/factories/offices/computers and tend to have a lot of people – high levels of labour (*L*). When *K* is small and *L* is large, the *MPL* is small. If you work for a firm with little equipment, your *MPL* is likely to be small, but if many people work for your company, your personal input is unlikely to be particularly important – again lowering your *MPL*.

In short, people tend to want to move to countries with high levels of capital and not many people, because their *MPL* will be high, assuring a relatively high real wage.

Calculating GDP: Assessing an Economy's Health

GDP is probably the single most useful statistic in appraising the health of an economy, so calculating it accurately is vitally important. Unfortunately, working out a country's GDP is no simple matter.

In this section we look at how GDP is calculated in the UK, why it's not always 100 per cent accurate and also how to take into account improvement in the quality of goods. Other developed economies calculate GDP in a similar way.

Introducing the basics

In the UK, the Office for National Statistics (ONS) is responsible for calculating GDP. It does so on a quarterly basis (every three months) by using three different ways of measuring GDP:

- ✔ **Calculating total income:** Basically adding up everyone's income in the UK, including people's wages from work and firms' profits paid out as dividends to their owners/shareholders. This figure is estimated by using data on firms' profits, individuals' weekly earnings, employer surveys and data from the UK tax authority (HMRC).

- ✔ **Calculating total output:** Working out the value of all final goods that firms produce. This is done by surveying thousands of firms to obtain a detailed picture of exactly what they're producing, in what quantities, using what inputs and for what price. To avoid double counting, only the value added by each firm is included. For this reason, this measure is often called *gross value added* (GVA). (See the section 'Adding up total value added' earlier in the chapter.)

- ✔ **Calculating total expenditure:** Adding up the amount of money that consumers, firms, the government and overseas buyers spend on final goods and services in an economy. The ONS carries out a number of expenditure surveys of households, firms and the government to estimate total expenditure.

 In Chapter 2 we discuss why an economy's total income, total output and total expenditure over a period of time must be identical. In reality, measurement errors mean that these three different measures give slightly different results. The ONS then combines the information from all three measures to give a single estimate for GDP that quarter.

Revising the estimates

Calculating the GDP of an economy is no easy business. Much of the data used is collected via surveys. These surveys sample only a relatively small proportion of individuals/firms in an economy and then use the insights gained to extrapolate to the economy as a whole. Calculating the GDP for a quarter that has just recently passed is especially hard – little data is available from which to make an estimate.

As time passes, more and more data becomes available, allowing for a more precise estimate of GDP:

- ✔ The first estimate for quarterly GDP is made 25 days after the end of the quarter. At this early stage, no data is available to calculate GDP using the income or expenditure approach. The only estimate available uses the data on total output and even this data is largely incomplete.

- ✔ The first estimate is then revised at the 55-day mark using income and expenditure data as well as new output data.

- ✔ Another revision is conducted at 85 days, which provides an even more accurate estimate.

Revisions regularly take place months or even years afterward. You can see these revisions in the *Blue Book*: the annual publication of national accounts in the UK (you can find it on the ONS website, www.ons.gov.uk). These revisions occur because of better data and improved methodology and changes in international accounting standards.

Accounting for quality improvements

One of the biggest problems when trying to compare real GDP across time is the fact that often the quality of products increases over time, especially in the technology industry. A laptop computer today is far superior to one from a decade ago. Furthermore, despite the higher performance, the real price of a laptop today is also much less than it was a decade ago. Simply comparing the total market value of laptops sold today compared to a decade ago would erroneously give you the impression that living standards (at least as far as laptops are concerned) have fallen. Whereas in fact the truth is that more people have access to high-performance laptops today than ever before!

Trying to take into account quality improvements isn't easy, and despite the best attempts of the good statisticians at the ONS, macroeconomists think that real GDP figures don't sufficiently correct for quality improvements (like improved computing performance). This means that living standards may in fact be rising faster than increases in GDP would suggest.

Measuring Living Standards with GDP and Other Methods

Perhaps the main reason macroeconomists are interested in GDP is that summarising the total amount of income in an economy in a year gives a good indication of living standards in that country. But wait a minute! China has a very large GDP, but living standards for the average person aren't that great. What about the fact that a £10,000 annual salary in the UK can't buy you as much as the same amount of money in Thailand?

Don't worry. Macroeconomists have the same concerns! In this section we look at how GDP can be used to reflect living standards in a country, but we also consider some other indicators that might do a better job of reflecting living standards than using GDP alone.

Using GDP per capita: How much cake per person?

If you think about real GDP as the total size of the cake, China has a truly massive cake: to be precise, more than $9 trillion worth of Victoria sponge! Even compared with a rich country such as the UK, this figure is huge (the UK's GDP is around $2.5 trillion). Why, then, are living standards in the UK so much higher than in China?

As you may have guessed, the total size of the cake is less important than how much cake each person gets: the size of each piece. To find out the average living standard in the UK, you need to divide the UK's GDP by the number of people in the UK. Then you find that on average every person in the UK has an income of around $40,000, while in China average income is around $7,000. These figures are known as the UK and China's respective *GDP per capita*. These are calculated using market exchange rates between the US dollar and the local currency, but market exchange rates don't reflect the real relative purchasing power.

Finding a fairer comparison: Purchasing power parity (PPP)

If the UK's GDP per capita is $40,000 and China's is $7,000, does that mean living standards are on average around six times higher in the UK than in

China? No, because per capita GDP doesn't take into account the fact that the cost of living in China is less than in the UK. To adjust for the different purchasing power of money in different countries, economists calculate a country's GDP per capita at *purchasing power parity* (PPP). This basically allows them to compare the amount of goods you can buy with your (average) income in different countries. Now the difference between the UK and China is much less stark.

The UK's GDP per capita (PPP) is around $36,000 while China's is around $12,000. So, when you adjust for the purchasing power of money in the two countries, UK average incomes are only three times more than average incomes in China. So, although people in the UK have on average a higher standard of living than people in China, the difference is much less when you take the different purchasing power of money into account.

Searching for a broader measure: Human Development Index (HDI)

The great thing about having a high GDP per capita (PPP) is that on average people in that country have high living standards. Furthermore, countries with high levels of income tend to have high life expectancy, low illiteracy, low infant mortality and lots of other good things. Even in 'happiness surveys', people in richer countries tend to report higher levels of happiness and well-being, even though people are on average no happier today than they were 50 years ago (when the world was much poorer).

But sometimes a country can have a relatively large GDP per capita (PPP) and at the same time not have all the other good stuff usually associated with having a high income. For example, Equatorial Guinea, a country in Central Africa, has a per capita income (PPP) of over $25,000. But the people of Equatorial Guinea don't have a decent standard of living. In fact, most of them don't have access to safe drinking water and around 1 in 5 children die before the age of five.

In order to focus more attention on the 'things that really matter' and not just on GDP, prominent development economists Amartya Sen and Mahbub ul Haq created an index that they argue does a better job of measuring living standards: the *Human Development Index* (HDI). The HDI combines information on three different indices:

- ✔ **Life Expectancy Index:** Calculated using how long someone can expect to live from birth
- ✔ **Education Index:** Calculated using the mean years of schooling and expected years of schooling
- ✔ **Income Index:** Calculated using income per capita

Even though Equatorial Guinea is the richest country in Africa (per capita), its HDI is way down the list at 144th in the world. Thus, HDI is a broader measure than GDP per capita and penalises countries (by way of lowering their world ranking) that have high incomes but don't convert these high incomes into positive outcomes for their people.

Despite HDI's appeal as a 'better' measure of living standards than income per capita, it never really took off. This is probably because countries such as Equatorial Guinea, with high incomes but low HDI, are very much an anomaly. Most countries with a high GDP per capita (PPP) have a high HDI. Similarly, most countries with a low GDP per capita have a low HDI. This is because countries with high incomes tend to have highly educated populations with high life expectancy and those with low incomes usually do not.

Recognising levels of inequality: The Gini coefficient

Related to the idea that a country can have a high average GDP per capita but low living standards for large numbers of people is *inequality:* how evenly a country's wealth/income is distributed across people. Inequality isn't necessarily 'bad': in fact, most economists think that some level of inequality is inevitable and indeed desirable if people are to exert effort in the workplace and in their studies. Nevertheless, very high levels of inequality are almost universally seen as undesirable.

The *Gini coefficient* is a numerical measure for the 'amount of inequality' present in a country. It's always a number between 0 and 1. A Gini coefficient of zero represents the case of perfect equality where everyone has the same income. As the Gini coefficient increases, incomes become more unequal until the Gini coefficient reaches a value of 1, which represents perfect inequality, that is, one person has everything. Of course, no countries score exactly zero or one, but some are more unequal than others. South Africa, for example, has a Gini coefficient of around 0.63, the UK is less unequal at around 0.35 and Scandinavian countries such as Denmark are even less unequal at around 0.25.

But where do these numbers come from? How are they calculated? Figure 4-5 shows the Lorenz curve for a hypothetical economy – a graphical representation of how income is distributed. On the horizontal axis is the percentage of households (ordered from poorest to richest). On the vertical axis is the percentage of the economy's income (or GDP) earned by that group. So, for example, point x on the Lorenz curve tells you that the poorest 50 per cent of households took home 25 per cent of the total income.

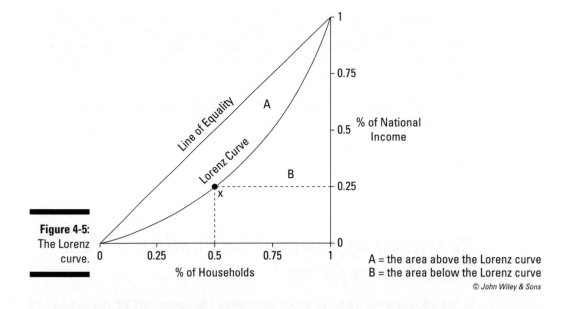

© John Wiley & Sons

Figure 4-5: The Lorenz curve.

A = the area above the Lorenz curve
B = the area below the Lorenz curve

The Lorenz curve must always go through the points (0,0) and (1,1), because by definition the 'poorest 0 per cent of households' (no one) must get nothing while the 'poorest 100 per cent of households' (everyone) must get everything.

When you have the Lorenz curve for an economy, you can calculate how unequal it is by comparing it to the situation where everyone has an equal share – represented by the 'line of equality' in Figure 4-5. The closer the Lorenz curve is to the line of equality, the more equally income is distributed. The Gini coefficient is a numerical measure for how 'close' the Lorenz curve is to the line of equality:

$$Gini\ coefficient = \frac{A}{A+B}$$

A and B are the areas above and below the Lorenz curve, respectively.

The Gini coefficient is a useful and widely used measure of inequality. Its strength is that it gives you a single figure that summarises the level of inequality in a country and allows comparisons across countries and across time. For example, both UK and US inequality has risen over the past 30 years and, as you would expect, so has the Gini coefficient.

Chapter 5

Facing the Fact of Increasing Prices: Inflation

*I*f you ask your grandparents how much things used to cost when they were young, most likely you hear them drone on endlessly (sorry, reminisce movingly) about how cheap things used to be in their day. If you're a grandparent, try the opposite: ask your grandchildren how much rent they pay – you're likely to be equally shocked!

Yet quite why the prices of things tend to rise over time isn't at all obvious. Why can't prices fall or even stay roughly constant? In modern times, what about prices causes them to go up over time in almost all countries? These questions are just some of the ones that macroeconomists attempt to answer.

The increase in the average level of prices in an economy is called *inflation*. It's one of those topics in macroeconomics that affects everybody and about which almost everyone has an opinion. Inflation is also a subject that confuses a lot of people, not least because of a big difference in the way economists think about the issues compared to the way laypeople often do.

In this chapter you discover how inflation is calculated, what influences and causes it and the different inflation measures used. You also find out why high inflation is bad but, perhaps surprisingly, why some inflation may be good. In addition, we let you in on how bad government policies can lead to extremely high inflation (called *hyperinflation*) and we talk briefly about the unusual problem of prolonged price falls (known as *deflation*).

Working Out Inflation: Looking into the Average Shopping Basket

Economists always express inflation as a percentage change over a year. So if inflation in the UK is currently 2 per cent, on average prices are now 2 per cent higher than this time last year. Sounds simple enough: the tricky bit is calculating by how much prices have risen. In the UK, this job falls to the Office for National Statistics (ONS).

In this section, we describe the process for calculating inflation and some factors that complicate it. We also discuss three different measures for inflation, detailing each one's strengths and weaknesses.

Compiling a basket of products and services

The main measure of inflation in the UK (and also many other countries, including the US) is calculated using the *Consumer Price Index* (CPI; see the later section 'Assessing different measures' for more details). The CPI measures the average price of goods and services that consumers bought (as opposed to firms or the government).

The rate of inflation affects so many things, such as state benefits, pensions, contracts, tax bands and salaries, that calculating it accurately is vitally important. The first task is to create a large 'representative basket' of goods and services on which people spend their money. This basket contains all sorts of items: chocolate bars (yum!), bleach (not so yummy), cinema tickets (what fun!), holidays (can we come?) and so on. Basically, the basket should include anything and everything that consumers typically spend their money on.

When the total cost of the basket increases, this change is reflected as an increase in the CPI. So, if the cost of purchasing the basket's contents goes up by 5 per cent, the CPI also increases by 5 per cent.

Of course, consumers' tastes change over time, so the composition of the basket also changes – every year it's updated to reflect the current spending patterns of the population. Equally important is the fact that some items make up a larger proportion of expenditure than others. So, for example, energy bills represent a large fraction of expenditure for most people, while postage stamps don't. In order to account for this, different goods are given different *weights*, so an increase in energy prices has a bigger impact on the CPI than an increase in the price of stamps.

When statisticians have decided on the basket and the weights, someone needs to collect data about prices. This job is a huge undertaking: every month around 100,000 prices for over 500 goods and services are recorded. Much of this data is now compiled electronically, but a substantial amount is still collected by an army of price collectors who physically visit local shops to record the prices!

Adjusting for quality and size

One of the principles for calculating inflation is that comparisons over time have to be 'like-for-like', which creates a problem when the quality of goods changes over time. For example, a family car you purchase today isn't the same as a family car you'd have purchased a decade ago. Today's car is likely to be more fuel efficient, safer and have more mod-cons. Looking to the future, you may be able to purchase a car that drives itself within the next decade.

Clearly, the family car of today, yesterday and tomorrow isn't the same animal (even if it's still called the Puma, Mustang, Chihuahua or whatever). Simply comparing the prices over time tends to overstate inflation, because part of any price increase can be attributed to the increase in quality (also see the later section 'Understanding why inflation is usually overestimated'). Statisticians at the ONS attempt to adjust for quality improvements, but doing so is incredibly difficult.

On the other side of the coin, you may have noticed that a number of items in your local supermarket have shrunk in recent years. World food prices have increased in recent years and a number of companies responded by reducing the size of their products instead of increasing the price! This method could potentially disguise inflation: if your favourite chocolate bar has halved in size but remains the same price, like-for-like it has doubled in price! Again, the statisticians at the ONS adjust for changes in the size of products when calculating inflation, and because the size of an item is easily quantifiable, doing so is much easier than adjusting for quality.

Assessing different measures

Economists use different ways of calculating inflation. In the earlier section 'Compiling a basket of products and services', we describe how the main measure of inflation in the UK, the CPI, is calculated. Luckily, the other measures are calculated in a similar way, though some important differences apply too.

Having more than one inflation measure raises an important question: which one is right? The truth is that economists don't think that one is 'right' and the others are 'wrong'. Instead, the different measures use different methodologies, and one is more appropriate in one situation and another in a different situation.

Here are the three most commonly used measures and some key information about each one.

CPI

As its name suggests, the Consumer Price Index (CPI) is an index. Therefore, the value of the CPI at any point in time on its own isn't very helpful. What really matters is the percentage change in the index over time: from one year to another or one month to the next.

The base year for the CPI is 2005, which means that its value was set to 100 in 2005. Statisticians chose this year arbitrarily; they could've picked any other year without impacting on the rate of inflation from one year to the next. The base year just provides a useful benchmark: for example, if the current CPI value is 130, prices are now on average 30 per cent higher than in 2005.

The CPI purposefully excludes a large component of many households' expenditure: mortgage interest payments. To understand why, read Chapter 10 on monetary policy. But for this discussion, just bear in mind that if policy makers want to reduce inflation, the key tool at their disposal is to increase the interest rate in the economy. For a number of reasons, this causes the prices of goods and services to fall (or increase by less). But, of course, it also means higher mortgage interest payments. If mortgage interest payments were included in the CPI, it might give the impression that inflation could increase after an increase in the interest rate. To avoid this effect, mortgage interest payments are excluded from the CPI calculation.

RPI

The *Retail Price Index* (RPI) is a much older measure of inflation than the CPI. In the UK it has been calculated since 1947 (with a current base year of 1987). In comparison, the CPI is a relatively recent measure going back only as far as 1996. Unlike the CPI, the RPI does include mortgage interest payments. Other items included in the RPI but not in the CPI include charges for financial services.

Historically, policy makers have used the RPI for a number of purposes, including the indexation of pensions (so they don't lose their real value), in wage negotiations and price increases in regulated industries. The RPI continues to be an important economic statistic, although its importance has diminished in recent years in favour of the CPI.

One of the reasons for the preference for the CPI is that many countries use it to calculate official inflation statistics. Therefore, comparing inflation across countries is easier with the CPI.

GDP deflator

Another widely used measure of inflation is the GDP deflator (check out Chapter 4 for all the gen on GDP). The *GDP deflator* is calculated in a quite different way to the CPI and RPI, because it uses the already available data on nominal GDP and real GDP in order to infer the rate of inflation.

As we describe in Chapter 4, *real GDP* is the total value of goods produced in a year using constant prices, and *nominal GDP* is the total value of goods produced in a year using current prices. By definition, they're equal in the base year.

Imagine that the base year is 2000 and that real and nominal GDP at that time equalled £1 trillion. Suppose that in 2001, real GDP comes in at £1.02 trillion and nominal GDP at £1.03 trillion. Can you say anything about how much inflation occurred between 2000 and 2001? Well, yes you can: nominal GDP has increased over the year by 3 per cent, potentially due to two factors:

- ✔ **Actual amount of goods and services produced increased:** That is, real GDP growth happened.
- ✔ **Average price level increased:** That is, inflation occurred.

The real GDP figures are available for all to see, so you can quite quickly tell that because real GDP increased by 2 per cent (from £1 trillion to £1.02 trillion), inflation must have been approximately 1 per cent in order to give a nominal GDP increase of 3 per cent (from £1 trillion to £1.03 trillion).

Extending this logic, the GDP deflator is defined as follows:

$$GDP\ deflator = Nominal\ GDP\ /\ Real\ GDP$$

This equation essentially creates an index that equals 1 in the base year. If inflation exists, nominal GDP increases by more than real GDP, which raises the level of the index. Similarly, deflation lowers the value of the index. If the index remains unchanged, the price level is unchanged, because nominal GDP and real GDP have increased by the same proportion. The percentage change in the GDP deflator from year to year is the rate of inflation that year.

A nice thing about the GDP deflator is that when you have data for nominal and real GDP, calculating it is straightforward – you don't need to go out and survey all the prices in the shops and so on. One major limitation, however, is that the GDP deflator picks up inflation only on domestically produced goods and not imported goods.

Understanding why inflation is usually overestimated

Many economists think that measures of inflation tend to overestimate the true increase in the cost of living. That is, if the inflation rate is quoted as being 3 per cent, economists think that the true cost of living has actually increased by less than 3 per cent.

Here are some of the reasons why:

- **The substitution effect:** Inflation at 3 per cent means that on average prices have increased by 3 per cent. But some prices will have increased by more and some prices will have increased by less (or even decreased). In response to these changes, people alter their behaviour by buying relatively more of the goods that haven't increased in price by much and relatively less of the goods that have increased in price by a lot: hence the name 'the substitution effect'. This means that inflation overestimates the true increase in the cost of living as people switch to relatively cheaper goods.

- **Unobservable quality improvements:** As we mention in the earlier 'Adjusting for quality and size' section, inflation needs to be calculated like-for-like. Although statisticians try to adjust for quality improvements, doing so fully is impossible. Thus some unobserved quality improvements remain unaccounted for. This means that inflation overestimates the true increase in the cost of living. An example helps make this clear: Suppose you had £1,000 to spend from either the 2015 Argos catalogue or the really cheap 1973 Argos catalogue your Grannie told you about. Which would you choose? Prices were much lower then, so you could buy lots more stuff, but it would be lots of low-quality stuff you would not want. So even though the 2015 selection is much more expensive, part of this is compensated by the higher quality.

- **Introduction of new goods:** As time passes, new goods or services are created that didn't exist in the past. When this happens, consumers are better off because they now have a new option to spend their money on. Although these new goods may eventually be included in the 'basket of goods' (see 'Compiling a basket of products and services' earlier in this chapter), the value of the new option isn't accounted for in the inflation statistics. This means that inflation overestimates the true increase in the cost of living because it doesn't take into account that consumers are better off due to the introduction of new goods.

Connecting inflation to interest rates

There is an intimate link between inflation and interest rates in an economy, which you can read about in detail in Chapter 10 on monetary policy. Here, we introduce two different interest rates: the real interest rate and the nominal interest rate, and show the relationship between the two and inflation.

Interest rates in an economy are important because they influence all sorts of things: how much it costs to borrow money, the incentives firms face to invest, the exchange rate and of course the rate of inflation.

Imagine that you're thinking about where to put your savings. You find a bank willing to pay you 5 per cent interest if you deposit your money for one year – you put your money there thinking that it's a pretty good deal. The only thing is, during the same period of time inflation is also 5 per cent. Now you're thinking: is this really a good deal?

When you come to withdraw your money at the end of the year you certainly have 5 per cent more money than you put in. The problem is that prices have also increased by 5 per cent, which means that the amount of stuff you can buy is completely unchanged!

As we reiterate throughout this book, a general theme in economics is that 'the real things in life are what count'. In this case, you shouldn't really care about the nominal value of the money you get back, but you should care about the real value of the money: that is, what it allows you to buy (check out Chapter 4 for more details).

To distinguish between these two things, economists talk about two kinds of interest rate:

- ✔ **Nominal interest rate:** Percentage return on your savings in terms of *money*. In the example, it's the interest rate the bank offers you (5 per cent).

- ✔ **Real interest rate:** Percentage return on your savings in terms of *goods*. In the example, it's equal to zero per cent, because inflation has completely wiped out your nominal gains.

Economists express the relationship of the real interest rate, nominal interest rate and inflation with the following simple equation, called the *Fisher equation* (note that, by convention, economists call inflation π [nothing to do with pi (3.14. . .)] you may remember from school):

$$i = r + \pi$$

This expression says that the nominal interest rate (i) is equal to the real interest rate (r) plus inflation (π). For example, if your bank offers you a rate of 4 per cent ($i = 4$), and inflation is 3 per cent ($\pi = 3$), your real interest rate is ($r = 1$). That is, you're able to purchase 1 per cent more goods after a year.

The real interest rate can even be negative. If your bank offers you a rate of 3 per cent ($i = 3$), and inflation is 4 per cent ($\pi = 4$), your real interest rate is ($r = -1$). That is, you're able to purchase 1 per cent fewer goods after a year.

Examining the Cause of Inflation: The Quantity Theory of Money

Is inflation an inevitable force of nature, or are there underlying causes that allow policy makers to have some control over it? In this section, you see that economists have a good idea about what causes inflation and how policy makers – if they are disciplined – can control it.

In this section we introduce you to the following:

- **The quantity theory of money:** Explains the underlying cause of inflation in the long run, which is the growth in the amount of money in the economy.

- **The quantity equation:** The relationship between money, how fast it circulates, prices and income.

We show what economists can discover from the quantity equation and why it isn't really an equation at all, but an identity!

Trying out the quantity equation

We derive the quantity theory of money as follows:

$$MV = PY$$

This quantity equation says that the amount of money (M) multiplied by the velocity of circulation (V) is equal to the price level (P) multiplied by total output (Y).

To see why this is true, take a look at the right-hand side of the quantity equation (PY). This is how much money you'd need in order to purchase all the output in the economy (at current prices). In other words, this is nominal GDP (check out Chapter 4).

In the left-hand side of the quantity equation (MV), V is the velocity of circulation, which measures how quickly money circulates around the economy, or in other words, how often money changes hands: the more that money changes hands, the more expenditure on goods and services in the economy. Therefore, MV represents the total amount of expenditure in the economy.

As we describe in Chapter 2, (the value of) total expenditure in an economy is just the same as (the value of) total output. The quantity equation expresses this idea succinctly.

The quantity equation is written in 'levels', however, whereas we want to know about the growth rate of prices (inflation), not the level of prices. But a simple trick allows you to go from levels to growth rates, which if applied to the quantity equation, yields:

$$g_M + g_V = g_P + g_Y$$

where g_X is the growth rate of variable X and g_P is the growth rate of prices (that is, inflation). Although the velocity of circulation (V) may vary from year to year, it's unlikely to grow in the long run. If you plug in $g_P = \pi$ and $g_V = 0$ and rearrange you have:

$$\pi = g_M - g_Y$$

This expression says that the rate of inflation (π) is equal to the rate of growth of money minus the growth rate of output.

Think about it this way: the price level tells you the rate at which you can convert money into goods. If the price level is high, you need a lot of money in order to buy goods and vice versa:

- ✔ If the amount of money in the economy (M) increases and the amount of goods (Y) stays unchanged, goods become relatively scarce and money is relatively abundant. This situation causes the prices of things to increase, because the rate at which you can turn money into goods worsens.

- ✔ If the amount of goods increases but the amount of money is unchanged, money becomes relatively scarce and goods are relatively abundant. This causes the price of things to fall because you're able to turn money into goods at a better rate.

Identifying the quantity equation as always being true

The quantity equation is a bit of a misnomer; really it should be called the *quantity identity*.

Converting the quantity equation from levels to growth rates

Here's the full derivation of how to convert the quantity equation from levels to growth rates. You need basic calculus to follow it.

The quantity equation links the money supply (M), the velocity of circulation (V), the price level (P) and real output (Y):

$$M_t V_t = P_t Y_t$$

The subscript t is added to make clear that these refer to the values of the variables at time t. Take the natural logarithm of both sides:

$$\ln(M_t V_t) = \ln(P_t Y_t)$$
$$\Rightarrow \ln(M_t) + \ln(V_t) = \ln(P_t) + \ln(Y_t)$$

Now, differentiate both sides with respect to time (t):

$$\frac{d[\ln(M_t)]}{dt} + \frac{d[\ln(V_t)]}{dt}$$
$$= \frac{d[\ln(P_t)]}{dt} + \frac{d[\ln(Y_t)]}{dt}$$

Using the chain rule:

$$\frac{d[\ln(M_t)]}{dM_t}\frac{dM_t}{dt} + \frac{d[\ln(V_t)]}{dV_t}\frac{dV_t}{dt}$$
$$= \frac{d[\ln(P_t)]}{dP_t}\frac{dP_t}{dt} + \frac{d[\ln(Y_t)]}{dY_t}\frac{dY_t}{dt}$$
$$\Rightarrow \frac{1}{M_t}\frac{dM_t}{dt} + \frac{1}{V_t}\frac{dV_t}{dt}$$
$$= \frac{1}{P_t}\frac{dP_t}{dt} + \frac{1}{Y_t}\frac{dY_t}{dt}$$

But these are just the growth rates of the respective variables:

$$g_M + g_V = g_P + g_Y$$

Here's the difference between an equation and an identity:

- **An equation:** Is true for *some* values of the variables (for example, $x + 5 = 7$ is an equation because it's only true for $x = 2$).

- **An identity:** Is *always* true whatever values the variables take (for example, the relationship between the temperature in Fahrenheit (F) and in Celsius (C): F = (9/5)C + 32 is always true by definition).

The quantity equation $MV = PY$ is an identity because it's true by definition – the left-hand side is total expenditure in the economy, and the right-hand side is the value of everything produced. These two things must always be equal no matter what values the variables take.

The relationship we derived from the quantity equation between inflation, growth in the money supply and output growth ($\pi = g_M - g_Y$) must, because it's derived from an *identity*, also always be true (assuming constant velocity).

Pointing the finger at policy makers for inflation

Milton Friedman, one of the great economists of the twentieth century, famously said, 'inflation is always and everywhere a monetary phenomenon'. To see exactly what he meant, we rearrange the quantity equation by dividing both sides by output (Y), which yields:

$$P = MV/Y$$

This expression reiterates that the price level can only increase for one of three reasons:

- ✔ An increase in the amount of money in the economy (M)
- ✔ An increase in the velocity with which money circulates (V)
- ✔ A fall in the total amount of output (Y)

In the long run (a period of more than a few years), economists think that government policy has little impact on V or Y:

- ✔ V is either relatively stable or, if it does change, it's not something that policy makers can easily control. For example, the introduction of credit and debit cards as well as online banking increased V because it made spending/transferring money easier.

- ✔ In the long run, output (Y) grows mainly due to technological progress – basically the economy becomes better at transforming factors of production such as capital and labour into output. Again, this isn't directly in the control of policy makers, although, of course, badly managed economies (for example, where corruption is rife and law and order weak) tend to do worse than well-managed ones. But when an economy is reasonably well managed, policy makers have difficulty boosting the long-run growth rate of output.

What policy makers *do* have a lot of control over is the amount of money in the economy (M), because the central bank has a monopoly over the creation of money in the economy. Therefore, policy makers can effectively choose M directly. (The full story is slightly more complicated, because the financial system has the ability to 'multiply' the amount of money through fractional reserve banking; see Chapter 14 for details.)

Thus, Friedman is really saying to policy makers: if your country is experiencing very high levels of inflation, it's your fault! It must be because you're increasing the money supply excessively. Furthermore, if you want to reduce the amount of inflation, you have to do one simple thing: stop printing so much money!

Although economists agree that in the long run growth in the money supply causes inflation, in the short run other things can cause inflation (see Chapter 9 for details).

Appraising Inflation: Good or Bad?

If you ask non-economists how they feel about inflation, they probably tell you that they hate (or at the very least, dislike) it. But despite agreeing that high levels of inflation are very costly and never a good idea, economists also see a couple of potential benefits in inflation.

In fact, although some economists suggest that the optimal inflation rate is zero, many believe that an economy should have a small positive amount, something that most central banks try to achieve.

In this section you discover the social costs and benefits of inflation.

Counting the costs of inflation

The reason laypeople typically give for not liking inflation is that it makes them poorer. This is a valid concern, especially because the wage specified in an employment contract is almost always the nominal wage – for example, 'this year you'll be paid £15/hour' – which will, of course, buy a lot less at the end of the year than at the beginning of the year, if inflation is high.

Economists, however, look at inflation slightly differently, because over time nominal wages (the wage in money terms) tend to at least keep up with inflation. In fact, most of the time, nominal wages tend to rise faster than inflation – which is the same as saying that the real wage (the wage in terms of goods) tends to rise over time.

Sometimes real wages do fall, though. For example, you may have noticed that in the years after the 2008 financial crisis, real wages fell for many people in the UK and other places. Although this represents a struggle for many families, economists discern a possible silver lining – more on this in the later section 'Appreciating two benefits of inflation'.

Shoe-leather costs

Cash is great. With cash you can easily purchase goods, which is why economists say that cash is highly *liquid*. What's not so good about cash is that holding it offers no return: a £10 note today is still a £10 note next year.

Without inflation the real value of cash would remain constant over time. But with inflation, the real value of cash falls over time: a £10 note buys you less next year than it does today. Economists care about this because inflation, especially high levels of it, means that people and firms have to spend time and effort continually adjusting their money holdings so inflation doesn't erode too much of their wealth.

Suppose that you have £50,000 of savings. You can decide to keep it all in cash (or, similarly, in a current account that pays little or no interest). The good thing would be that you always have cash handy to make a purchase. But this may not be a great idea – if inflation is high every year, your savings would be worth less and less.

Another possibility is that you keep all your savings in an illiquid savings account that pays you a good rate of return. This way you're maximising the return from your savings. But every time you want to buy something, you'd need to withdraw funds from your savings account, which is ridiculous. Can you imagine having to visit your bank before buying anything?

The best thing to do would probably be something in the middle. Keep most of your savings in a high-returning account while maintaining a reasonable amount as cash or in your current account. Nevertheless, even in this case you need to manage your finances carefully – making sure to transfer money as and when it's needed.

The time and hassle of thinking about and making these transfers to your money holdings comes under the heading *shoe-leather costs*. This funny name refers to the fact that travelling backwards and forwards to your bank wears down the leather soles of your shoes! Even though today people don't tend to visit their bank physically to withdraw funds, the name has stuck.

Menu costs

Imagine that you run a business that prints a catalogue of its prices for different goods and services (a restaurant menu is an obvious example). Without inflation, your life would be relatively simple: print the catalogue once and then use the same one for a long period of time. Whether customers buy something today or in ten years doesn't matter; the prices won't have changed!

Of course, even with no inflation and prices not rising on average, some items may still fall in price and others rise. But even then you probably don't have to update your prices that often. Contrast this with the case where inflation is, say, 10 per cent. Now, if you don't update your prices, the real price of your goods will fall by 10 per cent every year. Unsurprisingly, prices are updated much more often in countries experiencing high levels of inflation.

The time, effort and cost of continually having to update your prices due to inflation are called the *menu costs* of inflation.

Other costs

Here are some more costs of inflation:

- **Relative price distortions:** Linked to the idea behind menu costs, if some firms are changing their prices and others aren't, relative prices change from their 'true' value. So, for example, the 'true' relative price of milk versus eggs might be that 4 pints of milk costs the same as 6 eggs. Inflation means that milk and egg manufacturers should both increase their prices.

  But perhaps only the milk manufacturer increases its price, so that now 3 pints of milk = 6 eggs. Economists call this situation a *distortion*, because relative prices no longer reflect the correct trade-off between goods.

- **Arbitrary redistribution of wealth:** Because almost all contracts are set using nominal prices, inflation can arbitrarily redistribute between two parties in a contract. For example, if you take out a loan at a time when inflation is expected to be low, but inflation turns out to be high, the real value of your repayments to the lender will fall. Similarly, if you take out a loan when inflation is expected to be high and it turns out low, your real repayments increase.

  The same applies to wage contracts – if inflation is unexpectedly high, the real wage falls. Although one party always benefits when the other party loses, economists consider this situation to be costly to both parties, because it makes them more uncertain about the future.

- **Planning for the future becomes difficult:** High and volatile inflation causes problems, because how much money will be worth in the future in real terms isn't clear. As a result, retirement planning is especially difficult.

  Imagine that you plan your retirement carefully to ensure that you have exactly £2,000 per month. You're meticulous and 30 years later you achieve your goal, only to find that the money doesn't go nearly as far as you'd imagined in your youth.

Appreciating two benefits of inflation

Even the most awful thing can have benefits – the proverbial silver lining. Your football team losing in the Cup semifinals means that you save the exorbitant price of an FA Cup final ticket; the high cost of property in London means that the capital doesn't have to endure 'Brangelina' joining its ranks; James Blunt releasing a new album means . . . , means. . . , no, sorry, can't think of an upside there.

Economists identify at least two benefits of inflation: allowing otherwise 'sticky' prices to adjust and giving policy makers more room for manoeuvre by allowing them to set negative real interest rates.

Adjusting sticky prices

One of the great things about a well-functioning market economy is that prices adjust to ensure that supply equals demand. If a resource becomes relatively scarce, its price rises. Equally, if people's tastes change and they no longer want to buy a certain good, its price falls. In this way, resources are allocated optimally.

Economists have noticed that some prices are very 'sticky' as regards price falls. A good example is nominal wages. Sadly, sometimes, real wages in certain industries need to fall, perhaps because the demand for labour has fallen or the supply of people willing to work has increased. People tend to fight hard against any fall in their nominal wage (say, from £10/hour to £9.50/hour), but they don't seem to care so much if their nominal wage stays constant and inflation reduces their real wage (wages stay at £10/hour, but because of inflation this amount now buys less).

Inflation therefore allows the real wage to fall without cutting the nominal wage. This is a good thing, because if a fall in demand for labour occurs, instead of unemployment going through the roof (the likely outcome if the real wage isn't able to adjust), the labour market is able to adjust and keep unemployment low.

Another good example is house prices – people are very reticent to sell their house for a lower (nominal) price than the price they bought for. Imagine a fall in demand for houses, which dictates that real house prices should fall. In the absence of inflation, nominal house prices would also need to fall. But because nominal house prices are sticky downwards, sellers refuse to reduce their asking prices and buyers aren't willing to pay over the odds. Net result: the housing market stops functioning well.

If, however, inflation is 2 per cent and real house prices need to fall by 2 per cent, this can be achieved without a fall in nominal house prices. Without inflation, nominal house prices would need to fall by 2 per cent in order for real house prices to fall by 2 per cent!

Negative real interest rates

One of the main tools policy makers have at their disposal to boost the economy is lowering interest rates. (For a detailed look at monetary policy, see Chapter 10.) But here, briefly, we rearrange the Fisher equation ($i = r + \pi$; see the earlier section 'Connecting inflation to interest rates') to give:

$$r = i - \pi$$

In other words, the real interest rate (r) is equal to the nominal interest rate (i) minus inflation (π). In order to really boost the economy, policy makers would like to have a negative real interest rate. Among other things this would encourage households to spend now, because the real returns on saving are now negative.

If inflation is positive, achieving a negative real interest rate is easy: just set the nominal interest rate to be less than inflation. But with no inflation ($\pi = 0$), having a negative real interest rate is impossible; policy makers can't choose a nominal interest rate of less than zero – because it would mean putting £100 into your bank account and getting back, say, £95. People would prefer to keep cash under their mattress!

Rising to Extremes: Hyperinflation

Hyperinflation refers to extremely high inflation. No agreed precise definition exists of what constitutes hyperinflation, but people in an economy experiencing it typically notice that the prices of things rise on a daily basis. Something that costs £1 today may cost £1.20 tomorrow, £3 by the end of the week and £90 by the end of the month!

In this section you see how a government suffering from fiscal problems can fund itself in the short term by running the money printing presses and how this behaviour leads to inflation and then hyperinflation. We describe how this behaviour worsens the government's fiscal problems and leads to a vicious cycle whereby more and more money needs to be printed. In the end, the only way to stop hyperinflation is to fix the underlying fiscal problems that led to the need for printing money in the first place!

Seigniorage: Financing the government by printing money

When governments generally behave themselves, they fund their economies from the tax revenue they collect. If they're feeling slightly naughty, they fund themselves by borrowing money from whomever will lend it to them.

If they're feeling very naughty (or perhaps no one is willing to lend to them, because they're seen as a bad risk), governments fund themselves by printing money – known as *seigniorage* (and you thought it was the name of a French actress!). For more on the three potential sources of funds, turn to Chapter 11.

The bottom line is that a government usually turns to printing money when the following two situations apply:

- ✔ **It's running a budget deficit:** Government spending is greater than tax revenue.

- ✔ **No one is willing to lend it money on reasonable terms:** Potential lenders don't believe that they're likely to be paid back.

In other words, if the government wasn't running a budget deficit, it wouldn't have to borrow money, and if someone was willing to lend to it at reasonable rates it wouldn't have to print money to cover its budget deficit. As you can guess, governments tend not to use seigniorage unless it's the only remaining option, for the simple reason that seigniorage never ends well. . .

Seeing how seigniorage can lead to hyperinflation

As we describe in the earlier section 'Trying out the quantity equation', the quantity equation ($MV = PY$) means that the rate of inflation is equal to the rate of growth of the money supply minus the rate of growth of output:

$$\pi = g_M - g_Y$$

Seigniorage on any meaningful scale means a massive increase in the amount of money in the economy: that is, a massive increase in g_M. In turn, this causes a massive increase in inflation. The intuition is clear: if the government prints large amounts of money, it devalues the money already in existence by making it worth less.

Things might be okay if this was the end of the story. Unfortunately, it's not. High inflation makes collecting tax revenue very difficult, owing to a time lag in the collection of taxes. For example, you may work all year but only pay your income tax at the end of the year. Or a business may pay its VAT bill after a few months. In normal times these short delays have little impact, but in an economy with high levels of inflation, even short delays destroy the real value of tax receipts.

Now the government's initial problem is ten times worse: it has a worse budget deficit than it started with, financial markets still won't lend to it and inflation has taken off. In the short term, the government can do very little except to engage in even more seigniorage.

The vicious cycle is now in full motion, with large amounts of seigniorage leading to large amounts of inflation, which further reduces real tax revenue and requires even more seigniorage. Unchecked, hyperinflations can easily become explosive – where the price level doubles every couple of hours. Money stops functioning as a store of value, medium of exchange and unit of account, and people switch to bartering or using another country's currency – usually the US dollar.

Stopping hyperinflation after it starts

Milton Friedman was right when he said that 'inflation is always and everywhere a monetary phenomenon'. Hyperinflation is indeed always caused by a massive and sustained increase in the money supply.

But, in the case of hyperinflation, the underlying problem is the government's fiscal problems: it's spending more than it earns in tax revenue and is unable to borrow. Therefore, to stop hyperinflation in a country where it has taken hold, the answer is to attack the problem at its source – by reducing government expenditure substantially or increasing tax revenue. Because the latter is very difficult to do during hyperinflation, the only real option is substantial and massive cuts in government expenditure. Only when the government is again living within its means and doesn't need to fund its deficit by printing money can it rid itself of the scourge of hyperinflation.

If it doesn't do so, and quickly, the country's people will ultimately force the government's hand by no longer accepting any amount of local currency as payment. When people completely lose faith in the currency, they may switch to using US dollars for example, a phenomenon known as *dollarisation*. When this happens, even seigniorage isn't an option, which is sadly exactly what happened to Zimbabwe in the not-so-distant past.

Going Downwards: Deflation

Households, firms and policy makers tend to focus on the dangers of high inflation. Rarely do you hear people worrying about *deflation*, that is, falling prices, but it can be just as bad as high inflation.

The Japanese economy has been struggling with deflation since 1998. Although Japan is still one of the world's rich economies, enjoying high living standards, GDP per capita growth from 1998–2014 averaged a fraction of 1 per cent per year. Essentially, average real income in Japan today is very similar to that in 1998!

The Japanese stock market crash (for details see the nearby sidebar 'Riding a Japanese rollercoaster') saw the start of a prolonged period of economic stagnation that has essentially continued until today. (Currently Japan is trying to revive its economy through a number of policies called Abenomics, after the Prime Minister Shinzo Abe, but whether these reforms will succeed in revitalising the Japanese economy is still unclear.)

Very low output growth coupled with low inflation or deflation led to economists talking about Japan's 'lost decade', although that's far too generous – sadly, it's more like a 'lost quarter of a century' now. Although the causes of Japan's malaise are complicated, economists have noted that deflation played a significant part. The reason is the impact of deflation on the real interest rate.

Here's why. You can write the Fisher equation (from 'Connecting inflation to interest rates' earlier in this chapter) as follows:

$$r = i - \pi$$

Riding a Japanese rollercoaster

Japan has an unusual and interesting economic history. The Japanese economy was devastated by the Second World War – much of its capital stock had been destroyed. In the postwar period, Japan went from an economic disaster to one of the world's richest economies in under 30 years.

By the 1980s Japan hosted much of the world's most successful electronics companies. The 1980s also saw a massive asset price bubble

develop. The Nikkei, the index of the largest companies listed on the Japanese stock exchange, increased in value six-fold and reached a peak of close to 39,000 in 1989. Soon after, the bubble burst spectacularly and the Nikkei never recovered its previous high. In 2009, the Nikkei was at around 7,000, having lost about 80 per cent of its value over the previous 20 years!

Because the nominal interest rate (*i*) cannot be negative, deflation ($\pi < 0$) means that the real interest rate must be positive. What Japan really needed during these difficult years was an economic boost, which having a negative real interest rate could have provided. Instead, deflation meant that this was impossible and the resulting real interest rates led to falls in consumer confidence (why buy now, when things will be cheaper in the future?) as well as a fall in investment (firms could potentially earn more just by holding cash than from an investment project).

One of the main aims of Abenomics is to create inflation by massively increasing the money supply and thereby reducing real interest rates. Some evidence suggests that this approach is starting to work – Japan now has small but positive inflation. To ensure that deflation doesn't reoccur, Japan now needs to entrench inflation into people's expectations – no easy task when prices have been falling for around 15 years!

Chapter 6

Unemployment: Wasting Talent and Productivity

*I*f you've ever been unemployed, you know that it can be a disheartening experience. Despite being willing and able to do plenty of jobs in return for the market wage in that industry, for whatever reason no job materialises.

The 'standard logic' in economics is that the wage rate should adjust to ensure that the *supply of labour* equals the *demand for labour*. In other words, the number of people willing to work at the going wage should exactly equal the number of people that firms want to hire at that wage (we discuss this theory in more detail in this chapter). In theory, this logic eliminates all involuntary unemployment – the only people who are unemployed would be those who don't want to work at the going wage. But this situation is clearly not the case in reality. So the big question is: what stops the labour market from ensuring that everyone who's willing and able to work at the going wage gets a job?

This chapter gives you a good idea about the answer to this and other questions that may have been bothering you about unemployment. We describe two different ways of measuring a country's level of unemployment and two methods that economists use to classify unemployment. We also discuss how policy makers can use the information that economists provide to help combat unemployment.

Understanding the Importance of Unemployment: Opportunity Cost

Macroeconomists are highly preoccupied by the costs of unemployment, as well as ways in which it can be effectively reduced, for a number of reasons.

First and foremost, unemployment can be deeply distressing for those experiencing it. On average, people who are unemployed have worse mental and physical health, are more likely to experience divorce and report lower levels of life satisfaction in surveys. This reason on its own is sufficient incentive for policy makers to attempt to reduce unemployment.

In addition, unemployment involves a large economic cost: the additional output that would have been produced had these people been working. Economists call this the *opportunity cost* of unemployment. The unemployed person could've helped to build a road, produced something of value or taught someone a skill and so on. And even though they can do all these things when they eventually find a job, they never recover the time lost to unemployment.

Countries with high levels of unemployment, where perhaps 20 per cent or more of the labour force is unemployed, are wasting a huge amount of human talent and productivity. Just think about all the goods and services the unemployed could produce if they were able to find work.

Comparing Two Different Measures of Unemployment

In order to talk about the 'level of unemployment' in any meaningful way, you have to be able to measure the amount of unemployment in an economy. You may think that an obvious way is to count the number of unemployed people – and you'd be right. The only thing is that different definitions apply to what it means to be unemployed!

To give you some idea about the potential difficulties, think about whether you consider the following people to be unemployed or not:

   ✔ A 66-year-old person claiming a pension. Does it make a difference if the person is looking for work or not?

> ✔ Someone who has a few hours of work every week but would really like a full-time job.
>
> ✔ A full-time student. What about a part-time student?
>
> ✔ Someone who's too ill to work.

Any measure of unemployment has to clarify where each of these people (and others) should feature in the unemployment statistics. In this section we introduce and compare the two main measures of unemployment used in the UK: the International Labour Organization (ILO) measure and the Claimant Count.

ILO: Looking at the big picture

The International Labour Organization (ILO) is an agency of the United Nations (UN). The ILO definition of unemployment is standardised and used by all the major world economies.

The fact that it's standardised means that economists and others can make meaningful comparisons about unemployment in different countries. For example, in late 2014 unemployment in the UK was around 6 per cent while unemployment in Spain was much higher, at around 23 per cent. The fact that these figures are calculated using the same methodology allows people to make statements such as 'the unemployment rate in Spain is around four times the unemployment rate in the UK'.

The ILO classifies each person over the age of 16 into one of three categories:

- ✔ **Employed:** Someone who carries out more than an hour (yes, one hour) of paid work a week, or is temporarily away, for example on holiday. People on government training schemes are also considered employed as well as those who work for their family business.

- ✔ **Unemployed:** Someone who's not employed (by the above definition) is able to work and is actively seeking work. In the UK this means someone who has looked for work in the past four weeks and is available to start work in the next two weeks.

- ✔ **Economically inactive:** Not a person so broke that he can't afford to move, but someone who's neither employed nor unemployed (by the above definitions). Examples of people in this category include full-time students who aren't looking for work, the retired, the sick and disabled, and housewives/husbands.

Economists call people in the employed and unemployed categories *economically active*. They then define the unemployment rate as the proportion of the economically active who are unemployed, as follows:

$$unemployment\ rate = \frac{unemployed}{economically\ active} = \frac{unemployed}{unemployed + employed}$$

The unemployment rate isn't the proportion of the population that's unemployed or even the proportion of all adults who are unemployed. This means that a country can have a low unemployment rate but also many more people not working than working; for example, when it has a lot of retired people and children under the age of 16.

To calculate the unemployment rate, government statisticians carry out a survey called the Labour Force Survey (LFS). Every country in the European Union (EU) is legally obliged to carry out a Labour Force Survey.

In the UK, in any three-month period the LFS interviews around 41,000 households. They ask the members of the household a number of questions about their circumstances and how much they work. According to their answers, the people are placed in one of three categories: employed, unemployed or economically inactive.

In total, the LFS samples around 80,000 individuals over the age of 16. They then weight the results so they're representative of the UK as a whole. Finally, they adjust the results seasonally to take into account predictable variations in employment over the year (for example, many retail stores hire large numbers of people every year before Christmas).

Although a final number is quoted as the unemployment rate, it's just an estimate. If the LFS had interviewed different people, the results would have been slightly different.

Therefore, statisticians calculate a range of values called a *confidence interval*, where they're 95 per cent sure that the true level of unemployment lies somewhere in this range.

Claimant Count: Talking about benefits

The *Claimant Count* is another measure of unemployment that's used in the UK. To be included in the Claimant Count, you need to be receiving benefit payments primarily because you're unemployed. This typically means that you're claiming Jobseeker's Allowance (JSA).

People qualify for JSA in two ways:

✔ **Contribution-based JSA:** If you've made sufficient National Insurance (NI) contributions in the previous two years, you can claim this benefit for a period of six months. The payment isn't *means tested*, which means that your claim doesn't depend on your income or wealth.

✔ **Income-based JSA:** This benefit is means tested – if you have more than a certain amount of savings or your partner has a job, you may not be eligible.

Some people are counted in the Claimant Count but aren't receiving JSA: people who are unemployed and looking for work but not eligible for either type of JSA. Instead they claim NI credits (that is, national insurance payments are made on their behalf) so they don't lose their eligibility for a state pension.

But times they are a-changin'. The UK government is in the process of rolling together a number of benefits into a single payment called Universal Credit, which includes income-based JSA. So far only people living in certain areas have been switched to Universal Credit, but the intention – as its name suggests – is for it to be universal!

Regardless of the change, the principle remains that the Claimant Count counts the number of people claiming benefits primarily because they're unemployed. Thus the calculation of the Claimant Count is relatively straightforward: just add up the number of people claiming benefits. To get the unemployment rate according to the Claimant Count, divide by the economically active population (which we define in the preceding section).

Comparing the two measures

In many cases, someone who's unemployed according to the ILO definition is also unemployed according to the Claimant Count, and vice versa. But in certain cases, the two measures disagree, for example:

✔ A person working only a handful of hours a week, but looking for full-time employment. The ILO definition considers this person to not be unemployed (he's working more than one hour a week). However, this person can possibly be counted in the Claimant Count as unemployed if he's working less than 16 hours a week and has a low income.

✔ A person looking for work but whose partner is employed may not be eligible for unemployment benefits (and so not deemed unemployed by the Claimant Count), but would be unemployed according to the ILO definition.

> ✔ A person of retirement age looking for work is considered unemployed according to the ILO definition, but because he can't claim unemployment benefits, he wouldn't be included in the Claimant Count.

The total number of unemployed people according to the ILO definition tends to be much larger than according to the Claimant Count (see Figure 6-1) for a variety of reasons, including the following:

> ✔ Eligibility rules mean that a large number of people who are looking for work can't claim benefits.

> ✔ Some people eligible to claim unemployment benefits choose not to.

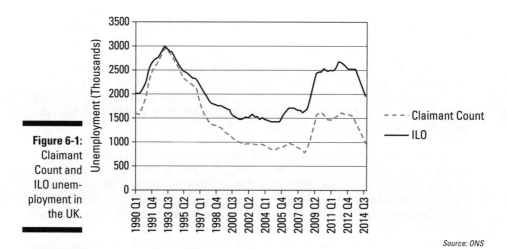

Figure 6-1: Claimant Count and ILO unemployment in the UK.

Source: ONS

Distinguishing Two Different Types of Unemployment

Economists classify unemployment into different types depending on the underlying cause of the unemployment. The actions that policy makers may want to take in order to reduce unemployment depend on the cause of unemployment.

We take a closer look in this section at two particular types of unemployment that stand out:

> ✔ **Frictional unemployment:** Unemployment that arises due to labour market *frictions* (issues or problems), such as potential employees not being well informed about all available jobs, employers not being able easily to observe the ability of potential employees and potential employees having limited geographical mobility.

✔ **Structural unemployment:** Unemployment that arises due to failure of the labour market to adjust to an equilibrium where the demand for labour is equal to the supply of labour. In other words, the failure of wages to adjust to ensure that the number of people willing and able to work at the market wage is exactly equal to the number of people that firms want to hire at that wage.

Figure 6-2 shows the theoretical position: the quantity of labour demanded at the wage rate w^* is exactly equal to the quantity of labour supplied at the wage rate w^*. Thus everyone willing and able to work at the wage rate w^* is employed. Sadly, the real-world labour market doesn't work like this.

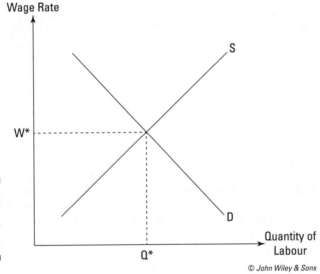

Figure 6-2:
Supply and demand for labour.

© John Wiley & Sons

Frictional unemployment: Finding a job is like finding a spouse

Not happy with simply analysing the economy, economists have also tried to apply economic reasoning to all kinds of areas not traditionally associated with the discipline. One of these areas is marriage. Strangely enough, it turns out that many of the difficulties people face when looking for a spouse are the same difficulties they face when looking for a job! Interested? Then read on!

The 'marriage market' is an example of a *two-sided matching market*: the market has two sides (men and women), each of whom is looking to match with someone from the other side of the market.

Figure 6-3 shows an example of a possible matching. Four men $\{m_1,m_2,m_3,m_4\}$ and four women $\{w_1,w_2,w_3,w_4\}$ want to match with each other. Man 1 and Woman 2 have decided to match; Man 2 and Woman 4 have decided to match and so on.

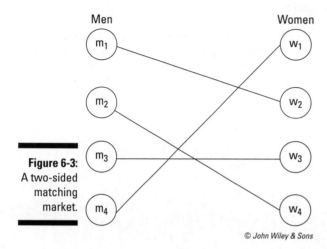

© John Wiley & Sons

Figure 6-3: A two-sided matching market.

In an ideal world all participants would be very well informed: they'd know a lot about all their potential matches – their personalities, what they look like, their job, their level of education and so on. With this information they should be able to form preferences regarding the other side of the market. So, for example, Woman 1 (w_1) may have the following preferences regarding the men:

$$m_2 > m_3 > m_1 > m_4$$

That is, her favourite man to be matched with is Man 2, and if not him then Man 3, and if not him then Man 1, and finally if all else fails, Man 4. Similarly, each man should be able to rank each of the women.

If everyone is well informed so they know not only their own ranking but also everyone else's rankings, the matching problem is relatively straightforward. You simply approach someone you like and whom you know also likes you. You match, get married, have kids and live happily ever after.

Of course, as you may have noticed, things aren't that simple! Or as an economist would say, the marriage market has frictions, such as:

✔ People aren't well informed about the other side of the market. Hence the reason people date each other – to find out more about them.

✔ Someone may be a really great match for you, but you don't even know the person exists. How sad!

✔ Two people who'd otherwise be a great match live too far away from each other and their commitments mean they can't easily move.

These frictions and others make the marriage market inefficient. A lot of good matches don't occur that otherwise should occur. Equally, some people get matched when they really shouldn't have been matched.

Like the marriage market, the labour market is also a two-sided matching market. Except this time the people who need to match are workers and employers. Workers have different preferences regarding the firms they'd like to match with – some would like an office-based job, others a job where they can travel, others a job at a small firm and so on. Firms also have preferences regarding the workers – an accountancy firm wants highly numerate workers, a tech firm wants people with advanced IT skills and so on.

Also like the marriage market, matching would be easy if workers had a lot of information about firms and firms had a lot of information about workers. Firms would be able to hire those workers who best fit with their needs and workers would be able to work for firms that complement their skills.

The problem is – like the marriage market – the labour market has frictions:

✔ **Firms don't have good information about workers and workers only have limited information about firms.** Hence the need for interviewing. But even an interview doesn't tell you that much: interviews are short and both sides are on their best behaviour.

✔ **A certain worker may be a very good match for a firm but doesn't hear about the vacancy.** Plus, the firm doesn't know about the worker's existence and thus they won't be matched.

✔ **Geographical constraints can stop a worker and a firm being an excellent match.** Workers often can't easily relocate.

These frictions make the labour market less efficient and increase the level of unemployment.

Policy makers have difficulty reducing frictional unemployment, but here are some possible ways:

✔ Making sure that jobs are widely advertised to the unemployed, for example at job centres.

✔ Encouraging people to gain respected qualifications that firms can use to identify good matches. For example, having a first-class degree in economics signals to an employer that you know your economics.

✔ Ensuring that unemployment benefits aren't so generous that they discourage workers from exerting effort in their job search. Generous unemployment benefits can increase unemployment because they reduce the incentive to look for work.

Structural unemployment: Experiencing a mismatch between labour supply and demand

The other major cause of unemployment is *structural unemployment*. This refers to a mismatch between the demand for labour and the supply of labour.

Figure 6-4 illustrates the situation. At the prevailing market wage w, firms would like to hire L_D amount of workers. However, many more workers are willing to work at the wage w; in particular, L_S people would like a job. The difference between the number of people willing and able to work (L_S) and the number of people firms want to hire (L_D) represents the structural unemployment in an economy.

If wages fell to the equilibrium wage w^e, demand for labour would exactly equal the supply of labour: in other words, everyone who wants to work is able to find a job and structural unemployment is eliminated. If only things were that simple!

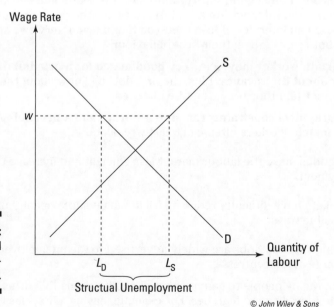

Figure 6-4: Structural unemployment.

Structural Unemployment

© John Wiley & Sons

Considering possible causes of structural unemployment

Structural unemployment has a number of possible causes. Here we discuss three that economists think are the most relevant: minimum wages, trade unions and efficiency wages. It would be wrong to suggest that economists think that these three always cause unemployment. Rather, excessively high levels of minimum wages, trade union power and efficiency wages are of potential concern. Here's why.

Minimum wages

The *minimum wage* is the legal minimum that a firm can pay a worker. In the UK, a firm must pay an adult over 21 at least £6.50 an hour, an adult aged 18–20 at least £5.13 an hour and someone under 18 at least £3.79 an hour (2014 rates).

The idea behind the minimum wage is a noble one – to increase the incomes of the lowest-paid workers and protect them from exploitation. However, a minimum wage can have unintended consequences. Here are two important points to note:

- ✔ **Not binding minimum wage:** When the minimum wage is below the equilibrium market wage for a given industry, it has no impact whatsoever (see where the diagonal lines for supply and demand intersect for Industry B in Figure 6-5). Everyone is already being paid more than the minimum wage.

- ✔ **Binding minimum wage:** In industries where the equilibrium market wage is below the minimum wage (where the supply and demand lines intersect for Industry A in Figure 6-5), the introduction of the minimum wage increases wages for those employed in that industry but at the same time it creates unemployment in those industries where the minimum wage is binding.

The minimum wage is lower for young people for good reason. On average young people tend not to be very experienced, which lowers their productivity and the wages that firms offer them. If the minimum wage for young people was the same as for all adults, high levels of unemployment would result among the young. That is, the market equilibrium wage would be far below the minimum wage for many young people.

Trade unions: Good for insiders, not so good for outsiders

One way of thinking about the role of trade unions is that they put pressure on firms to offer higher wages than the equilibrium wage. Firms are forced to do so because if they don't, the union may call a strike or take some other industrial action. Instead of risking costly industrial action, firms may well prefer to give in to the union's demand.

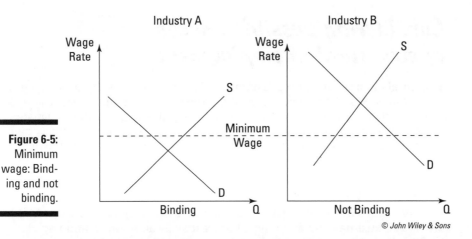

© John Wiley & Sons

Figure 6-5:
Minimum
wage: Bind-
ing and not
binding.

This is certainly good news for the union because its members now enjoy higher wages. However, the increase in the wage rate reduces the quantity of labour demanded by the firm. Furthermore, many people who'd be eager to work for the higher wage but are unable to are going to be unemployed. You can see this effect clearly in the earlier Figure 6-4.

For this reason, economists think that trade unions can be good for 'insiders' (those already employed who receive a higher wage) but bad for 'outsiders' (those who'd like to work in the industry but can't).

Efficiency wages: Paying more than you need to

A firm is said to pay *efficiency wages* when it voluntarily chooses to pay workers a higher wage than it needs to. This isn't necessarily due to altruism: paying efficiency wages can increase a firm's profits. It's also good for those workers who happen to receive the (higher) efficiency wage. However, in a similar way to trade unions, it's not so great for outsiders (those who would like to work at that wage but find there isn't enough demand for their labour at that higher wage).

In 1914, Henry Ford, the founder of the Ford Motor Company, did something that turned quite a few heads – he increased the wages of his workers to $5 per day. This was about double the market wage for similarly skilled workers at the time. Why would he do such a thing? He certainly didn't need to – the firm didn't have problems finding workers at the old wages.

Far from spelling disaster for the firm, Ford went from strength to strength over the next few decades. Economists have posited a number of theories about why a firm may want to pay over the odds to its workers:

✔ **Better nutrition:** Workers who are poorly paid tend to experience poor nutrition, which can result in low productivity. Boosting their incomes means they can afford to eat more nutritious food and do better work.

Of course, in rich countries today this argument doesn't seem that relevant, but in the past and in developing countries it could be the case.

✔ **Attract the best workers:** At the time Henry Ford introduced the $5-a-day wage, lots of mechanics were working for different firms in Detroit. When Ford started paying a lot more than its competitors, all the best mechanics in town looked to move to Ford – the firm could take its pick.

✔ **Give workers incentives not to shirk:** One of the problems that all firms face is how to ensure that workers exert sufficient effort. Watching everyone all the time is very difficult. So the firm needs some other way of incentivising employees. The ultimate sanction a firm can apply is firing someone. The thing is, losing your job isn't that big a deal if you can easily find another one paying a similar wage. By paying more than all the other firms, Henry Ford made sure that everyone was keen on keeping their jobs and thus keen on working hard.

Reducing the 'Natural' Rate of Unemployment

Unemployment varies from month to month and from year to year. Sometimes the economy is booming and firms are hiring a lot of people, and at other times they stop hiring or even let people go. This situation is normal and referred to as the *business cycle*. Unfortunately, policy makers can do little about short-term changes in unemployment caused by the business cycle.

What policy makers can influence, however, is the long-run average level of unemployment. Economists call this the *natural rate* of unemployment. Policies designed to reduce the natural rate of unemployment are called *supply-side policies*. This is because short-term fluctuations in unemployment tend to be due to the 'demand side' of the economy, while the average long-term level of unemployment is determined by the 'supply-side'. (More on this in Part III.)

Determining the natural rate of unemployment

Here's how economists work out the natural rate of unemployment. The labour force (L) is made up of those people who are employed (E) and those who aren't employed but would like to be (the unemployed, U):

$$L = E + U$$

Now, every month some of the employed people sadly lose their jobs and become unemployed. If *s* is the proportion of employed people who lose their job in any given month, then *sE* represents the number of people who lose their job: *s* is called the *rate of job separation*.

On the flipside, some of the unemployed will find work and become employed. If *f* is the proportion of employed people who find jobs in any given month, then *fU* represents the number of people who find a job: *f* is called the *rate of job finding*.

Clearly, if the number of people who find a job (*fU*) is greater than the number of people who lose their job (*sE*), unemployment falls and vice versa. Figure 6-6 shows the cyclical nature of employment numbers.

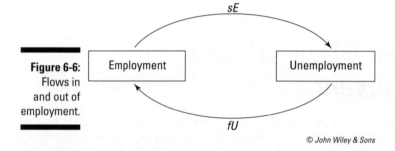

Figure 6-6: Flows in and out of employment.

© John Wiley & Sons

The interesting thing is, if in a certain month the flows from one state (employment or unemployment) to another are larger than the flows in the opposite direction, this impacts the flows in the following month. Eventually the flows in and out of employment (or unemployment) become equal.

For example, imagine starting in a situation with 1,000 unemployed and 1,000 employed. The rate of job finding is 0.2 and the rate of job separation is 0.1:

- ✔ In the first month, 200 unemployed people find a job, while 100 employed people lose their jobs. As a result, 900 people are now unemployed and 1,100 employed.

- ✔ In the second month, 180 unemployed people find a job, while 110 employed people lose their jobs. This leaves 830 unemployed and 1,170 employed.

- ✔ In the third month, 166 unemployed people find a job, while 117 employed people lose their jobs. This leaves 781 unemployed and 1,219 employed.

REMEMBER

This process continues. Notice that the number of unemployed people who find a job is falling every month and the number of employed people who lose their job is increasing every month. This is because the total stock of unemployed people is falling and the total stock of employed people is rising. Eventually, the number of people finding work is exactly equal to the number who lose their job:

$$sE = fU$$

Using this expression along with the fact that $L = E + U$ allows you to solve for the natural rate of unemployment (U/L): that is, the proportion of the labour force who are unemployed (for the full derivation, see the nearby sidebar 'Derivation of the natural rate of unemployment'):

$$\frac{U}{L} = \frac{s}{s+f}$$

From this equation, you discover that anything that increases the rate of job separation (s) increases the natural rate, while anything that increases the rate of job finding (f) decreases the natural rate.

Derivation of the natural rate of unemployment

The labour force (L) comprises the employed (E) and the unemployed (U):

$$L = E + U \qquad (1)$$

In equilibrium, the number of people finding a job is exactly equal to the number of people losing their job:

$$sE = fU$$

$$\Rightarrow E = \frac{fU}{s} \qquad (2)$$

Using equation (1), the unemployment rate can be written as

$$\frac{U}{L} = \frac{U}{E+U} \qquad (3)$$

Substituting equation (2) into equation (3) gives

$$\frac{U}{L} = \frac{U}{\dfrac{fU}{s} + U}$$

$$\Rightarrow \frac{U}{L} = \frac{1}{\dfrac{f}{s} + 1}$$

$$\Rightarrow \frac{U}{L} = \frac{1}{\dfrac{f+s}{s}}$$

$$\Rightarrow \frac{U}{L} = \frac{s}{s+f} \qquad (4)$$

Thinking about supply-side policies

Supply-side policies are ones designed to increase the productive capability of the economy. Applied to the labour market, supply-side policies attempt to reduce the rate of job separation (s) and increase the rate of job finding (f). (Check out the preceding section if these terms seem unfamiliar to you.)

Sometimes supply-side policies can be politically unpopular because they can negatively affect certain groups in the short run. However, in the long run, policy makers hope that by reducing unemployment (and increasing wages), the policies will benefit everyone. Here are some examples of supply-side policies to consider:

- **Curtailing trade union power:** As we mention in the earlier section 'Considering possible causes of structural unemployment', powerful trade unions can increase industry wages by threatening industrial action. This reduces the demand for labour and increases unemployment. Reducing trade union power should bring wages closer to the market equilibrium wage where everyone who's willing and able to work for that wage can find employment.

- **Reducing taxes on labour:** Taxes on labour such as income tax and National Insurance lead to *deadweight loss*, which means that they destroy some potential trades that would make both employer and employee better off.

  For example, suppose that Catherine is willing to work for you for £10/hour and you're willing to pay her £11/hour. Clearly, in this case you should employ her at £10.50 an hour – whereby you and Catherine both make a surplus of 50p/hour. However, now suppose that the government levies a 20 per cent tax on labour. Now you need to pay Catherine around £12/hour in order for her to take home £10/hour – something you're unwilling to do. Thus you don't employ her, and the potential surplus isn't realised and is lost forever.

- **Reducing taxes on capital:** Like taxes on labour, taxes on capital also lead to deadweight loss. Instead of firms investing in capital stock in the UK, they decide to place it elsewhere. This has a negative effect on real wages because it lowers the marginal product of labour. By reducing taxes on capital, the government can increase the demand for the labour needed to make use of the additional capital.

Of course, the government has to raise revenue from somewhere (to pay for the National Health Service, education, road building, defence and security, and so on). Whether it does so by taxing capital, labour or goods, some amount of deadweight loss is inevitable. The point is that policy makers should levy taxes carefully in order to minimise deadweight loss.

✔ **Being careful with benefits:** Overly generous benefits can be a strong disincentive to search for work. As a result, the rate of job finding reduces and the natural rate of unemployment increases. Of course, most people quite rightly want a fair benefit system that protects the most vulnerable in society, but economists start to worry when people able to work choose not to, or at least choose not to search seriously for work.

✔ **Ensuring labour market flexibility:** Perhaps surprisingly, making it very difficult to fire workers can increase the natural rate of unemployment. How? If firms know that firing someone who's unproductive is difficult, they become reticent to hire. This can reduce the rate of job finding and increase the natural rate of unemployment.

✔ **Removing subsidies:** Economists think that countries should specialise in producing those things that they can make comparatively better than other countries. For example, the UK is quite good at professional services such as consulting and accountancy but not very competitive at producing agricultural goods. Only the massive farming subsidies maintain the UK's reasonably large agricultural sector. Economists think that this situation diverts factors of production away from their most productive use. Not to mention the fact that it spends large amounts of taxpayers' money, leads to higher food prices (by blocking imports) and impoverishes farmers in poor countries. Removing subsidies reallocates capital and labour more efficiently and leads to lower unemployment and higher wages.

Part III
Building a Model of the Economy

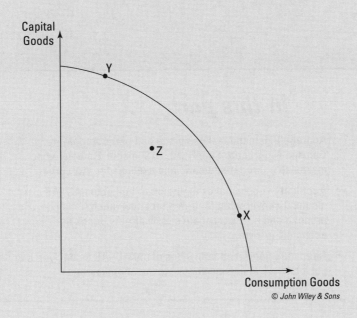

© John Wiley & Sons

The IS-LM model is an important model that shows how the economy responds to fiscal and monetary policy in the very short run. Check out the free article at www.dummies.com/extras/macroeconomicsuk for details.

In this part . . .

- ✔ Aggregate demand makes up one half of the Aggregate Demand–Aggregate Supply (AD–AS) model. Find out what makes up aggregate demand and examine the AD curve.

- ✔ Aggregate supply makes up the other half of the AD–AS model. Discover what factors affect how much firms can produce and how aggregate supply affects prices and economic growth.

- ✔ After you understand both sides of the AD–AS model, you can put it to work analysing shocks to the economy.

Chapter 7

Working Out a Country's Economic Demand

. . . .

In This Chapter

▶ Introducing aggregate demand

▶ Understanding its different components

▶ Looking at the aggregate demand curve

. . . .

*E*conomists love models. We don't mean the men and women who grace the world's catwalks (although some may – who are we to judge?), but models of how the economy behaves. The Aggregate Demand–Aggregate Supply (AD–AS) model is the workhorse model of macroeconomics. Economists love it because it's a simple model that can accurately predict how the economy will respond to different situations.

In this chapter you discover one half of the AD–AS model – aggregate demand (AD). As its name suggests, you can think of AD as representing the combined demand for goods and services of all economic agents: in other words, the combined demand of consumers, firms and the government. (To read about aggregate supply (AS), flip to Chapter 8.) We describe the various parts that make up aggregate demand and examine the AD-curve. Along the way you see why AD increases when the price level falls and how the exchange rate affects a country's net exports. Although we have to include a fair amount of maths, don't worry: we lead you through it and explain everything clearly step-by-step.

Looking into What Everyone Wants: Aggregate Demand

Economies run on people, firms and governments requiring and buying things. A need exists (demand) that firms fulfil (supply). Students of microeconomics spend time learning about the behaviour of supply and demand in individual markets. (See our other book *Microeconomics for Dummies*.)

Students of macroeconomics are interested in the economy as a whole, so the emphasis is on aggregate (that is, total) demand for goods and services and aggregate (total) supply.

More specifically, *aggregate demand* comprises the total demand for goods and services in an economy.

Aggregate demand is important because (along with aggregate supply) it determines a country's GDP and price level (and therefore its inflation rate). Changes in aggregate demand also impact the level of unemployment.

Without understanding aggregate demand, policy makers would not stand much of a chance of being able to control the economy. Indeed the main tools that policy makers have at their disposal (monetary and fiscal policy) work by influencing aggregate demand (see Chapters 9–11).

Meeting the Components of Aggregate Demand

Economists conveniently break aggregate demand down into four different components:

- ✔ **Consumption (*C*):** Household demand for goods and services.

- ✔ **Investment (*I*):** Firm demand for capital goods but also household demand for new housing.

- ✔ **Government purchases (*G*):** Government demand for goods and services.

- ✔ **Net exports (*NX*):** The demand of people living abroad for goods and services produced domestically, less domestic demand for foreign goods. That is, net exports (*NX*) = exports (*X*) – imports (*M*).

Adding all these components together gives total expenditure on goods and services. Now, the total expenditure on goods and services must equal total output or GDP (*Y*), and so the components of AD must add up to equal *Y*:

$$Y = C + I + G + NX$$

Or equivalently

$$Y = C + I + G + X - M$$

Taking imports out of the equation

One issue can easily seem a little confusing: why do imports (M) have to be taken away in $Y = C + I + G + X - M$ (equation [1])? After all, if Y is equal to total goods and services produced domestically, surely imports shouldn't feature here?

The reason is that total consumption (C) is actually equal to the consumption of domestically produced goods (C_D) and the consumption of imported goods (C_M):

$$C = C_D + C_M$$

The same is true for investment (I) and government spending (G):

$$I = I_D + I_M$$
$$G = G_D + G_M$$

Substituting these expressions into equation (1) gives:

$$Y = (C_D + C_M) + (I_D + I_M) + (G_D + G_M) + X - M$$

Really, the imported terms shouldn't be there because Y should equal total domestic output. The good news is that deducting all imports (M) takes them out of the equation. To see how, notice that:

$$M = C_M + I_M + G_M$$

Substituting this back into equation (2) gives:

$$Y = (C_D + C_M) + (I_D + I_M) + (G_D + G_M) + X - (C_M + I_M + G_M)$$

This cancels all the import terms, leaving:

$$Y = C_D + I_D + G_D + X$$

This expression makes clear that aggregate demand is the total demand for goods and services produced domestically. It includes domestic purchases by consumers, firms and the government ($C_D + I_D + G_D$) but also purchases by foreigners (X).

Tucking in! Consumption

Consumption (C) is the largest component of aggregate demand: in the UK it accounts for some two-thirds of output. In other words, around 60 per cent of everything produced in the UK ends up being consumed by households in one way or another. So whether you're slurping a soft drink, chomping on a chocolate bar or even gobbling some grapes, you're contributing to the country's consumption.

Consumption doesn't just include things you literally consume such as food and drink (and, if you're Homer Simpson, flowers!): all goods and services that households purchase are included in consumption. So the flat-screen TV you got for Christmas is consumption. That train ticket you bought last week – that's consumption. Even the rent you pay for your tiny overpriced flat in London counts as the consumption of 'housing services'.

Basically, if you buy something – and you aren't an entrepreneur buying something for your business – it's probably consumption.

Consumption function

The amount that households choose to consume depends on a number of different variables.

The most important is their *disposable income*, which is household income after tax. Total disposable income in an economy equals $Y - T$, where Y is total income (GDP) and T is total taxes households pay to the government.

You can express the relationship between consumption and disposable income mathematically with a *consumption function*:

$$C = C(Y - T)$$

In words, this expression says that consumption (C) is a function of disposable income ($Y - T$). Specifying the consumption function explicitly as a linear relationship shows how consumption varies with disposable income:

$$C = c_0 + c_1(Y - T)$$

c_0 is called the *level of autonomous consumption*, that is, consumption independent of the level of disposable income. c_1 is called the *marginal propensity to consume* and tells you how much consumption increases when disposable income increases by £1. It's a number between 0 and 1.

Figure 7-1 shows a graph of the consumption function. The line intersects the y-axis at c_0 and the slope of the line is equal to c_1. If autonomous consumption increases, this shifts the entire consumption function upwards, whereas an increase in the marginal propensity to consume makes the consumption function steeper.

You may be thinking, how can households consume even if they have no disposable income? Good question: they either use their savings or borrow against future income.

The consumption function makes clear that any increase in income (Y) raises consumption (C), but by less than the increase in income. Equally, any decrease in taxes (T) also increases consumption by raising disposable income: because the marginal propensity to consume is less than 1, this increase in consumption is less than the amount by which taxes have fallen.

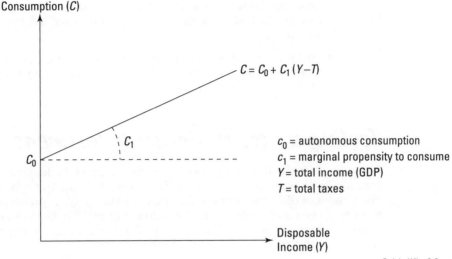

$$C = C_0 + C_1 (Y - T)$$

Consumption (C)

C_1

C_0

c_0 = autonomous consumption
c_1 = marginal propensity to consume
Y = total income (GDP)
T = total taxes

Disposable
Income (Y)

Figure 7-1:
The con-
sumption
function.

© John Wiley & Sons

Other determinants of consumption

A number of factors other than the ones we discuss in the preceding section also influence how much households consume:

- **Household wealth:** As well as the income households receive every year, they also have a stock of wealth: perhaps their house, their savings in the bank or their equity portfolio. The wealthier people are, the more you expect them to consume. As a result, when the stock market is performing strongly or house prices are increasing, consumption tends to rise.

- **Future income:** People don't just look at their current income when deciding how much to consume. Expectations about future disposable income can be just as important as disposable income today. For example, if Frieda is poor today but expects high income tomorrow, she may well consume a lot today. Similarly, if taxes are low today but you expect them to be high tomorrow, you may consume less today to pay for your impending taxes.

- **Interest rate:** The rate at which people can borrow money has a large impact on household consumption for a few reasons:

  - Low interest rates mean that borrowing money to fund higher consumption today is attractive.

  - Low interest rates mean that saving for the future is less attractive compared to consuming now.

- Low interest rates tend to increase the value of assets such as shares and houses, which increases household wealth and consumption.

- Low interest rates mean lower monthly mortgage interest payments for homeowners, which increases the money they have available for consumption.

Tooling up for business: Investment

Investment (*I*), the third-largest component of aggregate demand, accounts for roughly 15 per cent of GDP in the UK – though, being the most volatile component of GDP, this amount can vary substantially. Typically, during a *boom* (a period of above-average economic growth) investment can rise sharply, whereas during a *bust* (a period of below-average or negative economic growth) investment can fall sharply.

Investment is one of those words that economists use substantially differently to laypeople. To the latter, investment often refers to the purchase of shares in a company or buying a house in the hope that it will appreciate in value. To an economist, investment is the purchase of new *capital goods*, which are goods used to produce other goods and services in the future.

Examples of capital goods include machines, computers, buildings and so on. Firms carry out most capital goods investment; after all, they're trying to make stuff to sell to people, and in order to make stuff, they need capital goods. (Turn to Chapter 2 for further discussion on what economists mean by the terms *investment* and *capital*.)

There is one case where economists count purchasing a house as investment: buying a newly built house (more precisely they call it *residential investment*). The idea is that purchasing a new house provides you with a stream of 'housing services' in the future. In order to count as investment, the house has to be a newly built one. A second-hand house doesn't count because this entails the transfer of an already existing stream of housing services from one person to another.

If you think about it, deciding that buying a new house counts as investment whereas, say, buying a new car counts as consumption is a little strange. After all, a new car provides a stream of 'car services' in the future. The problem is, why stop there? Buying a new washing machine provides a stream of 'washing services' in the future, but that's also counted as consumption and not investment. What about a new pen? Doesn't that provide 'writing services' in the future?

As you can see, all sorts of little ambiguities arise, and economists had to draw the line somewhere. For whatever reason – perhaps because housing is such an economically important service – buying a new house is recorded as investment whereas almost anything else a household would buy is considered consumption.

Investment and the interest rate

The most important determinant of investment is the interest rate. When the interest rate is low, firms like to carry out relatively large amounts of investment, but a high interest rate deters them from doing so. To help you remember that investment is highly sensitive to the interest rate, the *investment function* makes it explicit:

$$I = I(r)$$

This equation says that investment (I) is a function of the interest rate (r). In fact, it's a negative function of the interest rate, because a fall in the interest rate leads to an increase in investment.

Why is this the case? Well, imagine that you work for a firm and you have a great idea for a new investment project. You carefully draw up a proposal and pitch it to your boss. One of the first questions she asks is 'How much will it cost?', closely followed by 'How much return will it make the company?'. You reply that it'll cost £1 million and that you estimate that if the project goes well the firm will see a 5 per cent return in one year. Your boss replies that interest rates are 6 per cent and the company would be better off just putting that money in the bank! If, however, interest rates are only 2 per cent, your investment project suddenly becomes attractive.

This leads to an important observation: the interest rate tells you the *opportunity cost* of investment. That is, if a firm has some money to invest in new capital stock, the opportunity cost of doing so is the interest rate it misses out on by just keeping it at the bank.

Figure 7-2 displays the investment function graphically. Notice that as the interest rate falls, more investment projects start to look attractive and firms purchase more capital stock.

Residential investment by households is also very sensitive to the interest rate. Typically, people need to take out a mortgage in order to purchase a new home. If the interest rate is high, new houses become unaffordable to many people.

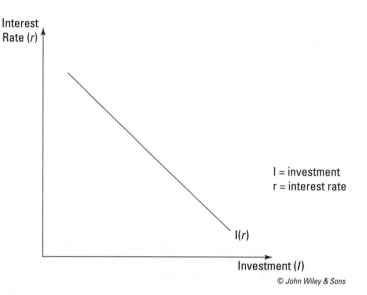

© John Wiley & Sons

Figure 7-2:
The
investment
function.

Other determinants of investment

Four other factors can affect the level of investment in an economy. Because investment is one of the key drivers of economic growth (see Chapter 8), countries that want to grow their economies need to think carefully about the following points:

- ✔ **Tax rates:** High tax rates reduce the incentive to invest. If firms know that, say, 50 per cent of any profit they make from a new machine is going to be paid as tax, they're going to be less likely to buy it.

- ✔ **Secure property rights:** Firms want to know that if they buy capital goods, they'll retain the use of those goods now and in the future. That is, they want secure property rights and assurances that their property isn't going to be expropriated either by the state or anyone else. In developed economies this is now relatively rare – but that's probably why their economies are developed! The safer firms feel, the more likely they are to invest in a country.

- ✔ **Efficiency of the legal system:** Often in business, firms enter into contracts with other firms and consumers. A contract is a legal agreement whereby parties agree to certain binding obligations. They're very important in market economies to ensure that people and firms do what they say they're going to do. When one party fails to meet its obligations, the other party attempts to seek redress through the legal system. Unfortunately, in some countries enforcing a contract is extremely difficult and arduous, which makes doing business difficult. This situation makes firms reluctant to invest.

✔ **Availability of workers:** A firm needs workers in order to use the capital it's purchased – no point having machines if no one's around to work them. (Although if some technology enthusiasts are to be believed, robots will eventually make human workers redundant.) All other things being equal, firms prefer to invest in countries with a large potential workforce and where wages are relatively low. Formally, if the existing capital stock is small and lots of people are willing to work, the marginal productivity of capital is high, making investment attractive.

Factoring in government purchases

Government expenditure (*G*) is the second-largest component of aggregate demand and accounts for around 20 per cent of GDP in the UK. It refers to the government purchasing goods and services. The idea is that these goods and services are eventually provided to households in some shape or form. Examples of government purchases are spending on healthcare, education, defence, roads and so on.

Social security spending on benefits and welfare payments aren't counted as part of government purchases. This is because they're *transfer payments* from one group of people to another group: they don't involve the government purchasing any goods or services.

Government expenditure is usually *exogenous* in macroeconomic models, which means that the model doesn't attempt to explain it. It just equals what it equals. This makes sense, because the level of government spending is a political decision taken by politicians – within certain constraints, of course. For this reason *G* is assumed to be fixed, unless it's specifically changed by policy makers.

To show that a variable is fixed, you can put a 'bar' above it:

$$G = \bar{G}$$

Of course, *G* does change over time depending on the particular preferences and constraints of the government at the time. But unless you're explicitly told that government spending has changed, you can assume that it's constant and unaffected by other macroeconomic variables.

Coming in, going out: Net exports

Net exports (*NX*) are exports (*X*) minus imports (*M*). The term represents the net demand from overseas for domestic goods. Imports need to be subtracted so their inclusion in *C*, *I* and *G* is taken out – this is to ensure that AD only includes demand for goods and services produced domestically.

The UK tends to import more than it exports, which means that net exports is usually a negative component of aggregate demand and GDP. Net exports as a whole tends to be only a few percentage points of total GDP. You may think that this means that trade is insignificant, but in fact *open economies* (countries that make it relatively easy to trade with others) such as the UK engage in huge amounts of trade. In 2014, UK exports were worth around £0.5 trillion, which is a substantial chunk of the country's GDP. But because UK imports of foreign goods was more than this (although not a huge amount more), the overall trade balance is small compared to GDP.

The main macroeconomic variable that affects net exports is the *exchange rate*, which tells you the rate at which you can convert one currency into another. For example, if the exchange rate is £1 = $1.50, you can go to the foreign exchange market and convert £1 into $1.50 or alternatively $1.50 into £1. If the exchange rate changes to £1 = $2, it's called an *appreciation* of the pound and a *depreciation* of the dollar. Basically, £1 now buys you more dollars.

If the pound appreciates, it becomes relatively cheaper for people in the UK to buy US goods; this causes an increase in imports (*M*). Equally, UK goods are now relatively more expensive to people in the US; this causes a decrease in UK exports (*X*). These effects lead to a fall in net exports ($NX = X - M$). (Strictly speaking, something called the Marshall–Lerner condition needs to hold for a depreciation to increase net exports. In this book we always assume that the condition holds. (See the nearby sidebar 'Delving into the Marshall–Lerner condition' for more details.)

Mathematically, you can express the relationship between net exports and the exchange rate as follows:

$$NX = NX(e)$$

In words, this expression says that net exports (*NX*) are a function of the exchange rate (*e*).

Figure 7-3 illustrates this situation graphically. You can see that, as the exchange rate depreciates, net exports increase. The dashed line at 0 (zero) represents the case of balanced trade, that is, imports are exactly matched by exports. To the right of the dashed line, net exports are positive and the economy has a trade surplus: exports are greater than imports. To the left of the dashed line, net exports are negative and the economy has a trade deficit: imports are greater than exports.

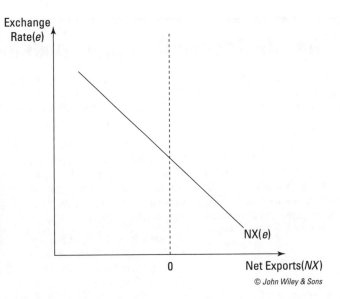

Figure 7-3:
Net exports
(*NX*) and the
exchange
rate (*e*).

© John Wiley & Sons

Nominal and real exchange rates

Two types of exchange rate exist:

- ✔ **The nominal exchange rate (*e*):** The rate at which you can convert between the *currencies* of two countries. For example, 1.5$/£ (that is, $1.50 per £) is a nominal exchange rate. This is usually the rate that you see quoted in the news or in bureau de change.

- ✔ The **real exchange rate** (*ε*): The rate at which you can convert between the *goods* of two countries.

The real exchange rate is defined as:

$$\varepsilon = e\frac{P}{P^*}$$

Here, *P* is the domestic price level and *P** is the price level abroad. If the real exchange between the UK and the US is equal to 1, a certain amount of pounds buys you just as much in the UK as it would if you were to exchange those pounds for dollars and spend them in the US. If the real exchange rate is equal to 2, you can buy twice as much in the US as in the UK with the equivalent amount of money.

In the short run, macroeconomists think that prices are 'sticky' and don't change very much. This means that the nominal exchange rate and the real exchange rate move together. Thus when the exchange rate depreciates (nominal or real), you expect net exports to rise.

Delving into the Marshall–Lerner condition

The Marshall–Lerner condition says that a depreciation of an economy's currency leads to an increase in net exports (*NX*) so long as:

$$|PED_X| + |PED_M| > 1$$

PED_X is the *price elasticity of demand for exports* (that is, how responsive the quantity of exports are to a change in their price [in other words, the exchange rate]) and PED_M is the price elasticity of demand for imports; |.| is the *absolute value* function, which keeps any positive number unchanged and turns any negative number into its positive equivalent (for example, |3| = 3, and |–5| = 5).

The price elasticity of demand tells you how responsive demand for something is to a change in its price. Formally

$$PED = \frac{\%\Delta Q_d}{\%DP}$$

In words, the price elasticity of demand is equal to the percentage change in the quantity demanded divided by the percentage change in its price. Basically, when the price of something rises, the quantity demanded falls. The PED tells you by how much the quantity demanded falls in response to an increase in price.

Price and quantity demanded are inversely related (when price goes up, demand goes down and vice versa), so PED is a negative number. This is why the Marshall–Lerner condition uses the absolute value function – to turn it into a positive number.

The larger is |PED|, the more responsive is demand to price. The Marshall–Lerner condition says that in order for a depreciation to lead to an increase in net exports, the demand for exports and imports needs to be sufficiently responsive to a change in its price. One way of thinking about it is that a depreciation is equivalent to an increase in the price of imports and a fall in the price of exports. Because *NX* is the *value* of net exports (in the domestic currency), the quantities need to respond sufficiently in order to ensure that the depreciation leads to an increase in *NX* overall.

Real exchange rate and purchasing power parity

Recall that net exports (*NX*) is a component of aggregate demand. The real exchange rate has an impact on the level of net exports and therefore on AD also.

In the long run, economists think that the real exchange rate is what really matters. People don't care about how much foreign currency they can buy per se: instead, they want to know how much they can buy with their foreign currency in goods. All other things being equal, if a country's goods are relatively cheaper than other countries' goods, it's likely to run a trade surplus. If it's more expensive, that country is likely to run a trade deficit.

When the real exchange rate between two countries is equal to 1, goods can be exchanged one-for-one. That is, whether you buy in your home country or whether you convert your currency and buy abroad, you can purchase exactly the same amount of goods. For this reason $\varepsilon = 1$ is called the case of *purchasing power parity* (PPP).

If *free trade* exists between two countries (that is, goods can be traded between them with few restrictions), an economic force called *arbitrage* acts to ensure that the real exchange rate doesn't stray too far from PPP ($\varepsilon = 1$).

An arbitrage opportunity arises when the same item is available for sale at two different prices. An enterprising individual can buy the item at the low-price location and then sell the item at the high-price location, locking in the difference as profit. Doing so increases demand at the low-price location and increases supply at the high-price location, which increases the lower price and decreases the higher price. The *arbitrageur* (the person engaging in arbitrage) can continue to make a profit until the two prices become equal.

You can apply the same idea to two different countries: if the same goods cost a lot less in one country than another, individuals can buy something from the cheaper country and sell it in the more expensive country. By doing so, they increase the price in the former and decrease the price in the latter.

Of course, a number of reasons exist why arbitrageurs can't perfectly close the gap between prices in two countries:

- ✔ **Not all goods are tradable:** Many goods just can't be traded. Haircuts for example are much cheaper in some countries than in others. But you can't buy a haircut in one country and export it to another!

- ✔ **Lack of free trade:** Despite the best efforts of economists, most countries still don't trade freely with the rest of the world. Even in the UK, a relatively open economy, restrictions apply to importing goods.

- ✔ **Transportation costs:** Even if arbitraging between two countries is possible, the transportation costs may make it prohibitively expensive. This means that only sufficiently large departures from PPP can be arbitraged effectively.

For these and other reasons, deviations from PPP can and do persist. Nonetheless, economists still think that the possibility of arbitrage ensures that exchange rates don't deviate too far from PPP. So, the real exchange rate has a big impact on the level of net exports because it determines the terms that countries trade with one another. This in turn impacts aggregate demand because *NX* is a component of AD. And finally, in the long run, the real exchange rate shouldn't deviate too far from PPP because of the possibilities for arbitrage.

Following the Aggregate Demand Curve

As the preceding section describes, economists break down aggregate demand into its four constituent components of consumption, investment, government purchases and net exports:

$$AD = C + I + G + NX$$

Here you discover how to represent aggregate demand graphically by using the aggregate demand curve (see Figure 7-4) and the importance of distinguishing between a *movement along* the AD curve and a *shift of* the AD curve.

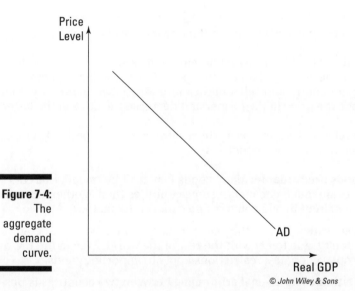

Figure 7-4:
The aggregate demand curve.

© John Wiley & Sons

The AD curve shows how total demand for goods and services in an economy varies as the *price level* (the average level of prices in the economy) varies. The AD curve is of interest because it shows the level of demand in an economy at a particular moment in time. A change in economic policy or a change in consumer/firm sentiment is likely to shift AD – thus allowing economists to analyse the effect of different changes.

Even though it's called an 'AD curve', economists often draw it as a straight line – because they're lazy like that. But seriously, it doesn't matter whether you draw it as a straight line or a curve; the important thing is that it is downwards sloping and shows that the total demand in an economy increases as the price level falls while holding everything else fixed. Of course if other things change (like economic policy or sentiment), this will result in a shift in the AD curve.

Figure 7-4 shows that, as the price level falls, aggregate demand increases. This happens for a number of reasons:

- **The Pigou effect (also called the real balance effect):** When the price level falls, the value of individuals' money holdings rises. That is, you can buy more with the same amount of money. Thus, individuals become wealthier and they respond by consuming more (*C* increases).

- **The Keynes effect:** The fall in the price level leads to a reduction in the demand for money. Because things are cheaper, you don't need to hold as much money in order to make purchases. This fall in demand for money reduces the interest rate. A lower interest rate stimulates investment by firms and consumption by households (*C* and *I* increase).

- **The Mundell–Fleming effect:** The fall in the (domestic) price level makes domestic goods relatively more attractive compared to foreign goods. This stimulates exports and reduces imports, leading to an increase in net exports (*NX* increases).

If you've come across the supply-and-demand model in *micro*economics before, you may have learnt that the demand curve for a good slopes downwards because 'more people are willing to buy at a lower price'. It's easy to think that the AD curve slopes downward for the same reason. But no: the AD curve slopes downwards due to the three effects we list above.

Observing movement along the AD curve

A movement along the AD curve represents the change in aggregate demand caused *only* by a change in the price level. You assume that everything else remains as it was (called the *ceteris paribus* assumption, fact fans – Latin for 'all other things equal').

Figure 7-5 shows that at the price level P_1, aggregate demand is equal to Y_1. If the price level falls to P_2 – so that on average things are cheaper – aggregate demand increases from Y_1 to Y_2 due to the three effects outlined in the preceding section. Assuming that everything else remains as it was means that this increase in aggregate demand can be attributed just to the fall in the price level (and the direct effect this fall has on other variables in the economy).

Similarly, if the price level were to rise from P_2 to P_1, the AD curve tells you that aggregate demand will fall from Y_2 to Y_1.

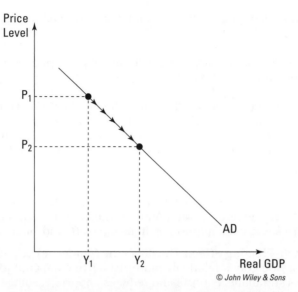

© John Wiley & Sons

Figure 7-5: Movement along the AD curve: at price level P_1, aggregate demand is equal to Y_1; at price level P_2, aggregate demand is equal to Y_2.

Tracing a shift of the curve

Anything that causes aggregate demand to change other than the price level leads to a shift of the AD curve.

In Figure 7-6, aggregate demand has increased from AD_1 to AD_2, which means that at any given price level, aggregate demand is now greater. For example, at the price level P_1, aggregate demand used to be equal to Y_1. After the shift of the AD curve, aggregate demand would equal Y_2 if the price level were to remain at P_1.

Many things can cause the AD curve to shift in this way, including the following:

- **Increased consumer confidence:** At any given price level, households want to consume more (an increase in C).

- **Increased confidence of firms:** At any given price level, firms want to invest more (an increase in I).

- **Increase in government purchases:** Perhaps the government decides that it wants to spend more on healthcare (an increase in G).

- **Increase in demand for exports:** Caused by a fall in the value of the pound (an increase in NX).

- **Lower taxes:** Encourages spending by households and firms (an increase in C and I).

- **Increase in the money supply reduces the interest rate:** Stimulates spending by households and firms (an increase in C and I).

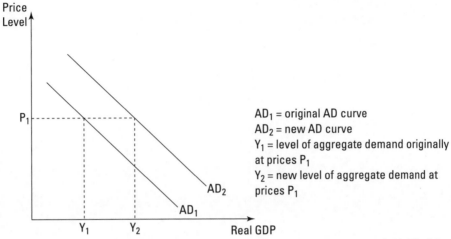

AD$_1$ = original AD curve
AD$_2$ = new AD curve
Y$_1$ = level of aggregate demand originally at prices P$_1$
Y$_2$ = new level of aggregate demand at prices P$_1$

Figure 7-6:
A shift of the
AD curve.

© *John Wiley & Sons*

Clearly, all these factors also work in the opposite direction so that a fall in consumer confidence or a fall in government expenditure leads to a decrease in aggregate demand, which shifts the AD curve to the left (see Figure 7-7).

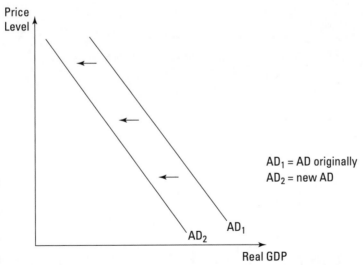

AD$_1$ = AD originally
AD$_2$ = new AD

Figure 7-7:
A fall in
aggregate
demand.

© *John Wiley & Sons*

Chapter 8

Determining How Much Stuff an Economy Can Produce

*W*hen people are demanding something, someone else needs to fulfil that demand to avoid disappointment all round: whether it's a crying baby after milk, football fans baying for a goal or TV viewers lobbying for the return of their favourite, cancelled show (apparently plenty of people still miss *Cagney and Lacey!*).

Chapter 7 introduces the idea of *aggregate demand* (the total demand for goods and services in an economy). But clearly, people demanding a certain amount of output isn't enough; someone needs to supply that output. In a market economy, this important job falls to firms (the total amount of produced goods and services is called *aggregate supply*). But these companies face constraints on how much they can produce.

In this chapter you discover what determines how much firms can produce, in the short run and the long run. We discuss important related topics, including economic growth and the flexibility (or otherwise) of prices.

Producing What People Demand: Aggregate Supply

In order to fulfil the demand from people, firms and governments, companies have to produce and supply goods and services.

Aggregate supply (AS) is the total amount of goods and services that firms produce in an economy. It's the other half of the Aggregate Demand–Aggregate Supply (AD–AS) model, which is the central model of macroeconomics (we cover AD in Chapter 7). Aggregate supply (together with aggregate demand) determines how much a country can produce (its GDP or output) and how much on average those goods will cost to purchase (the price level) as well as how much unemployment an economy experiences.

Because AS impacts the price level, it also impacts the rate of inflation in an economy. As you will see, AS also determines a nation's output and living standards in the long run (while AD only impacts output in the short run). If policy makers want to increase living standards sustainably, then their focus must be on aggregate supply.

Looking at Long-Run Aggregate Supply

Economists distinguish between the short run and the long run because the economy behaves in a different way depending on the time frame you're looking at. The important thing about the long run is that prices are fully flexible (they can change a lot), whereas in the short run prices are *sticky* (in the sense that they don't change by very much; check out the later section 'Pulling apart why prices can be sticky' for some suggested causes for this stickiness).

In this section we look at aggregate supply in the long run, which is more succinctly called *long-run aggregate supply* (LRAS).

Deciding on output in the long run

In the long run, two things determine aggregate supply (the total output that firms supply):

- ✔ **Available factors of production:** Such as land, labour and capital.
- ✔ **Available technology:** So that firms can convert factors of production into goods and services that households, firms and the government want to buy.

Factors of production: Inputs

Factors of production are the basic inputs that firms need to use in order to produce outputs (goods and services) that households, other firms and the government want to buy. Here are the three classic examples of factors of production:

✔ **Land:** If you want to produce something, one of the first things you need is a place where the production can take place. Whether it's a factory, an office or whatever, you need some place to put it! Furthermore, any raw materials that you're going to use ultimately must come from the resources available on Earth – again from the land. Until humans colonise other planets, you can think about the total amount of land being fixed.

✔ **Labour:** Firms need workers to supply their labour in order to help turn the inputs into outputs. Whether that's operating the machines, talking on the phone to customers or sending emails to clients, all firms require workers and their labour to get things done. The more labour firms have available to them, the more they can produce. The total quantity of labour (in a country) can change: it can increase, for example, as a result of population growth or immigration; or it can decrease, for example, when demographic changes mean that more people are of retirement age.

✔ **Capital:** Firms need machines, buildings, offices or some other kind of equipment that workers can use in order to produce things. The more capital firms have, the more output they can produce, all other things being equal. The amount of capital can increase or decrease over time: it can decrease due to *depreciation*, that is, the natural wear and tear that occurs over time; it can increase due to investment, in other words, the purchase (and creation) of new capital goods.

What economists mean by capital is different to the layperson's usage. You can read more about the difference in Chapter 2.

In this chapter we focus on the two factors of production, labour (L) and capital (K) – we leave out land because it is easier to work with just two factors, and all of the points below apply equally to land. Yes, we know, capital begins with a C, not a K, but because economists use C to represent the level of consumption, the quantity of capital is called K!

Production function: Turning inputs into outputs

Firms are constrained by the available technology for turning inputs (factors of production) into outputs (goods and services).

A convenient way of representing the technology available to firms is the *production function*. For a detailed look at the properties of the production function, check out Chapter 4. For now, take a look at the *aggregate production function*:

$$Y = f(K, L)$$

This expression is the production function for the economy as a whole. In words, it says that total output (Y) is a function (f) of the total quantity of capital (K) and labour (L) available to firms.

The better the available technology, the more efficient is the economy at turning inputs into outputs. Here's another way of thinking about this: better technology means that more output can be produced from the same amounts of capital and labour.

Drawing the LRAS curve

The long-run aggregate supply (LRAS) curve shows graphically the total amount of output that an economy can produce, which is sustainable in the long run: it's called the *natural level of output* ($\bar{Y}$). The level of output results when the factors of production are used at a normal intensity (for example, workers/machines don't work 24 hours a day). Furthermore, some factors of production are going to be underemployed at the natural level of output.

Importantly, if output is at $\bar{Y}$, unemployment in the labour market is also at its natural rate. (Chapter 6 provides a detailed explanation of the natural rate of unemployment.) At any given point in time, output (and therefore unemployment) can deviate from its natural rate, but the idea is that over time it tends to gravitate towards the natural rate.

The natural level of output is determined by the production function:

$$\bar{Y} = f\left(\bar{K}, \bar{L}\right)$$

$\bar{K}$ and $\bar{L}$ emphasise that, at any given point in time, the amount of labour and capital is fixed. When output is at its natural rate $\bar{Y}$, the factors of production are also being employed at their natural rate.

Figure 8-1 shows the LRAS curve, which is a vertical line showing that the natural level of output is independent of the price level. Essentially it illustrates how much stuff the economy can sustainably produce with its current level of technology and inputs.

If you've studied microeconomics before, you may be surprised to see that the LRAS curve is a vertical line and not upward sloping like the traditional supply curve. The reason is that in the microeconomic supply-and-demand model, only the price of the particular good you're looking at changes: all other prices remain constant. In the macroeconomic AD–AS model, however, when the price level falls, it means that *all* prices fall, including the price of firms' inputs, which includes their employees' (nominal) wages. Therefore, firms' real profits are unaffected by a fall in the overall price level.

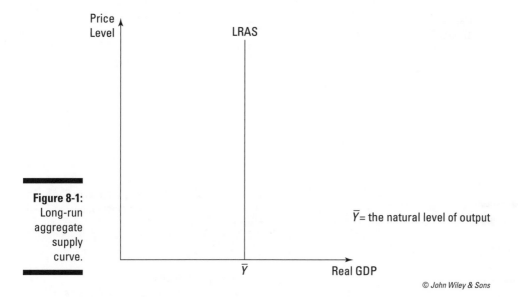

© John Wiley & Sons

Figure 8-1:
Long-run
aggregate
supply
curve.

Considering economic growth

A country experiences *economic growth* when its productive potential increases. You can represent an economy's productive potential in the following two ways:

✔ Production possibility frontier (PPF)

✔ Long-run aggregate supply (LRAS) curve

Both the PPF and LRAS shift with economic growth.

Production possibility frontier (PPF)

Figure 8-2 shows a PPF, including all possible combinations of consumption and capital goods that the economy can sustainably produce.

For example, if the economy was at point X, it would be producing quite a lot of consumption goods and not very many capital goods; whereas at point Y, the opposite is true. Point Z is also feasible, but because it's below the PPF, it's *inefficient*. This is because the economy could be producing more of both types of goods but isn't. In contrast, any point on the PPF (such as X and Y) is *efficient* because increasing the amount of one good without decreasing the other is impossible.

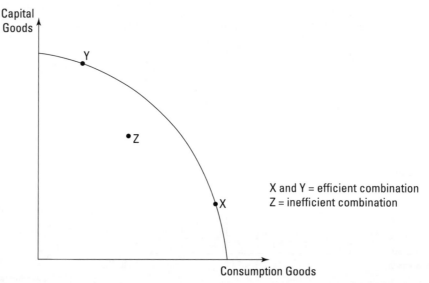

© John Wiley & Sons

Figure 8-2:
Production
possibility
frontier.

Economic growth causes the PPF to shift out so the economy can now produce combinations of consumption and capital goods that were previously impossible.

In Figure 8-3, economic growth means that the PPF has shifted out. Previously the economy wouldn't have been able to operate at point A – it was unfeasible. Now, point A is within the PPF, which means the economy can produce that combination of consumption and capital goods.

Doing so, however, would be inefficient, because producing more of both goods is possible by moving even closer to the PPF.

Shifting long-run aggregate supply (LRAS)

Although the PPF specifies the output mix – the kinds of goods being produced and in what proportions – LRAS is informative about the natural level of total output.

Economic growth means that the LRAS curve shifts to the right, because now the economy is able to produce more output sustainably.

From the production function and the definition of the natural level of output $\bar{Y} = f(\bar{K}, \bar{L})$ (see the earlier section 'Deciding on output in the long run'), you can identify two main sources of economic growth:

> ✔ An increase in the available factors of production.
>
> ✔ Better technology, represented by a 'better' production function $f(.,.)$: that is, one able to turn the same quantity of inputs into more output.

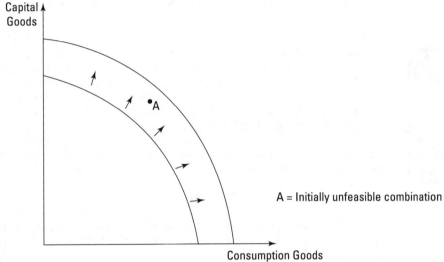

Figure 8-3:
Economic
growth
shifts the
PPF.

A = Initially unfeasible combination

© John Wiley & Sons

In Figure 8-4, economic growth has shifted long-run aggregate supply from LRAS$_1$ to LRAS$_2$.

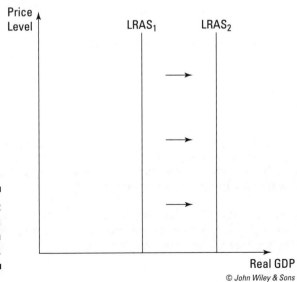

Figure 8-4:
Economic
growth
shifts LRAS.

© John Wiley & Sons

A couple of things to note:

- ✔ Although most of the time countries experience economic growth, the natural level of output $\bar{Y}$ can also fall. An extreme example is when a country experiences war. At their worst, wars can lead to the destruction of a large amount of a nation's capital stock (K) as well as its labour force (L).

- ✔ The source of economic growth is important in determining the effect on living standards. For example, an increase in L due to population growth leads – through the production function – to economic growth. It's unlikely to lead to higher living standards, however, because these depend on output *per capita*. Conversely an increase in K is likely to lead to higher living standards because it's likely to increase per capita income (not just total income).

We can show the second point formally. Economists commonly assume that the production function is *constant returns to scale* (CRS):

$$f\left(\lambda K, \lambda L\right) = \lambda f\left(K, L\right) = \lambda Y$$

In words, scaling up the inputs by a factor $\lambda > 0$ also scales up output by λ. For example, doubling the amount of capital and labour ($\lambda = 2$) also doubles the amount of output.

The justification for this assumption is that if you're able to produce a certain amount of output (Y) using a certain quantity of inputs (K, L), you should be able to *replicate* it if all your inputs are doubled (or tripled, or whatever!).

Setting $\lambda = 1/L$ gives:

$$Y/L = f\left(K/L, 1\right)$$

This expression says that output per person is equal to an (increasing) function of capital per person.

You can write this more simply as

$$y = f\left(k\right)$$

where y denotes output per person (Y/L) and k denotes capital per person (K/L). This expression is called the production function in *intensive form*. It tells you that output per person (and therefore average living standards) depends upon how much capital exists per person.

All other things being equal, an increase in L reduces k = K/L and so reduces $y = f(k)$; whereas an increase in K increases k and so increases y. Equally, any improvement in technology $f(.)$ also sees an increase in y.

Getting to Grips with Short-Run Aggregate Supply

In the short run, aggregate supply doesn't need to equal the natural level of output. Output can be temporarily above or below the natural level of output $\bar{Y}$, because prices are sticky in the short run and take some time to adjust to changes in aggregate demand (AD). (You can read more about $\bar{Y}$ in 'Deciding on output in the long run', earlier in this chapter.)

Producing more in the short run

Firms are able to produce more than $\bar{Y}$ in the short run by hiring more people or using the people and machines they already have more intensively. Even at $\bar{Y}$ some unemployment exists, so increasing output beyond this causes unemployment to fall temporarily below the natural rate. These additional workers increase L in the production function and allow firms to produce more output.

In Figure 8-5, you can see that the short-run aggregate supply (SRAS) curve is upward sloping, which means that as the average price level in the economy rises (due to an increase in AD), firms produce more output in the short run.

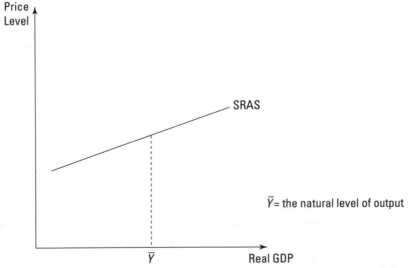

Figure 8-5:
Short-run
aggregate
supply.

© John Wiley & Sons

In the long run, though, output has to return to its natural level, $\bar{Y}$. To see how this works in practice, consider the increase in aggregate demand shown in Figure 8-6.

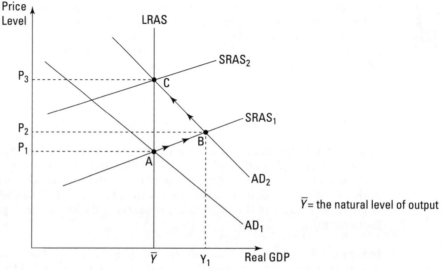

© John Wiley & Sons

Figure 8-6: Aggregate demand increase in the short and long run.

$\bar{Y}$ = the natural level of output

Aggregate demand has increased from AD_1 to AD_2. If prices had been fully flexible, this would've left output unchanged at $\bar{Y}$ and caused the price level to increase to P_3 (point C). In the short run, however, prices are sticky and the increase in AD causes output to increase from $\bar{Y}$ to Y_1 (a movement along the SRAS curve from point A to point B). You can also see that, even though prices are sticky in the short run, they aren't completely fixed: the short-run price level increases from P_1 to P_2.

Moving to the long run, prices in the economy are able to adjust more fully to the increase in AD and the economy moves from point B to point C. This shifts the SRAS curve gradually from $SRAS_1$ to $SRAS_2$. When the economy is at point C, it has responded fully to the increase in AD, which has resulted only in an increase in the price level and not in real output.

Notice that in the movement from A to B, output increases above its natural level. This leads to a fall in unemployment to below the natural rate of unemployment. As the price level adjusts fully (from B to C), output falls back to $\bar{Y}$, which means unemployment also returns to its natural rate.

Pulling apart why prices can be sticky

Saying that prices are sticky in the short run is all very well, of course, but what causes them to be so? The answer to this question is important, because without sticky prices output would always be at its natural level $\bar{Y}$.

Economists have come up with a number of theories to explain this stickiness of prices; in other words, the upward-sloping SRAS curve.

Some firms are just slow to adjust prices

Adjusting prices isn't a costless activity for firms. At a basic level, going round updating all the prices in your store regularly is likely to be expensive and not a particularly good use of time. This is especially true when the required increase in price is small.

These so-called menu costs are likely to differ between firms:

- ✔ For firms that need physically to change each price manually, such as a local corner shop, menu costs are likely to be relatively high.
- ✔ For large online retailers with sophisticated automated systems, menu costs are likely to be small.

If only a few firms change their prices in the short run, on average the price level doesn't increase by much. At the same time, those firms that have sticky prices and haven't changed their price are now relatively underpricing their goods compared to the 'true' market price. This results in an increase in demand from households and firms for the underpriced goods.

Another reason for sticky prices is that most contracts are written using the nominal price. For example, if a consumer has signed a contract with a firm that promises to provide some service over the year at a certain (nominal) price, he expects that price to be honoured even if an increase in AD means that the price should increase.

Also, evidence suggests that some industries are slow to change prices even when doing so would seem relatively easy. The newspaper/magazine industry is a good example. It often keeps prices unchanged for years even though changing cover prices of newspapers and magazines would be relatively easy.

Misperceptions about the price level

This suggested reason for sticky prices is a clever one. Essentially, people confuse an increase in the nominal price of whatever they're selling for an increase in its real price. This mistake causes them to oversupply the market with goods. Only when they realise that the real price is unchanged do they return to their earlier production.

Imagine that you're a baker. Every day after baking your loaves of bread, you take them to the marketplace to sell. Unknown to you, aggregate demand has increased, causing the price level to increase. Therefore the price that you can sell your bread for has also increased. You respond by singing 'Happy days are here again!' and rushing home to bake as many loaves as you can in order to sell to market.

What you don't realise, however, is that *all* prices in the economy have also increased and so the real price you're receiving for your bread is unchanged. Only the *nominal* price has increased.

At the end of the week, you go to do your weekly shop and notice that the prices of all goods have risen. Only then do you understand that the real price of bread is the same as it was last week. Armed with this understanding, the following week you go back to your usual amount of bread production, muttering 'I knew it was too good to be true'!

The same thing can happen in the labour market. An increase in AD causes the price of all things to rise. Workers notice that their nominal wage has increased, which causes them to supply more labour (that is, existing workers work more hours or previously unemployed workers start working) and allows firms to produce more output. Eventually workers realise that the real wage is unaffected and so they return to their original labour supply.

Sticky nominal wages

Here, the argument for sticky prices goes something like this: in the short run the nominal wage (w) is fixed – firms are able to hire as many workers as they like at this wage. An increase in AD raises the price level (p) but not the nominal wage, which causes a fall in the real wage (w/p). Firms take advantage of this fall in real wages by hiring more labour, which allows them to produce more output.

Over time the nominal wage adjusts, raising firms' costs and shifting the SRAS up and to the left (see the earlier Figure 8-6). Eventually, the nominal wage adjusts fully and the real wage is the same as it was before the increase in AD.

Although some workers may be in this situation, at the aggregate level this explanation is less convincing to economists than those in the preceding two sections. Here's why: this analysis implies that the real wage is *countercyclical*, that is, it should fall during booms (when output is above the natural level) and rise during recessions (when output is below its natural level). But in fact empirically the opposite is true: the real wage is *procyclical* – it rises during booms and falls during recessions.

Rounding on the Russian rouble

2014 was a tough year for the Russian currency (the rouble): it lost around half its value against the US dollar. This decline earned it the unenviable title of the world's worst-performing currency of that year. Analysts provide a number of reasons to explain the large fall, including the dramatic tumble in world oil prices (the Russian economy is heavily dependent on oil exports) and the effect of economic sanctions placed on Russia following the crisis in Ukraine.

The rouble had been steadily losing value throughout 2014, but in December something quite extraordinary happened: within 48 hours it lost around 20 per cent of its value. Equally extraordinary was that immediately after the depreciation, consumers in Russia went on a shopping spree like no other. Car showrooms and furniture stores were bulging with customers desperate to buy anything they could get their hands on.

This behaviour may seem strange for a country experiencing an economic crisis, but it was for a very simple reason: people wanted to buy before firms had a chance to raise their prices in response to the depreciation. This is a perfect example of the effect of so-called sticky prices: the fact that prices didn't respond immediately meant that consumers bought much more than they'd have bought otherwise.

Chapter 9

Using the AD–AS Model to Analyse Shocks to the System

*L*ike a jittery politician waiting to start a TV interview with a rottweiler of a journalist, the economy never stands still. For example, interest rates, government policy and consumer confidence are always changing, impacting the economy in different ways. Macroeconomists often call these changes *shocks*, probably because they can't easily predict them. The Aggregate Demand–Aggregate Supply (AD–AS) model (which we discuss in detail in Chapters 7 and 8) comes into its own when you use it to analyse how macro-economic shocks impact the economy.

In this chapter you discover how to use the AD–AS model to analyse different shocks as well as how they affect key macroeconomic variables, including inflation, unemployment and real GDP. More specifically, we discuss the following impacts:

✔ **On the demand side:** Consumer and company confidence, fiscal and monetary policies, and the multiplier effect

✔ **On the supply side:** Energy prices and technological advances

Discovering What the AD–AS Model Does and Doesn't Explain

Although the AD–AS model is of great importance in macroeconomics, no single model attempts to explain everything.

In economic modelling, analysts make a key distinction between endogenous and exogenous variables:

> ✔ **Endogenous:** Variables that the model attempts to explain
>
> ✔ **Exogenous:** Variables determined outside the model

For example, in the AD–AS model, the price level and real GDP are endogenous variables (see Figure 9-1). The increase in aggregate demand from AD_1 to AD_2 (for some as-yet unspecified reason) has, in the short run, caused the price level to increase from P_1 to P_2 and real GDP to increase from Y_1 to Y_2. Thus the AD–AS model has 'explained' the change in the price level and real GDP: the increase in AD caused them both to increase.

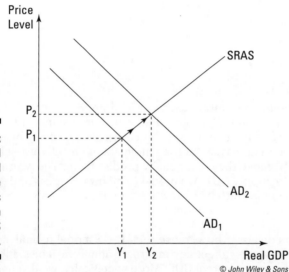

Figure 9-1: Price level and real GDP are endogenous variables in the AD–AS model.

© John Wiley & Sons

The increase in AD could be the result of a number of changes in the economy, for example a fall in the interest rate or an increase in government spending. These two changes are examples of exogenous variables in the model, because the model doesn't attempt to explain *why* the interest rate has changed or *why* the government has increased spending, it just uses the fact that it has.

So, in general, economic models can say how endogenous variables are affected by changes in exogenous variables. We're not implying that macroeconomists are uninterested in what determines the interest rate or government spending, simply that explaining them requires a different model in which those variables are endogenous instead of exogenous.

Economists model in this way because building knowledge in economics is an incremental process. Instead of trying to work out in one go how an extremely complicated system such as the economy functions, it makes more sense to try slowly to understand a few things at a time!

Delving into Demand-Side Shocks

Demand-side shocks are anything that impacts on aggregate demand. So anything that affects consumption (*C*), investment (*I*) or net exports (*NX*) would count as a demand-side shock. So too would a change in government expenditure (*G*). Demand-side shocks are important because they have an impact on real GDP, inflation and unemployment (as least in the short run).

We cover how changes in confidence, investment, fiscal and monetary policies, and the multiplier effect can change the level of aggregate demand. All of these have a different impact on the economy depending on whether you're looking at the short run or the long run. Be sure to bear that in mind when looking at each one.

Testing your faith: Confidence in the economy

In life, confidence matters. It can mean the difference between landing your dream job and not, winning that crucial business contract and not, or between coming first in the race and coming second. Similarly, consumer and firm confidence can have a large impact on the economy, in the short and the long run (sometimes in surprising ways).

Changes in consumer confidence directly impact on consumers' spending decisions. While watching news stories about the economy, you may hear how boosting consumer confidence is a 'good thing' for the economy. Although often true in the short run, over longer periods it's not necessarily the case.

John Maynard Keynes, one of the fathers of macroeconomics, attributed much of human behaviour to what he called their *animal spirits*. That is, sometimes people are just more confident about the future than at other times, and it doesn't have to be for any discernible reason. This makes understanding the economy more difficult for economists but also more interesting!

In this section we use the AD–AS model to show you how changes in consumer and firm confidence impact the economy.

Short run

In the short run, increased consumer confidence raises the demand for consumption (C). Along with investment (I), government expenditure (G) and net exports (NX), C is a component of AD ($= C + I + G + NX$), so this raises aggregate demand in an economy. Now, at any given price level, more goods and services are demanded. We represent this in Figure 9-2 by a shift in the AD curve from AD_1 to AD_2.

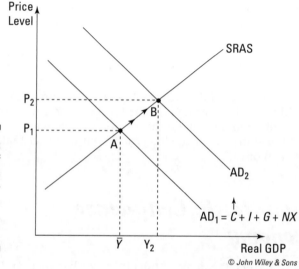

Figure 9-2: Effects of increased consumer confidence in the short run.

© John Wiley & Sons

As we discuss in Chapter 8, in the short run prices are sticky, which causes the economy to move along the short-run aggregate supply (SRAS) curve from point A to point B.

The increase in AD caused the price level and real GDP to increase, and because real GDP rose beyond the natural level of output $\bar{Y}$, unemployment also fell below its natural rate. Thus increased consumer confidence appears to be a 'good thing' for the economy in the short run.

Long run

In the long run, prices become flexible and are able to adjust fully to the increase in AD, meaning that the increased consumer confidence has far less real impact on the economy. The quantity of available factors of production doesn't increase and no technological advance happens, so output must return to its natural level $\bar{Y}$: as prices begin to increase, SRAS begins to shift up and to the left until finally output falls back to $\bar{Y}$ (see Figure 9-3).

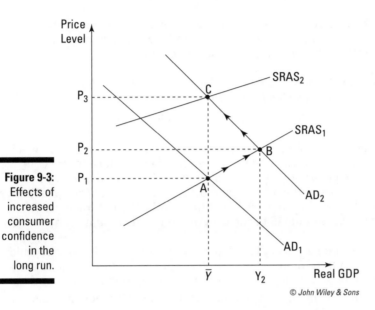

© John Wiley & Sons

Figure 9-3:
Effects of
increased
consumer
confidence
in the
long run.

The increase in AD took the economy from point A to point B in the short run. Prices rose a little, but not much. In the long run, prices increase further, shifting SRAS up and to the left from $SRAS_1$ to $SRAS_2$. The economy moves along the AD_2 curve from point B to point C. Real GDP and unemployment are unchanged and only the price level has increased.

The 'really long run'

Here we consider what effect the increase in consumer spending has on the natural level of output $\bar{Y}$ in the really long run: the answer may surprise you!

Output can increase in the long run in two main ways:

- ✔ **Improved technology:** Innovations that allow firms to make more/better goods and services from the same quantity of inputs.

- ✔ **Increased factors of production:** Examples include capital and labour. Increases in the capital stock are especially important for increasing living standards.

Although increased consumer confidence may not affect firms' technological advances, it does impact indirectly on capital accumulation. Every year, some part of the existing capital stock *depreciates*, that is, wears away. *Investment* as economists use the term refers to the purchase of capital goods, which adds to the capital stock. Consumer confidence has quite a lot to do with investment.

In the long run, increased consumption due to increased consumer confidence actually *reduces* investment and may reduce living standards. Think about it this way. Firms produce two types of goods:

- ✔ **Consumption goods:** Made to be consumed – almost all goods that households purchase fall into this category.

- ✔ **Capital goods:** Made to produce other goods in the future.

At one extreme, firms could produce only consumption goods, which would mean very high levels of consumption now but would reduce future consumption due to the lack of new capital goods. Every year that this continued, the capital stock would depreciate further and the country's productive capacity would be further impaired. In other words, the natural level of output $\bar{Y} = f\left(\bar{K}, \bar{L}\right)$ would fall because of the reduced amount of capital (K).

At the other extreme, firms could produce only capital goods, which would mean no consumption today (!) but higher output in the future due to the large amount of new capital goods. Over time the capital stock would grow substantially and the natural level of output $\bar{Y} = f\left(\bar{K}, \bar{L}\right)$ would increase. (Whether anyone would be around to enjoy all that output after not consuming anything for years is another matter!)

Clearly, neither of these extreme options is likely to be optimal. Instead, the optimum policy involves devoting some proportion of output to consumption goods and some proportion to capital goods.

The more of a nation's output that's devoted to consumption goods, the less capital goods it produces, and this reduction is one-for-one. This reduces living standards in the long run – compared to the case where consumption is lower and investment (new capital goods) is higher.

Feeling confident enough to invest?

How confident firms are about the future has a large impact on their investment decisions (whether to purchase capital goods). Firms only want to make such purchases in the following circumstances:

- ✔ They're confident that the additional goods and services they can produce with the new capital goods are demanded.

- ✔ They think that their future profits aren't going to be taxed heavily.

- ✔ They believe that their capital won't be taken from them. Although rarely a problem in advanced economies, it's still a problem in many developing countries.

Short run

In the short run, an increase in firms' confidence increases investment (I) demand. As we explain in the earlier section 'Testing your faith: Confidence in the economy', investment is a component of aggregate demand ($AD = C + I + G + NX$), so it raises aggregate demand (see Figure 9-4).

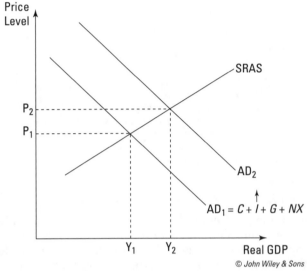

Figure 9-4:
Effects of
increased
investment
in the
short run.

© John Wiley & Sons

AD has increased from AD_1 to AD_2. In the short run, because prices are sticky, this change causes the price level to increase slightly from P_1 to P_2 and real GDP to increase from Y_1 to Y_2. The increase in investment demand means that the economy is now producing more output and that more investment is taking place by firms.

Long run

Earlier in the chapter (the 'Long run' section under the 'Testing your faith: Confidence in the economy' section) we show that in the long run increased demand for consumption (C) has no effect on output (Y), because as the price level rises, SRAS shifts up and to the left until output returns to its natural level. In the case of the impact of additional investment in the long run, things are different, because the new capital goods increase the country's productive capacity and therefore increase the natural level of output $\bar{Y}$.

In Figure 9-5, you can see that the new capital goods have shifted long-run aggregate supply from $LRAS_1$ to $LRAS_2$. Therefore, output stays higher and the price level has no need to rise further. Thus the increased confidence of firms that led to higher investment is able to increase living standards!

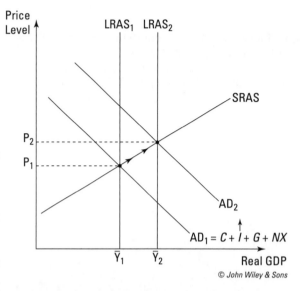

Figure 9-5:
Effects of
increased
investment
in the
long run.

© John Wiley & Sons

The 'really long run'

Even though greater investment today can increase living standards in
the future, macroeconomists think that the underlying level of investment
is determined by the level of savings, which (rather confusingly) doesn't
depend on firms' choices. What really matters is how much of national
income is left after consumers and the government have taken their portion.
A little bit of maths is helpful here.

Assume a closed economy: one that doesn't trade with the rest of the world
($NX = 0$). Total output (Y) must comprise consumption (C), investment (I)
and government expenditure (G):

$$Y = C + I + G$$

A simple rearrangement yields the following:

$$I = Y - C - G$$

In other words, investment is what's left over after consumption and government expenditure are taken away. To see why intuitively, think in terms of
private saving and *public saving*. Private saving (S_{PRI}) is what private households have left after they pay for their consumption (C) and their taxes (T):

$$S_{PRI} = Y - T - C$$

Public saving is any savings made by the government; it's equal to tax
revenue (T) less government expenditure (G):

$$S_{PUB} = T - G$$

That is, if the government receives more in taxes than it spends, public saving is positive. But if it spends more than it receives in taxes, public saving is negative (in other words, the government is having to borrow).

Therefore, total saving (*S*) is the sum of private and public saving:

$$S = S_{PRI} + S_{PUB}$$
$$S = (Y - T - C) + (T - G)$$

which simplifies to

$$S = Y - C - G$$

Notice that this is exactly equal to the expression for investment ($I = Y - C - G$). Thus in a closed economy, savings must equal exactly investment:

$$S = I$$

because, in the long run, output (*Y*) is determined by the available factors of production and technology (see the earlier section 'Testing your faith: Confidence in the economy'). The only way, really, of boosting investment is to have low levels of consumption (*C*) and/or low levels of government expenditure (*G*). For this reason, you hear economists sometimes say things like 'government spending crowds out investment'. They mean that greater government spending lowers public saving, which lowers total saving, which lowers investment.

Impacting demand via fiscal policy

Fiscal policy refers to government policy as it relates to government expenditure and taxation. Fiscal policy matters because it determines how much tax everyone in an economy pays and what goods and services the government provides for the country and its people. Changes in fiscal policy have the potential to cause large impacts on the economy.

Fiscal policy impacts aggregate demand. As such, changes in fiscal policy are considered 'shocks' in the AD–AS model. We discuss fiscal policy in detail in Chapter 11, but here we take a look at it in the context of the AD–AS model and shocks.

Expansionary fiscal policy

Expansionary fiscal policy is an increase in government expenditure or a decrease in taxation. Either of these policy changes affects the economy by increasing aggregate demand.

Government expenditure (G) is a component of aggregate demand (AD = $C + I + G + NX$) (see the earlier section 'Testing your faith: Confidence in the economy'), so any increase in G directly leads to an increase in AD. A reduction in taxes also impacts on AD through two main mechanisms:

- ✔ **Increased consumption (C):** Consumption is highly influenced by the amount of disposable income people have (that is, income after tax, $Y - T$). By reducing taxes in an economy, the government increases disposable income. When people have more disposable income, they consume more.

- ✔ **Increased investment (I):** When firms make investment decisions, one of the key things they want to know is how much of any future profit they're likely to be able to keep. The more they can keep, the more they want to invest in capital goods today. Thus lower taxes boosts investment today.

Whether the reason is due to an increase in G or a fall in T (or both), the impact on the economy is to raise AD (see Figure 9-6). Aggregate demand has increased from AD_1 to AD_2, which in the short run caused output and the price level to rise. You can see this as a movement from point A to point B: because prices are sticky in the short run, the price level hasn't risen by much. As time passes and prices become more flexible, short-run aggregate supply (SRAS) shifts up and to the left, raising the price level and reducing output until eventually output is unchanged at point C.

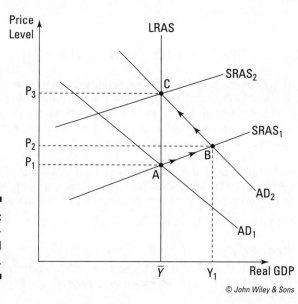

© John Wiley & Sons

Figure 9-6: Expansionary fiscal policy.

Thus, expansionary fiscal policy gives the economy a short-term boost and raises incomes and reduces unemployment. But this boost is short-lived. After prices adjust, output falls to its natural level and unemployment rises to its natural rate.

Depending on the particular fiscal policy change you're considering, long-run aggregate supply (LRAS) can increase and shift to the right.

Imagine that the government increases spending on education, leading to a more skilled, more productive workforce and increasing the natural level of output. Equally, if taxes fall and firms are encouraged to invest more, increasing the capital stock, the natural level of output also increases.

Contractionary fiscal policy

Contractionary fiscal policy is a decrease in government expenditure or an increase in taxation. Either of these policy changes affects the economy by decreasing aggregate demand.

Government expenditure (G) is part of aggregate demand (AD = $C + I + G + NX$), so any decrease in G directly leads to a decrease in AD. An increase in taxes also impacts on AD through two main mechanisms: increased taxes reduce consumption due to the reduction in disposable income. Equally, increased tax rates can reduce investment, because firms keep less of the fruits of their investment.

Automatic stabilisers

Automatic stabilisers, as their name suggests, act to stabilise the economy by bringing output back towards its natural level. Furthermore, this process happens automatically, that is, without any change in fiscal policy by policy makers.

To see how this works, consider that output is higher than its natural level – for example, after a positive AD shock. Higher output (in the short run) means that people are earning more income and firms are making more profits, which will automatically increase the amount of tax that the government collects. This puts the brakes on the economy – in much the same way as would contractionary fiscal policy; however, the big difference is that it happens automatically. Policy makers don't actually have to do anything, the taxes just pour in!

The stabilisation process works in the other direction too. Consider the case where output is less than its natural level, perhaps due to a negative AD shock. This situation leads to a fall in output and an increase in unemployment. But it also reduces the amount of tax revenue that the government collects. This automatically boosts the economy, much like expansionary fiscal policy would boost the economy, except that, very conveniently, it happens automatically!

In both cases aggregate demand falls, as you can see in Figure 9-7. Contractionary fiscal policy has caused aggregate demand to fall from AD_1 to AD_2. In the short run, sticky prices caused a fall in output and a relatively modest fall in prices. The fall in output also means that in the short run unemployment increases beyond its natural rate.

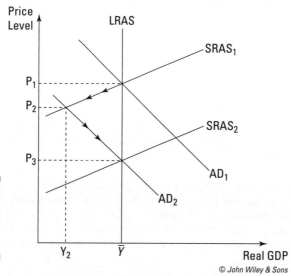

Figure 9-7:
Contraction-
ary fiscal
policy.

© John Wiley & Sons

In the long run, however, prices become flexible, causing the short-run aggregate supply to shift from $SRAS_1$ to $SRAS_2$. The price level falls more substantially and output increases back to its natural level. Similarly, unemployment falls back to its natural rate.

Thus contractionary fiscal policy can be painful in the short run because it reduces living standards and increases unemployment. But if the government is patient and waits for the price level to adjust, output increases back up to its old level.

In a similar way to expansionary fiscal policy (see the preceding section), contractionary fiscal policy can also potentially impact the supply side of the economy. In particular, falls in important areas of expenditure, such as education and health, can reduce the productivity of workers and reduce the natural level of output. Equally, higher taxes can cause investment to fall, which can mean that the new capital goods aren't enough to cover the depreciation of the existing capital stock. The result is also to cause LRAS to shift to the left and reduce the natural level of output. For more on supply-side shocks, read the later section 'Bumping into Supply-Side Shocks'.

Setting the interest rate: Impacts through monetary policy

Monetary policy is when policy makers (usually the central bank) use the money supply to influence the economy. (For a detailed look at monetary policy, check out Chapter 10.) Here we look at how monetary policy impacts on aggregate demand, including expansionary and contractionary policies, as we do for fiscal policy in the preceding section. Again, changes in monetary policy 'shock' the AD–AS system and cause the price level, real GDP and unemployment to change.

The central bank is a powerful institution because it has a monopoly over the creation of new money: it can create money out of thin air by simply printing more! Central banks typically use their ability to change the money supply in order to affect the interest rate in an economy. To see how, you need to understand how the money market works.

The *money market* is like any other market: the price of money is determined by supply and demand. When you think of the interest rate as the price of holding money, you can see exactly what we mean by the 'price' of money.

Holding money is great: it allows you to purchase goods and services easily. Economists say that money is very *liquid* (no doubt you've noticed how it drips away when you go shopping!). But this liquidity comes at a cost: money doesn't give you any return. The £10 note you're carrying around with you will still be a £10 note tomorrow, next year and so on. In fact, if inflation is positive (which it usually is) your money buys less and less the longer you hold onto it. In addition, if instead of holding the money you deposit it in a savings account, you'd earn a return equal to the interest rate. Therefore, by holding money you're giving up the opportunity to earn a return on it.

The (nominal) interest rate is the *opportunity cost* of holding money. This important observation means that when the interest rate is high, the demand for money is low: people don't want to hold very much cash. As the interest rate falls, people become more willing to hold larger amounts of cash. The money demand curve in Figure 9-8 represents this effect.

As the interest rate falls, so too does the opportunity cost of holding money, which means that people demand more money. Because the central bank can choose the supply of money in an economy, it can effectively set the interest rate by varying the money supply (see Figure 9-9). The central bank sets the money supply equal to M_S, which determines the interest rate in equilibrium (equal to i_0 in Figure 9-9).

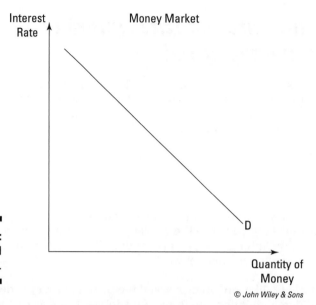

© John Wiley & Sons

Figure 9-8:
The demand
for money.

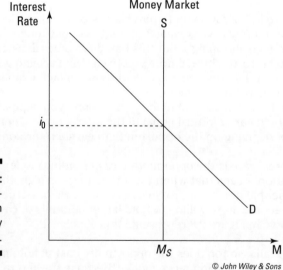

© John Wiley & Sons

Figure 9-9:
Equilib-
rium in
the money
market.

Expansionary monetary policy

In order to carry out an expansionary monetary policy, the central bank increases the money supply to reduce the interest rate in the money market. In Figure 9-10, the central bank has increased the money supply from M_0 to M_1, which reduced the interest rate from i_0 to i_1.

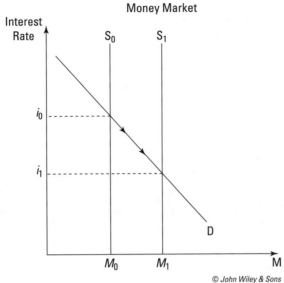

Money Market

Figure 9-10:
Expan-
sionary
monetary
policy: the
money
market.

© John Wiley & Sons

This reduction in the interest rate is going to affect aggregate demand in the economy in a number of ways:

- **Increased consumption (C):** Reduced interest rates make borrowing cheaper and saving less attractive. Consumers respond by borrowing more for current consumption and by saving less, which also boosts consumption. Furthermore, people on variable rate mortgages see their monthly repayments fall and have more disposable income to spend on consumption.

- **Increased investment (I):** The interest rate reflects the opportunity cost of investment, so any fall in the interest rate boosts investment. That is, more investment projects yield a greater expected return than the market interest rate.

- **Increased net exports (NX):** When a country lowers its interest rate, people are more reticent to keep their savings in that country. This reluctance reduces the demand for the domestic currency, which results in a depreciation of the currency in the foreign exchange markets. Buying the country's exports is cheaper for foreigners, and buying imported goods is more expensive for residents. These effects act to increase net exports.

Consumption, investment and net exports are all components of aggregate demand (AD = $C + I + G + NX$), so expansionary monetary policy boosts AD. You can model the effect on the economy using the AD–AS model (see Figure 9-11).

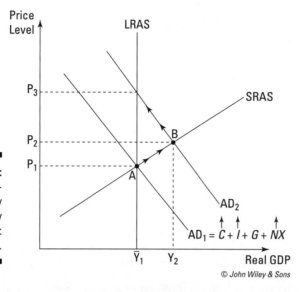

Figure 9-11:
Expansionary
monetary
policy:
AD–AS.

© John Wiley & Sons

In a similar way to expansionary fiscal policy, expansionary monetary policy has boosted aggregate demand from AD_1 to AD_2, in the short run causing output and the price level to rise (a movement from point A to point B in Figure 9-11). Sticky prices in the short run mean that the price level hasn't risen by much. In the long run, prices become more flexible and the SRAS curve shifts up and to the left, raising the price level and reducing output until eventually output is unchanged.

The caveat is that the increase in investment caused by the fall in the interest rate typically increases the capital stock, so LRAS may well also increase and shift to the right.

Contractionary monetary policy

To carry out a contractionary monetary policy, the central bank reduces the money supply (typically by selling government bonds; for more on the exact process, flip to Chapter 10). The reduction in the money supply drives up the interest rate. A higher interest rate means lower consumption, investment and net exports, and because these are all components of aggregate demand, AD falls. We don't reproduce all the diagrams for these because they're exactly the opposite of the expansionary monetary policy ones! We show the AD–AS diagram for contractionary monetary policy in Figure 9-12.

In Figure 9-12, contractionary monetary policy has reduced aggregate demand from AD_1 to AD_2, which in the short run causes output and the price level to fall (the movement from point A to point B). Owing to sticky prices in the short run, the price level falls relatively little and output falls relatively a lot. In the long run, prices become flexible and the SRAS curve shifts down and to the right. This move reduces the price level and increases output until eventually output is unchanged at point C.

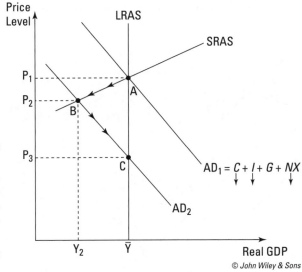

Figure 9-12: Contractionary monetary policy: AD–AS.

© John Wiley & Sons

Increasing demand with the multiplier effect

As well as monetary and fiscal policies impacting directly on aggregate demand, there are also second-order (and third-order and higher) effects.

We're talking here about something called the *multiplier effect*. Any positive shock to AD increases output (Y) in the short run (see, for example, Figure 9-11). But consumption itself is a function of disposable income, $C(Y - T)$: when disposable income increases, consumption increases. Therefore the initial increase in output increases consumption, which increases aggregate demand further. This is the second-order effect. But then this second-order increase in aggregate demand increases output by a little bit more, which in turn increases consumption a little, which shifts AD further and so on. Hence the name, the *multiplier effect*. Ultimately these effects get smaller and smaller and eventually peter out.

In Figure 9-13, you can see that initially aggregate demand increases from AD_1 to AD_2, but due to the multiplier effect, aggregate demand increases further, to AD_3, and keeps increasing through successive rounds until eventually it stops at $AD_\sim$. The same idea applies to a fall in aggregate demand: the initial fall in AD reduces output, which reduces consumption, which reduces AD further and so on. As a result, the short-run change in output and the price level is greater than it would otherwise be. However in the long run, when prices are flexible, output still returns to its natural level, although at a higher price level.

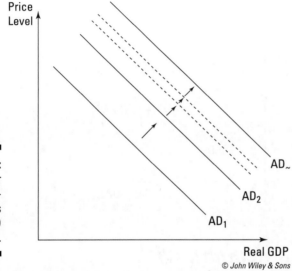

Figure 9-13:
Multiplier effect: multiple rounds of AD increase.

© John Wiley & Sons

Suppose that the government increases expenditure (G) by £1 million, directly increasing output in the short run by £1 million. This extra £1 million is spent on goods and services, which increases the incomes of the producers of those goods by £1 million. Some portion of this additional income will be spent. You can write the consumption function as follows:

$$C(Y-T) = c_0 + c_1(Y-T)$$

so an increase in income (Y) of £1 million increases consumption by $c_1 \times £1$ million (the second-order effect). But this increase in consumption further increases income by $c_1 \times £1$ million, which increases consumption by $c_1 \times c_1 \times £1$ million (the third-order effect). These rounds of effects continue so that the overall impact on output is equal to:

$$\Delta Y = £1m + c_1 \times £1m + c_1^2 \times £1m + c_1^3 \times £1m + \dots$$

Mathematicians call this an *infinite geometric series* and thankfully you can sum all these terms in a very easy way:

$$\Delta Y = \frac{£1m}{1 - c_1}$$

Notice that the larger the marginal propensity to consume (c_1), the greater is the total impact on output when some component of aggregate demand increases. Equally, when the marginal propensity to consume is low, the successive rounds of extra consumption become very small very quickly. The expression $1/(1 - c_1)$ is called the multiplier, because it multiplies up any initial increase (or decrease!) in aggregate demand.

Bumping into Supply-Side Shocks

In many ways supply-side shocks are more important than those hitting the demand side (which we discuss in the earlier section 'Delving into Demand-Side Shocks'). Demand-side shocks typically have only a temporary impact on the economy – usually the price level adjusts and the economy goes back to its natural level of output.

But supply-side shocks can have a permanent impact on the economy. Indeed, the only way for an economy to experience persistent growth is by increasing long-run aggregate supply (LRAS).

In this section we take a look at two important supply-side shocks: changes in energy prices and technological progress. Many other things can affect aggregate supply, and you can read about them in Chapter 6.

Examining the impact of energy prices

A fall in the energy price increases aggregate supply. Why? Well, energy is one of the basic inputs that firms use to produce goods and services, so the cheaper it is, the more easily firms can produce output. Low energy costs make turning factors of production, such as labour and capital, into goods and services, relatively easy.

Whether the impact on the economy is permanent or temporary depends, of course, on whether the fall in energy prices is permanent or temporary.

Check out Figure 9-14. In the short run, a fall in energy costs increases aggregate supply from SRAS$_1$ to SRAS$_2$ and takes the economy from point A to point B by reducing the price level and increasing output. If energy prices were to return to their original level, short-run aggregate supply would shift back from SRAS$_2$ to SRAS$_1$, meaning that the price level would go back up and output would fall to its original level. If, however, the fall in energy prices was permanent, you'd expect long-run aggregate supply to also shift from LRAS$_1$ to LRAS$_2$, meaning a permanently higher level of output.

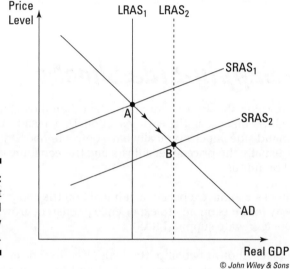

Figure 9-14:
The effect
of a fall
in energy
prices.

© John Wiley & Sons

But what about countries whose economies are major energy producers, such as Saudi Arabia or Russia? Here, things are a little different. Although domestic firms that use energy still find producing output easier, you need also to take into account that the energy being produced makes up a substantial portion of the goods and services being produced domestically. When the price of energy falls, the *value* of the goods and services being produced falls, and because real GDP is defined in terms of the *value* of goods and services, it also falls.

Here's another way of thinking about it. Russia produces a lot of energy – more than it can reasonably consume. When energy prices are high, it can convert that surplus energy into other goods and services at an attractive rate. But when energy prices are low, it can only convert energy into other goods at a poor rate, so reducing living standards and aggregate supply.

Innovating to effect change: Technological advances

As we describe in the earlier section 'Testing your faith: Confidence in the economy', a country's economy grows in two main ways: factor accumulation (more capital and more labour) and technological progress (finding better ways of producing outputs from inputs).

Rich countries already have large amounts of capital, and adding more people is unlikely to raise income per capita. This situation leaves technological progress as the only real means of increasing living standards over prolonged periods of time.

The natural level of output ($\bar{Y}$) is defined by $\bar{Y} = f\left(\bar{K}, \bar{L}\right)$; so any improvement in technology (represented by the function f) increases the natural level of output. The LRAS curve is vertical at $\bar{Y}$ and so shifts to the right. In Figure 9-15, technological progress has increased the natural level of output and shifted long-run aggregate supply from $LRAS_1$ to $LRAS_2$, increasing output and reducing the price level.

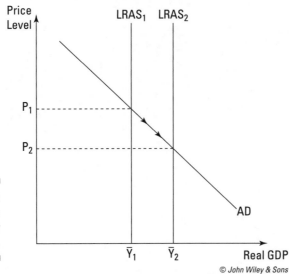

Figure 9-15: A positive technology shock.

© John Wiley & Sons

To invent or not to invent

Technological progress usually follows the generation of new ideas, so economists think that having clear *intellectual property rights* is important: they ensure that those who create new technologies are sufficiently rewarded. Otherwise, little incentive may exist to invest in the research and development. Firms would prefer to free-ride on the ideas of other firms.

On the other side of the coin, intellectual property rights can't be excessively generous: for example, giving monopoly rights to a firm to produce something for hundreds of years would shield them from competition and allow them to charge high prices to consumers. A balance is required between giving good incentives to generate new ideas and having competition between firms.

Part IV
Examining Macroeconomic Policy

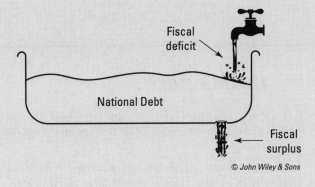

Fiscal deficit

National Debt

Fiscal surplus

© John Wiley & Sons

web extras

The Bank of England holds billions of pounds in bonds purchased by the UK government. The free article at www.dummies.com/extras/macroeconomicsuk explains why the Bank doesn't just cancel the payback of these bonds.

In this part . . .

- ✔ Take a look at how monetary policy determines the amount of money in circulation and what effect this has on the economy and inflation.

- ✔ See how policy makers influence the economy through the government's fiscal policies of expenditures and taxation.

- ✔ Examine the Phillips curve to understand how unemployment and inflation are related in the short run and the long run.

- ✔ Jump into the debate about whether policy makers should follow policy rules or use their discretion to control the economy.

Chapter 10

Using Monetary Policy to Influence the Economy

In This Chapter

▶ Understanding how monetary policy works

▶ Targeting the level of inflation

▶ Stimulating the economy with quantitative easing

▶ Discussing what monetary policy does (and doesn't) influence

*I*magine a world in which you can print your own money. If you're a little short of cash one day, you simply fire up the printing press and, voilà, problem solved! That house you always wanted but could never afford? No problem, just run the printing press for an hour or so and you're fine. In fact, in an age of electronic money you needn't even do that – with the touch of a button you'd just create the money!

Staying in your dream world for a minute, think about this question: if you print, say, £1 million and buy the house of your dreams (or in London the small flat of your dreams), who's actually paying for the house? Certainly not you: you just conjured up the money from thin air and so acquired the house 'for free'. Equally, the seller doesn't care that you printed the money – so long as it's genuine and has the Queen's head printed on it, he's happy. So who's paying for your luxury pad, if not you or the seller?

The answer is everyone who holds cash (in this case, pound sterling), and that's pretty much everyone (in the UK). By printing extra money, you effectively devalued all the existing money out there. This devaluation is reflected in now slightly higher prices for goods and services – in other words, inflation. (Check out Chapter 5 to discover exactly how printing money leads to inflation.)

What you discover from this slightly far-fetched scenario is that whoever has the ability to create money is effectively able to tax all the existing holders of cash. Whoever has the right to create money is awesomely powerful and needs to be trusted to exercise that power carefully. In most countries, the central bank has a monopoly over the creation of money. In this chapter you discover how the central bank increases (or decreases) the amount of money in circulation (called monetary policy) and what effect this behaviour has on the economy and inflation.

Seeing Monetary Policy in Action

Monetary policy refers to the use of the money supply by policy makers (usually the central bank) to influence the economy. We present a first look at how monetary policy impacts the economy in Chapter 9, but here we delve deeper into the inner mechanics of how monetary policy works.

To understand monetary policy you need to understand how the money market works, how the central bank can in effect choose the interest rate by varying the money supply and how it achieves this aim in practice. Luckily, we cover exactly these topics in this section!

Taking a stall at the money market

The money market is like any other market in that the price is determined by supply and demand. Things can get a little confusing, though, because you may be thinking: sure, a certain car or house can have a particular price, but how can money have a 'price'? Isn't money just money?

The price of money is the interest rate: or more precisely, the nominal interest rate (we compare the meaning of nominal versus real in Chapter 2). Cash is the most *liquid* of assets, which means that you can easily convert it into goods and services. But when you hold cash, you give up the return that you could get by holding a less liquid asset (say, government bonds or a savings account). Thus the *opportunity cost* of holding cash is the return on government bonds/savings account – that is, the nominal interest rate. So, if the nominal interest rate is 2 per cent, by holding cash you're effectively paying 2 per cent per year for the liquidity.

At high interest rates the demand for money tends to be low, whereas at low interest rates the demand for money is relatively high, because holding cash is very costly (in terms of opportunity cost) when the interest rate is high. That is, people hold only as much cash as is necessary to get them through the next few days (or even hours). Conversely, when interest rates are low, holding cash isn't that costly and people demand relatively a lot of it.

Bearing in mind that the central bank controls the money supply, equilibrium in the money market occurs when the quantity of money demanded is exactly equal to the quantity of money the central bank supplies. The interest rate adjusts to ensure that demand and supply are equal, as Figure 10-1 shows:

✔ The downward-sloping demand curve (D) shows that people want to hold more money as the interest rate falls (because the opportunity cost of holding money is reduced).

✔ The supply of money (S) is a completely vertical line – think of this as the central bank choosing exactly how much money is in circulation.

✔ The equilibrium interest rate (i^*) is the precise interest rate that ensures that the demand for money equals the supply of money.

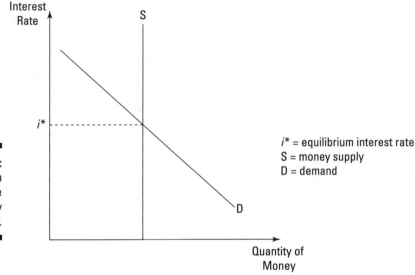

Figure 10-1:
Equilibrium
in the
money
market.

i^* = equilibrium interest rate
S = money supply
D = demand

© John Wiley & Sons

Changing the money supply affects the interest rate

The demand and supply of money determines the equilibrium interest rate, and the central bank controls the supply of money (see the preceding section). Therefore, the central bank can change the interest rate by varying the money supply:

✔ To reduce the interest rate, it increases the money supply.

✔ To increase the interest rate, it reduces the money supply.

In Figure 10-2, initially the supply of money corresponds to S_0, which leads to an equilibrium nominal interest rate of i_0. When the central bank increases the money supply to S_1, it reduces the equilibrium interest rate to i_1, because at the original interest rate (i_0) more money is now being supplied than demanded. This puts downward pressure on the price of money (the interest rate), causing the interest rate to fall to i_1 and bringing the money market back into equilibrium.

Similarly, the central bank can increase the interest rate by reducing the money supply to S_2, leading to an equilibrium interest rate of i_2. The rate increases because at the original interest rate (i_0) more money is now being demanded than supplied, putting upward pressure on the price of money (the interest rate). Therefore, the interest rate rises to i_2 and brings the money market back into equilibrium.

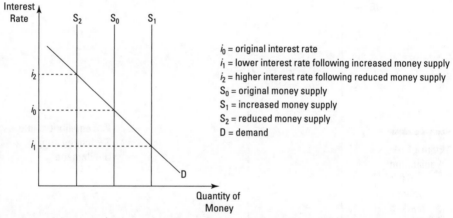

Figure 10-2:
Varying the
money
supply.

i_0 = original interest rate
i_1 = lower interest rate following increased money supply
i_2 = higher interest rate following reduced money supply
S_0 = original money supply
S_1 = increased money supply
S_2 = reduced money supply
D = demand

© John Wiley & Sons

Influencing the money supply:
Open market operations

In practice, the central bank varies the money supply using *open market operations*. These involve the bank going to the government bond market and buying and selling government bonds (see Figure 10-3):

✔ To increase the money supply, the central bank buys up some of the government bonds in circulation, paying for them with money. In doing so, it increases the amount of money in circulation.

✔ To decrease the money supply, the central bank sells some of the government bonds that it holds in return for money. In doing so, it decreases the amount of money in circulation.

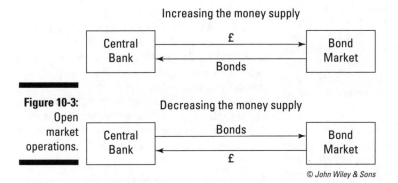

Figure 10-3:
Open
market
operations.

© John Wiley & Sons

The effects that open market operations have on the money market change the equilibrium interest rate as shown earlier in Figure 10-2.

The central bank isn't the same as the government. The central bank still expects to be paid by the government Treasury when the bonds it owns mature. The fact that the central bank owns some of the bonds doesn't relieve the government of its liabilities. Indeed the only reason the central bank is trading on the bond market is to affect the supply of money and thereby change the interest rate.

Another way of thinking about open market operations is to consider the effect on the bond market directly, because the money and bond markets are two sides of the same coin.

Many different kinds of bonds exist, some issued by governments and others by firms. Some bonds are seen as quite risky, because the probability of default (not repaying) is relatively high, whereas other bonds are less risky, because their probability of default is low. Bonds also differ in terms of their maturities: some have short maturities (they must be repaid quickly) and others have longer maturities.

Open market operations focus on buying and selling short-dated government bonds, because doing so allows the central bank to influence the price of those bonds. The price of a bond determines its yield, so the central bank is able to affect the implied interest rate on those bonds.

Bonds and how they work

Bonds are basically IOUs. Governments and firms routinely issue bonds in order to borrow money. So, for example, the UK Treasury may issue a bond that guarantees to pay the holder £1 million in ten years' time when someone is willing to pay the Treasury money *today* in order to own the bond (it's a valuable asset). In effect, the bond buyer is giving a loan to the government. When the bond *matures*, that is, it's time to pay up, the government is obliged to pay the bondholder the *face value* of the bond (in this case, £1 million).

Potential bondholders are probably only willing to pay some amount less than £1 million in order to secure themselves a return but also to compensate them for the risk. When bonds are initially sold, an auction is used to maximise revenue for the seller (in this case, the Treasury).

Clearly the government wants to sell the bond for as much as possible: the higher the price it achieves, the lower the interest rate it's paying to borrow money. For example, if the Treasury can sell the bond for a cool million today, it's not paying any 'interest' on its loan. If, however, it can only sell it for £0.5 million, it's paying over

7 per cent interest every year. The closer it gets to £1 million, the less interest it has to pay.

But this isn't the end of the story, because a thriving *secondary market* exists for bonds. So a bondholder doesn't have to wait until maturity in order to get paid. He can sell the bond today to someone else who's willing to hold the bond for a little while longer. Bond prices on the secondary market vary from day-to-day and from hour-to-hour, which means that the bond's *yield* also varies. The yield of a bond is the implied rate of interest bondholders are paid if they hold the bond until maturity (based on the current bond price, not the price it initially sold for).

Bond prices and bond yields are inversely related. So if for some reason the bond price falls today, the bond's yield increases, because the current bond price is lower but the face value is unchanged. Notice that this doesn't impact the interest rate that the government pays the bondholder, which was 'locked-in' when the bond was initially sold. But it does typically affect the rate of interest the government has to pay if it issues new bonds today.

Figure 10-4 makes this clearer. Initially the supply of short-dated government bonds is at S_0. When the bond price is high (yield is low), not many people want to hold bonds, but when the bond price is low (yield is high), many people want to hold them. Equilibrium in the bond market occurs when the quantity demanded is equal to the quantity supplied, which occurs at price p_0.

If the central bank wants to engage in *expansionary* monetary policy, it increases the supply of money by buying bonds in the secondary market, which reduces the supply of bonds available to everyone else. Think of this as reducing the supply of bonds from S_0 to S_1. Note that this causes the price of bonds to rise, which means a fall in bond yields: in other words, a fall in the interest rate!

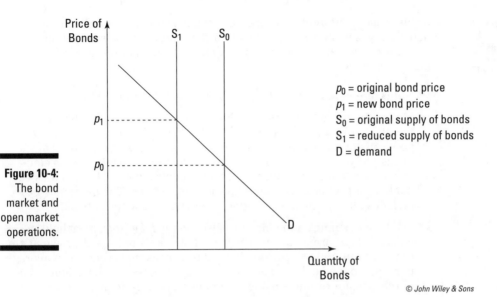

Price of Bonds / Quantity of Bonds

p_0 = original bond price
p_1 = new bond price
S_0 = original supply of bonds
S_1 = reduced supply of bonds
D = demand

Figure 10-4:
The bond market and open market operations.

© John Wiley & Sons

In a similar way, *contractionary* monetary policy reduces the supply of money by selling government bonds. In the secondary bond market this increases the supply of bonds and reduces their price, causing an increase in bond yields: in other words, an increase in the interest rate!

Controlling the supply of some types of money

The analysis that we present in the preceding sections assumes that the central bank has full control over the money supply, but this helpful simplification isn't entirely true. The central bank has control over only some of the different types of money. Everyone agrees that notes and coins are forms of money, but does your bank balance count as money? Does it make a difference if it's in a savings account or a current account? If you write a cheque, is that money? Are your credit or debit cards as good as money? When you start thinking about this issue, what precisely counts as money isn't at all clear.

For this reason, different measures and categories exist regarding how much money is in an economy. The first three measures are sometimes called *narrow money*, because they're quite restricted in terms of what counts as money:

- ✓ **Notes and coins:** Simply the notes and coins in circulation.

- ✓ **M0 (or the monetary base):** Includes notes and coins but also commercial banks' claims on the central bank. In a modern economy, when you transfer money to your friend, your bank doesn't send over a wad of cash to your friend's bank. Instead, commercial banks use an electronic payment system managed by the central bank. Think of it as each bank having a bank account with the central bank. The monetary base includes all this 'electronic money' held with the central bank.

- ✓ **M1:** Includes notes and coins but also *demand deposits*, ones held by individuals or firms in accounts that allow funds to be withdrawn at any time without notice. The idea behind this measure is that, to an average person, money held in an account that can be used to make immediate purchases, for example using a debit card, is as good as cash.

The next three measures are more liberal about what counts as money, and so are sometimes called *broad money*:

- ✓ **M2:** Includes the items in M1 but also savings deposits and small time deposits held by people. The money held in these accounts typically pays interest, and depositors may incur penalties if they want to access their funds at short notice.

- ✓ **M3:** Includes the items in M2, but also large time deposits and some *money market funds*. These large funds combine savings from many different individuals and try to get a good return without taking on (much) risk.

- ✓ **M4:** Even broader than M3, you get the idea. . . !

Although the central bank has a good amount of control over narrow measures of money, it has not much control over broad measures of money. For this reason central banks have to use a number of different strategies in order to change the interest rate:

- ✓ **Open market operations:** Buying and selling bonds to affect the supply of money and the yield on government bonds (see the preceding section).

- ✓ **Allowing commercial banks to borrow from the central bank at a certain rate:** Usually very short-term loans (overnight). The idea is that making it cheaper (or more expensive) for banks to borrow from the central bank impacts the rates at which banks are willing to lend money.

✔ **Allowing banks to deposit excess reserves at the central bank and earn a certain rate:** Banks can guarantee a certain return if they deposit money. In the UK, the Bank of England calls this rate the *bank rate*.

✔ **Repurchase agreements:** The central bank buys government bonds from a bank but at the same time enters into a contract to sell those bonds back to the bank in a week's time at a slightly higher price. Think of it as the central bank lending money to the commercial bank at a certain interest rate (called the *repo rate* in the UK).

Deciding who can borrow at the base rate: Hint, it's not you!

In 2009, the Bank of England reduced interest rates to 0.5 per cent. They're still at that level as of 2015 and may stay that low for some time. The thing is, if you go to your local bank or building society and ask for a loan with an interest rate of 0.5 per cent, they'll probably collapse in fits of laughter. Why can't individuals and firms borrow at the official interest rate?

The interest rate set by the central bank is only available to commercial banks and not to private individuals or firms because the government hopes that an official low interest rate will encourage commercial banks to lend at lower rates of interest. If the official interest rate is high, it increases borrowing costs for everyone else.

Commercial banks charge higher rates partly because they can, but also because costs are involved in assessing who should be lent money and who shouldn't: that is, who's likely to repay and who isn't. Furthermore, when lending, commercial banks need to add a *risk premium* depending on how risky they think a borrower is. If a good chance exists that someone won't repay a loan, banks are only willing to lend at a relatively high rate. On the other hand, someone seen as a 'good risk' usually gets a better rate.

Competition between commercial banks is meant to ensure that people don't pay over the odds to borrow money and that any change in the central bank's official interest rate filters through the financial system.

Exerting Control over Inflation

By using monetary policy, the central bank is able to set the interest rate. The interest rate impacts on a number of macroeconomic variables, including the price level, output, unemployment, consumption, exchange rate and so on. The big question is what the objective of monetary policy should be: to reduce unemployment, increase economic growth, support the exchange rate? And what problems are involved in achieving the stated aim?

Targeting inflation for price stability

The last few decades have seen a growing consensus among policy makers that the primary objective of monetary policy should be to control the rate of inflation (central banks often call this objective *price stability*). That's not because policy makers don't care about other macroeconomic variables, just that, in the long run, monetary policy is rather useless at influencing, say, economic growth or unemployment. Anyone who tries to use monetary policy to achieve objectives other than controlling inflation is likely to find themselves in hot water pretty quickly. (You can read more about the dangers of using monetary policy to reduce unemployment in Chapter 12.)

The acceptance that monetary policy should be devoted to achieving price stability means that many central banks have adopted an explicit policy of inflation targeting, including the central banks of New Zealand, Chile, Canada, Israel, the UK, Sweden, Australia, Korea, Norway, the EU and the US. The latter was quite late to the party, only adopting an official inflation target in 2012, although unofficially economists understood that it had been targeting inflation for some time before then.

Inflation targeting involves announcing a target level (or range) of inflation that the central bank aims for. It then uses monetary policy to achieve (or attempt to achieve) the target level of inflation. The central bank must publicly announce the target and not keep it to itself, because doing so puts the bank's reputation on the line and makes it more likely to hit the target. (You can read more about an important debate related to this point [the rules versus discretion debate] in Chapter 13.)

In theory, inflation targeting should be pretty simple to implement:

- ✔ **Inflation above target:** Raise the interest rate to reduce aggregate demand and reduce inflation.
- ✔ **Inflation below target:** Lower the interest rate to boost aggregate demand and increase inflation.

As you can guess, however, in reality things aren't quite so simple.

Accounting for policy time lags

Interest rate decisions today take around 18–24 months to have their full effect on the economy. Therefore, policy makers have to be forward-looking when making monetary policy decisions today and think about what inflation is likely to be around two years in the future.

Central banks do have sophisticated models for predicting what future infla-tion is likely to be, but it's a notoriously difficult task, so policy is made under conditions of uncertainty. Achieving the target for sure is impossible, but the bank hopes that it'll be close most of the time.

In the UK, for example, the target rate of inflation is currently 2 per cent. But achieving this target exactly and at all times is neither possible nor desirable (trying to do so would involve very large movements in the interest rate). Instead, only if inflation is more than 1 per cent away from target (that is, out-side the range 1–3 per cent) does the Bank of England have to explain in an open letter (which you can read on its website) why it failed to meet the target.

Identifying the underlying cause of the shock

The central bank has to consider the *cause* of inflation before deciding whether to act:

- ✔ If inflation is too high compared to the target due to aggregate demand increasing too much, increasing the interest rate sounds like a good plan: it's likely to reduce inflation and bring output back to its natural level.

- ✔ If inflation is too high due to a temporary supply-side shock, such as high energy prices, the central bank will be wary of increasing interest rates, because doing so will reduce output even further. The bank may be better off waiting for output to return to its natural level.

In Figure 10-5a, the economy has experienced a positive aggregate demand shock that increased AD from AD_1 to AD_2. This event increased the price level from p_1 to p_2 and if policy makers do nothing, the price level is likely to rise further to p_3. To stop this, the central bank can increase interest rates and bring aggregate demand back down to AD_1.

In Figure 10-5b, the economy has experienced a negative aggregate supply shock that increased the price level and simultaneously reduced output. This rather unpleasant phenomenon is sometimes called *stagflation*. If policy makers are worried that inflation is too high, they can increase interest rates (reducing AD), but doing so would reduce output even further. Instead, they may wait and hope that the supply shock is temporary and that the economy will return to its natural level of output.

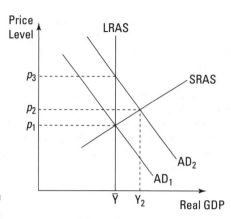
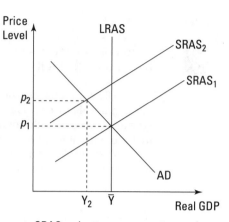

Figure 10-5:
Monetary
policy:
(a) demand
shock;
(b) supply
shock.

p_1 = original price level
p_2 = new short-run price level
p_3 = new long-run price level
$\bar{Y}$ = natural level of output
Y_2 = new short-run output
LRAS = long-run aggregate supply

SRAS = short-run aggregate supply
$SRAS_1$ = original SRAS
$SRAS_2$ = new SRAS
AD = aggregate demand
AD_1 = original aggregate demand
AD_2 = new aggregate demand

(a)　　　　　　　　　　　　　　　(b)

© John Wiley & Sons

Spotting the Liquidity Trap and Quantitative Easing

Sometimes traditional monetary policy (reducing the interest rate) becomes ineffective because the interest rate is already at (or near) zero – this is known as the *liquidity trap*. In recent times this has meant that some central banks have turned to *quantitative easing* (creating large amounts of new money) in order to stimulate the economy. In this section you discover more about both of these.

Zeroing in on the liquidity trap

The *liquidity trap* (often also called the *zero lower bound* problem) has been a big headache for policy makers worldwide for a number of years. It goes something like this. At some point conventional monetary policy becomes ineffective, because increasing the money supply further has no impact on the nominal interest rate; people are already willing to hold as much money as the central bank chooses to supply at that interest rate.

This problem occurs when the nominal interest rate is equal to zero, because the opportunity cost of holding cash is now zero. When you can't earn a return on your funds anyway, you may as well hold them in cash. After all, cash is the most liquid of all assets, and when the nominal interest rate is equal to zero, you can't do better than cash anyway.

In Figure 10-6, the money supply is initially represented by S_0 and the equilibrium nominal interest rate is already at zero. Increasing the money supply further to S_1 has no impact on the interest rate, because people are willing to hold unlimited cash if the nominal interest rate is zero! Compare this to the situation in Figure 10-2 where an increase in the money supply does result in a fall in the interest rate when there is no liquidity trap.

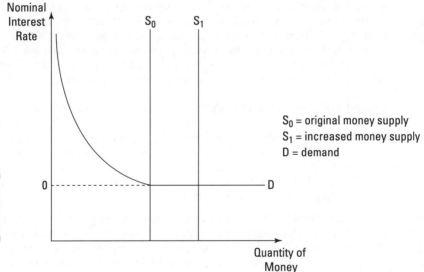

Figure 10-6:
Liquidity
trap.

© John Wiley & Sons

 Another way of thinking about this situation is as follows: if nominal interest rates are below zero, that is, negative, and you give someone £10, in the future he'd give you back less than £10. You'd be paying him for lending him money, which is crazy! You'd do better keeping hold of your cash.

 If you follow the news closely, you may smell a rat here! Highly unusually, recent years have seen a few cases where the nominal interest rate (yield) on some government bonds has been very slightly negative. Therefore, instead of being paid, people were effectively paying those governments for the privilege of lending them money. Why would anyone do that? They must have been so worried that they thought it was safer than putting the money in the bank or even under the mattress! But this situation is exceptionally rare and in 'less interesting times' you don't expect it to happen.

It does leave a problem, however: what are policy makers to do if the nominal interest rate is already at zero (or very close) and they want to stimulate the economy using monetary policy? Enter quantitative easing!

Querying the nature of quantitative easing

Quantitative easing (*QE*) involves the central bank creating new money and using it to purchase assets such as government bonds from the private sector. In many ways this behaviour is similar to conventional open market operations in that it increases the supply of money (check out the earlier section 'Influencing the money supply: Open market operations'). What's different is that the central bank isn't trying to reduce the official interest rate (in the UK, the *bank rate*), because that's already at or very close to zero.

Instead, QE is meant to stimulate the economy in a number of ways:

- ✔ **Reducing the yield on assets:** By buying up large amounts of assets, the central bank hopes to increase their prices. In doing so it decreases the yield on these assets. For example, if QE increases stock prices, the dividend yield on equities falls. Equally, if bond prices increase due to QE, holding bonds is less attractive.

  The central bank is attempting to make lending money relatively more attractive than purchasing financial assets. You can think about the return (yield) on financial assets as the opportunity cost of lending money. By acting to reduce the yield, the central bank reduces the opportunity cost of lending money.

- ✔ **Boosting consumption:** Related to the point above, if asset prices such as shares and property increase, household wealth also increases, which should increase consumption.

- ✔ **Reducing the real interest rate:** The Fisher equation (which we discuss in detail in the following section) links the nominal interest rate (i), the real interest rate (r) and inflation (π):

$$i = r + \pi$$

Rearranging, you can see that the real interest rate is equal to the nominal interest rate minus inflation:

$$r = i - \pi$$

Policy makers can reduce the real interest rate in only two ways:

- Reduce the nominal interest rate.

- Increase inflation.

But the nominal interest rate is already near zero, which leaves only the second option. By injecting large amounts of new money into the economy, the central bank can increase inflation. (Read more about how increasing the supply of money leads to inflation in Chapter 5.)

✔ **Flooding the financial system with liquidity:** Even though the official interest rate is close to zero in many advanced economies, the rate at which individuals and firms can borrow is substantially higher. Flooding the financial system with liquidity aims to bring all other interest rates in the economy closer to the official interest rate.

Reeling in the Fisher Effect

Like most things in macroeconomics, monetary policy has a different impact in the short run and the long run. In the short run monetary policy has real effects: it changes the level of real GDP and unemployment. However in the long run monetary policy has no real effects. The Fisher effect (explained in this section) makes this clear.

The *Fisher effect* says that in the long run an increase in the growth rate of the money supply by one percentage point leads to a one-percentage-point increase in the nominal interest rate and the inflation rate. However, it has no effect on the real interest rate or the growth rate of output.

Quite a lot is going on in that paragraph, but by a great stroke of luck we devote this section to making sense of it!

Discovering the real interest rate in the long run

The real interest rate in the long run is determined by the *market for loanable funds*, which is where savers meet investors: more precisely, it's where people with excess money lend to those with investment projects that need financing. Of course, savers and investors don't usually meet each other directly – the financial system acts as a convenient intermediary between them.

Saving and investment in a closed economy

An intimate link exists between the amount of savings (S) and investment (I) in an economy. In fact, in a *closed economy* (one that doesn't trade with the rest of the world), they must be exactly equal to each other (Chapter 9 explains why):

$$S = I$$

This expression is quite peculiar when you think about it. Why should the total amount of savings in a country exactly equal the new capital stock being purchased that year? What ensures that they're equal? The answer is the interest rate, which is the price that adjusts to ensure that the amount people want to save is exactly equal to the amount people want to invest.

In Figure 10-7, I(r) is investment that's a function of the real interest rate: the lower r, the more investment firms want to undertake. I(r) also represents the demand for loanable funds. The vertical line S is savings, that is, what's left over from output after consumption and government spending (Y − C − G). S also represents the supply of loanable funds. The interest rate adjusts to ensure that the demand for loanable funds is exactly equal to the supply of loanable funds.

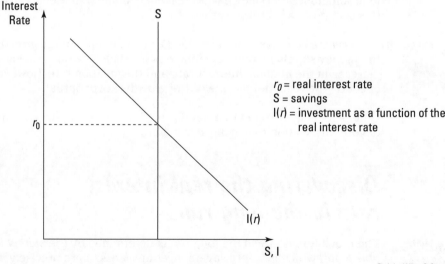

r_0 = real interest rate
S = savings
I(r) = investment as a function of the real interest rate

Figure 10-7:
Market for
loanable
funds.

© John Wiley & Sons

Saving and investment in an open economy

You may be concerned that savings only equals investment in a closed economy. This is a reasonable concern, because most countries engage in large amounts of international trade. In an open economy, the correct relationship between savings and investment is:

$$S - I = NX$$

NX is net exports and so, in words, savings less investment must exactly equal net exports.

This simple expression has a rather 'deep' interpretation: if a country has more savings than investment (S – I > 0), the excess savings flow abroad, which is why S – I is called *net capital outflow*. You can think of this net capital outflow as the country lending money to the rest of the world.

Interestingly, the money lent abroad is exactly equal to net exports: that is, the net demand for goods and services from abroad. For example, if the UK's net capital outflow is equal to £1 billion, all that money would be used by foreigners to buy UK exports. In return, people in the UK effectively receive a claim on (that is, ownership of) £1 billion worth of capital stock abroad.

So what determines the real interest rate in an open economy? Answer: the global market for loanable funds. The interest rate adjusts to ensure that global savings is exactly equal to global investment. This isn't surprising, because the world economy as a whole is a closed economy (at least until humans find alien life and begin trading with them!).

Call r^* the equilibrium world interest rate. Then for a small open economy (small relative to the world economy as a whole) the following must apply:

$$r = r^*$$

That is, the domestic real interest rate (r) must exactly equal the world interest rate. If not, arbitrageurs could make a riskless profit. For example, if $r > r^*$, arbitrageurs could borrow domestically at rate r and then lend abroad for rate r^*. Doing so would increase the demand for domestic savings (increasing r) and increase the supply of savings in the global market (reducing r^*). Arbitrage would continue until $r = r^*$. You can apply a similar argument for $r < r^*$.

Monetary policy doesn't affect saving and investment

Whether you're looking at an individual economy or the world economy as a whole, in the long run, the supply of savings and the demand for investment in the market for loanable funds are unaffected by monetary policy. You can see this because savings is equal to (see Chapter 9):

$$S = \bar{Y} - C\left(\bar{Y} - \bar{T}\right) - \bar{G}$$

Savings is what's left over from output after taking away consumption and government spending. In the long run, output is independent of monetary policy and equals its natural level $\bar{Y}$. Consumption is a function of disposable income (Y – T), which is also independent of monetary policy, $Y = \bar{Y}$, and taxes are set by the government, $T = \bar{T}$. Equally, government spending is independent of monetary policy, $G = \bar{G}$.

Similarly, the demand for capital goods/investment is a function of the real interest rate (r). This rate is determined by equilibrium in the loanable funds market (the domestic loanable funds market for a closed economy and the global loanable funds market for an open economy). And because monetary policy affects neither savings nor investment in the long run, the real long-run interest rate is also independent of monetary policy.

The nominal interest rate in the long run

The preceding section shows that the *real* interest rate is independent of monetary policy in the long run. In this section, you see that increasing the growth rate of the money supply does have a one-for-one impact on the *nominal* interest rate. Understanding these two phenomena is key to understanding the Fisher effect: in the long run, expansionary monetary policy only increases inflation and the nominal interest rate; it has no effect on the real interest rate or output.

We start with the quantity equation:

$$MV = PY$$

where M is the stock of money, V is the velocity of circulation (how fast money travels around the economy), P is the price level and Y is output. We can easily convert that into growth rates (see Chapter 5):

$$g_M + g_V = g_P + g_Y$$

Assuming that the velocity of circulation doesn't grow over time ($g_V = 0$), and noticing that inflation is by definition the growth rate of prices ($\pi = g_P$), yields:

$$g_M = \pi + g_Y$$

Rearranging for inflation gives:

$$\pi = g_M - g_Y$$

So the rate of inflation is equal to the growth of the money supply minus the growth rate of output. Note that in the long run output growth is independent of monetary policy (as we discuss in Chapter 8), because technological progress drives increases in living standards. A reasonable assumption is that technological progress is independent of monetary policy, which means that g_Y is independent of monetary policy. Thus, increasing the growth of the money supply increases inflation one-for-one:

$$\pi = g_M - \overline{g_Y}$$

where $\overline{g_Y}$ is the 'natural' growth rate of output in the long run.

In the long run, changes in the growth rate of the money supply (g_M) have no effect on the real interest rate (r). They do, however, increase inflation (π) one-for-one: that is, an increase in g_M by one percentage point increases inflation by one percentage point. Using the Fisher equation you can see that inflation rising by one percentage point means a one-percentage-point increase in the nominal interest rate (i):

$$i = \overline{r} + \pi$$

where $\overline{r}$ is the real interest rate determined in the market for loanable funds. Thus, in the long run, increasing the growth rate of the money supply increases inflation one-for-one, which increases the nominal interest rate one-for-one!

Understanding that money is neutral in the long run

Throughout this chapter and indeed this book you may notice that monetary policy has little effect on the economy in the long run. It has no effect on output (Y) or the real interest rate (r) or the level of unemployment. Neither does it have any effect on consumption (C), investment (I), the real wage or the real exchange rate.

This is no accident! In fact, it's a reflection of a very important result in macro-economics: the *classical dichotomy*, which says that in the long run, money has no effect on *real* variables, like output, unemployment or the real interest rate – it only affects nominal variables.

Monetary policy can, however, affect real variables in the short run. To convince yourself, consider an increase in aggregate demand caused by expansionary monetary policy. This typically increases output, reduces unemployment and reduces the real interest rate in the short run.

Monetary policy does influence nominal variables, such as the price level, nominal interest rate, inflation rate and nominal exchange rate in the long run. To see why, consider what would happen in the long run if the quantity of money in an economy doubled: all prices including nominal wages would double too. But no one would be any richer, because everything you could buy before, you could still buy now. Furthermore, the relative prices between different goods (for example, two bananas cost the same as one pear) would remain unchanged.

Chapter 11

Fiscal Policy: Balancing the Books – Perhaps

Fiscal policy refers to policy makers' policy (that's a lot of 'policy'!) as it relates to government expenditure and taxation: it impacts your own and everyone's lives in profound ways:

- ✔ When you receive your monthly pay (and sigh heavily because it's always less than you want), the amount of your salary that you get to keep after taxes depends on fiscal policy.

- ✔ When you spend your salary, fiscal policy impacts the price you pay for goods and services, whether you're renting the latest Hollywood blockbuster on DVD or buying tickets for the opera. For example in the UK, value added tax (VAT) adds 20 per cent to the price of most goods and services (including that Channing Tatum action flick, but not fruit and veg).

- ✔ When you get sick and visit your doctor (and you're lucky enough to live in a country where the government provides health services), the quality of the treatment you receive depends on fiscal policy.

- ✔ When you send your children to a state school, you're receiving a transfer that pays for their education due to fiscal policy.

Very few areas of economic life aren't impacted by fiscal policy, so changes in it have the potential to create large impacts on individuals and the economy. To see how fiscal policy affects aggregate demand and supply, check out Chapter 9. Here you discover how fiscal policy affects the economy and the constraints that policy makers face when undertaking it.

Delving into Fiscal Policy

Turn on the news and you're likely to see some politician talking about fiscal policy, or more accurately what should happen to government spending or taxation. If you listen carefully to what's said, you may notice that what's promised is higher spending on some social programme or lower taxes for the public.

These statements sound peculiar to economists, because higher government spending has to be paid for somehow, either by reducing spending elsewhere or by increasing taxes now or in the future. Similarly, lowering taxes means less revenue for the government and therefore less government spending now or in the future.

In this section we show you why this restriction on a government's freedom of choice has to exist, the details of debt and deficits (often the result of the constraint) and how governments can raise their revenue.

Acknowledging that governments face budget constraints

The fact that politicians tend to focus on the positives and ignore the negatives isn't surprising, but people need to be clear about the following:

✔ Promising more government spending is equivalent to promising higher taxes, now or in the future.

✔ Promising lower taxes is equivalent to promising lower government spending, now or in the future.

But why can't the government just increase spending without increasing taxes at some point in the future? The reason is that the government, much like a household, faces its own *intertemporal budget constraint* (*intertemporal* just means 'across time'), which constrains the kinds of choices it can make.

Thinking of a household's budget constraint

The easiest way to explain the intertemporal budget constraint is to think about it in terms of a household that lives for two time periods, $t = 1, 2$:

✔ In time period 1, the household receives income equal to y_1 and has to decide how much to consume, c_1.

✔ In time period 2, the household receives income equal to y_2 and has to decide how much to consume, c_2.

✔ If the household decides to save some of its income in time period 1, this amount $(y_1 - c_1)$ is put into a savings account and *earns* an interest rate equal to r. (Alternatively, the household could decide to borrow in period 1 from its period 2 income, in which case it would have to *pay* interest at rate r.)

The question is: what's the relationship between all these variables? Well, in period 2 the household has to decide how much to consume: after all, it's the final period and so no point saving anything – it may as well consume as much as it possibly can! With this in mind, period 2 consumption must equal:

$$c_2 = y_2 + (1+r)(y_1 - c_1)$$

In words, this equation says that in period 2, the household should consume all its income in that period plus all its savings.

Notice that the savings term $(y_1 - c_1)$ is multiplied by $(1 + r)$ because of the return it earns. For example, if the interest rate is $r = 5$ per cent and the household saves £100 in period 1, by period 2 its savings would've grown to £105 = (1.05)(£100).

This equation must still be true even if the household borrows in period 1: that is, it consumes more than its income ($c_1 > y_1$). Except that now $y_1 - c_1$ is negative and represents the household's borrowing in period 1. It's also multiplied by $(1 + r)$, because interest must be paid on the loan.

If you divide both sides of the equation by $(1 + r)$ and rearrange, you get:

$$c_1 + \frac{c_2}{1+r} = y_1 + \frac{y_2}{1+r}$$

This equation says something interesting: the net present value (NPV) of consumption better be equal to the NPV of income. The NPV of something is the equivalent value of it in terms of money *today*.

For example, the NPV of getting £100 today is clearly £100. But what about the NPV of £100 in one year's time? Is it still £100? Well, what would you prefer: £100 today or £100 in a year's time? Most people go for the £100 today – therefore, the NPV of £100 in a year's time is less than £100. Getting £100 next year just isn't as good as getting it today.

But then how good is getting £100 next year in terms of money today: in other words, what's the NPV of £100 next year?

Looking to the household's future

One way of discovering the NPV of £100 next year is to ask another question: how much money would you need today in order to turn it into £100 next year? Well, if you have £X today and you save it at interest rate r, next year you have £$(1 + r)X$. Setting this expression equal to £100 gives you the following:

$$(1+r)X = £100$$

$$\Rightarrow X = \frac{£100}{1+r}$$

That is, you need exactly £100/(1 + r) today in order to turn it into £100 next year, which is why the NPV of £100 next year is £100/(1 + r).

Applying this logic more generally, the NPV of £X in t years' time is equal to:

$$\frac{£X}{(1+r)^t}$$

Notice that the farther away in the future something is, the more heavily it's discounted. That is, the NPV of £100 in two years' time is less than the NPV of £100 in one year's time. But they're both much larger than the NPV of £100 in 100 years' time!

So what the earlier equation

$$c_1 + \frac{c_2}{1+r} = y_1 + \frac{y_2}{1+r}$$

is really saying is that the NPV of all the household consumption better be equal to the NPV of all your income, otherwise:

- ✔ **If the NPV of consumption is greater than the NPV of income:** The *consumption stream* (the consumption over time taken as a whole) is unaffordable.

- ✔ **If the NPV of consumption is less than the NPV of income:** The household could increase its consumption.

Moving from a household to the government

The government is much like a household in that every year it gets some income in the form of taxes (T) and every year it has to decide how much to spend (G). Like a household, the government can choose to spend less than it earns and save the difference or (more commonly) spend more than it earns and borrow the difference. So, from year-to-year, no reason exists for $T = G$.

But the government's intertemporal budget constraint does put a constraint on what kind of fiscal policy is feasible. It says that the NPV of all the tax revenue better equal the NPV of all its spending:

$$G_1 + \frac{G_2}{1+r} + \frac{G_3}{(1+r)^2} + \ldots = T_1 + \frac{T_2}{1+r} + \frac{T_3}{(1+r)^2} + \ldots$$

On the left-hand side of this equation is the NPV of an infinite stream of government purchases and on the right-hand side is the NPV of an infinite stream of taxes. (You may think that assuming that the government is going to be around forever is a bit far-fetched, but because knowing how long is impossible and because cash flows very far in the future have a negligible NPV, the simplification is useful.)

Therefore, looking at this equation you can clearly see that increasing government spending today (G_1) must either coincide with a fall in future government spending or an increase in taxes at some point. Equally, a fall in taxes today (T_1) must be made up for either by an increase in taxes in the future or a fall in government spending at some point. In short, there's no free lunch (though we hear the MPs' restaurants in the Houses of Parliament come close!).

Distinguishing between deficit and debt

The economic crisis of the late 2000s meant that large amounts of private sector liabilities were transferred to the public sector. (You can read more about this in Chapter 16.) Ever since then, governments around the world have been trying to deal with the fiscal repercussions.

The UK in particular has seen a strong focus on 'getting the deficit down'. Politicians regularly justify their decisions with reference to the effect that they'll have on the fiscal deficit and the national debt. Therefore, more than ever, people need to have a good understanding of what exactly these terms mean and how they're related. Luckily, that's precisely what we provide in this section!

Fiscal deficit

A *fiscal deficit*, often just called *a deficit* for short, refers to the case where the government is spending more on government purchases (G) than it earns through taxation (T). The opposite of a deficit is a *fiscal surplus*, where the government spends less than it earns through taxation.

Sometimes thinking about the *fiscal balance* is useful: the amount of tax revenue less government spending ($T - G$). When the government runs a surplus, the fiscal balance is positive, and if it runs a deficit, the fiscal balance is negative.

The fiscal deficit is a *flow variable*, which means that you need to specify the period of time you're talking about. Just saying that the deficit is £1 billion doesn't mean anything unless you also say something like 'the deficit was £1 billion in 2015 or £600 million in the first quarter of 2015'.

Nevertheless, sadly, you still hear people quoting the amount of the deficit without reference to the time period. In this case, usually the person is referring to the most recent quarterly or annual deficit (or surplus).

Figure 11-1 shows the UK fiscal deficit from 1970 to the present day – and it's not a pretty sight! Except for a few years in the late 1980s and late 1990s/early 2000s, the UK has been running fiscal deficits. Furthermore, in the recent past (since the late 2000s), the fiscal deficit has been large, and despite all the cuts in government expenditure since then, it has persisted.

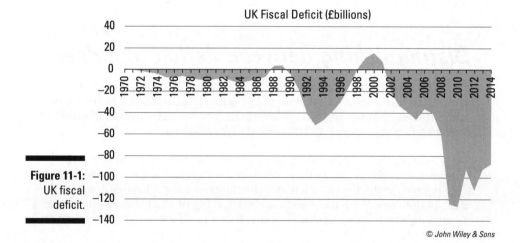

Figure 11-1: UK fiscal deficit.

© John Wiley & Sons

These numbers make sense when you consider that one of the consequences of the financial crisis and the long recession that followed was to make it much harder for the government to collect tax revenue – people and firms just weren't making as much money. At the same time, increased unemployment put pressure on government welfare programmes.

National debt

Whereas the fiscal deficit is a flow variable, the *national debt* is a stock variable. It tells you how much money the government owes at any given time to its creditors (the people who've lent it money over the years). For example, in early 2015 the UK national debt was around £1.5 trillion, which means that at some point the government will have to pay this amount back (plus interest) from future tax revenue.

An intimate relationship exists between the fiscal deficit (when government spending is greater than tax revenue) and the national debt (see Figure 11-2). The national debt is basically the accumulation of all past fiscal deficits. Think about it like bathwater (bear with us):

- ✔ **The fiscal deficit is like the clear water that flows from the tap:** Whenever government spending is more than tax revenue, this situation causes the tap to run and the bathwater to increase. The difference between spending and tax revenue must be covered by new borrowing, which adds to the national debt.

- ✔ **The national debt is the dirty bathwater as a whole (that causes your skin to wrinkle like a prune):** It's an accumulation of all the previous fiscal deficits. But if the government runs a fiscal surplus (government spending is less than tax revenue), some of the bathwater can drain away; that is, the difference between spending and tax revenue can be used to pay off existing debts, which reduces the national debt.

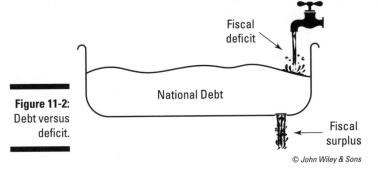

Figure 11-2: Debt versus deficit.

© John Wiley & Sons

In the UK, much of the political debate over the past few years has focused on austerity, the deficit and national debt. Politicians vie with each other as to who will balance the books and reduce the deficit the quickest. Despite all the bluster (and the spending cuts), you might be surprised to learn that in 2014 the UK ran a budget deficit of £87 bln. That is, not only did the UK not manage to pay off any of its debts, it added to them substantially!

Running deficits every year: Debt-to-GDP ratio

The preceding section makes clear that if a government runs a deficit today and funds it by borrowing, at some point in the future it has to pay it back. If that's the case, surely in some years the government needs to run fiscal surpluses in order to balance the years of fiscal deficits.

But hang on a minute. The earlier Figure 11-1 clearly shows that isn't the case in the UK (and indeed in most countries) – instead the tendency has been to run persistent deficits with only the occasional surplus. How is that possible?

The argument goes as follows. Although any year with a fiscal deficit increases the national debt, at the same time, countries tend to experience economic growth over time. People shouldn't be concerned about how indebted a country is in absolute terms; they should consider how indebted the country is relative to how rich it is.

For this reason economists often look at what's happening to the debt-to-GDP ratio over time. If it's falling, most likely the country's debt is sustainable. If it's persistently rising, the country may have difficulty meeting its liabilities if it's not careful.

Figure 11-3 shows that over time UK debt has tended to increase and that in recent years it has increased substantially. This is consistent with Figure 11-1, shown earlier, which shows that the UK has tended to run fiscal deficits and that these have been particularly large recently.

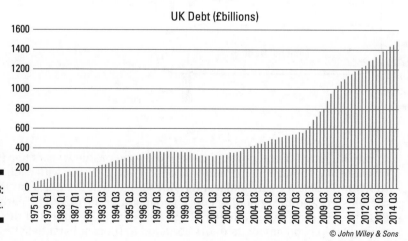

Figure 11-3: UK debt.

© John Wiley & Sons

In Figure 11-4, you can see that no clear trend exists in the UK's debt-to-GDP ratio: at certain times (the 1980s) it fell; at other times (the 2000s) it rose.

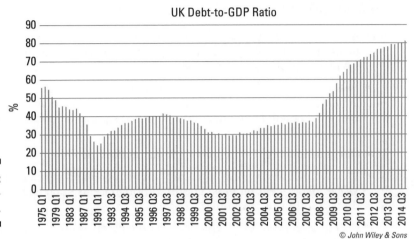

UK Debt-to-GDP Ratio

Figure 11-4: UK debt-to-GDP ratio.

© John Wiley & Sons

Notice that even though UK debt has been steadily increasing over the years (with a few minor exceptions), the debt-to-GDP ratio has fallen at times because during those periods, GDP increased faster than the national debt:

- ✔ A *falling* debt-to-GDP ratio is always good news, because it means that a nation's finances look sustainable even if it's running persistent deficits.

- ✔ An *increasing* debt-to-GDP ratio is a matter of concern, because it indicates that a country's debts are becoming less and less affordable.

So even though the UK's national debt continues to increase, so too has GDP. You can see in Figure 11-4 that the UK's debt-to-GDP ratio, although historically high, appears to be stabilising at around 80 per cent. And because the UK government is still able to borrow from financial markets at very low interest rates, it seems that investors think the UK Exchequer will pay back their loans eventually.

Raising a government's revenue

In essence, a government can raise revenue to fund its expenditure in three ways: taxes, bonds (which we argue are just delayed taxes) or *seigniorage* (printing money, which we argue leads to an inflation tax). Therefore, if bonds and printing money equate to taxes anyway, in practice a government has only one way to raise revenue: through taxation! Nonetheless, looking at each of these ways separately is useful.

Taxes

In the UK, annual government tax revenue equals around one-third of the country's gross domestic product (GDP). Here are a few of the ways in which taxes are collected:

- ✔ **Income tax:** The tax payable on earned income. For most people, earned income is their salary from working, but it also includes income from savings, rental income and dividend income from shares.
- ✔ **National insurance (NI):** Originally paid to fund certain state benefits, NI is paid by workers and firms. Nowadays it's similar to income tax, except that entitlement to the full state pension requires a certain number of years of NI contributions.
- ✔ **Corporation tax:** Taxes paid by firms on their profits.
- ✔ **VAT:** A tax levied on the consumption of goods and services. In the UK, VAT is 20 per cent on most goods, although items such as food and children's clothes are excluded.
- ✔ **Duties:** Ever wondered why petrol and cigarettes are so expensive? That's right, a large portion of the price is a tax. Duties are a serious source of revenue for governments: for example, fuel duty earns the Exchequer more than £25 billion per year!
- ✔ **Taxes on capital:** Taxes on things you own – includes capital gains tax, inheritance tax and stamp duty.

The revenue raised from taxes allows the government to purchase goods and services for the public, pay public servants and so on. It's also used to redistribute income, typically (though not always!) from richer people to poorer people.

Strictly speaking, the revenues raised for redistributive purposes aren't called taxes but *transfers*. Equally, when economists talk about government expenditure, they usually exclude transfers, because transfers only involve the transferring of purchasing power from some individuals to others – they don't involve the purchase of goods and services.

Bonds

When the government runs a fiscal deficit, it has to make up the difference between spending and revenue somehow. Issuing bonds is the main way in which governments fund deficits. A *bond* is like an IOU, a piece of paper that promises to pay the owner some amount of money at a certain date in the future.

For example, the UK government could issue a bond that promises to pay the owner £10 million in 2025. It would sell the bond today in order to raise money. But how much would it be sold for? Well, in normal times, probably not more than £10 million because that would be silly (though see the nearby sidebar 'Buying bonds doesn't always make sense!'). Similarly, buying the bond today for exactly £10 million isn't a particularly attractive prospect – the buyer would make nothing in nominal terms, and if inflation were positive, the holder would make a loss in real terms.

So the government is only likely to be able to sell the bond for less than its face value (£10 million), because bondholders expect compensation for lending the government money.

The lower the price the bond is sold for today, the higher the interest rate the government is paying for the loan.

Economists think of issuing bonds as deferred taxes, because when a government borrows money by issuing bonds, that money has to be repaid at some point in the future. And how will it be repaid? Well, by future taxes of course.

Seigniorage

A government can fund itself through *seigniorage* – the printing of money – but it's a slightly dodgy business and can get out of hand very quickly; few governments today consider it a serious source of revenue.

Here's how seigniorage works: if the government runs a deficit ($G > T$) that it can't fund through borrowing, it can print an amount of money equal to $G - T$. Doing so allows the government to pay for all its spending today without the need to borrow or collect additional taxes.

But that sounds too good to be true. Surely someone must be paying to fund the deficit. The question is, who? The answer is surprising: everyone in the economy pays a little bit. By printing money the government creates some additional inflation, which acts to reduce the real value of people's nominal assets, such as their cash and savings. So undertaking seigniorage is like levying an additional tax on people.

Seigniorage is a slippery slope. If a government becomes reliant on raising revenue using seigniorage, the ultimate result is the horror of hyperinflation (which you can read about in Chapter 5).

Taking in Two Views of Fiscal Policy

Most economists agree that in the long run, expansionary fiscal policy can't lead to sustained economic growth (flip to Chapter 9 for all about expansionary – and indeed contractionary – fiscal policy). The reason is that in the long run the economy is constrained by its factors of production and level of technology.

Economists also agree that expansionary fiscal policy can boost output and reduce unemployment in the short run, because short-run prices are 'sticky', which means that output doesn't have to equal its natural level.

What economists disagree about is how effective fiscal policy is at boosting output in the short run. Here we present two different views:

- ✔ **Standard view:** Fiscal policy can have large impacts on the economy in the short run.
- ✔ **Ricardian view:** Fiscal policy is ineffective in the long run and not very effective in the short run.

Studying the standard view

In the *standard view*, fiscal policy impacts the economy in the short term. Consider the case of a tax cut: a fall in taxes (T) influences both consumption (C) and investment (I).

Consumption should increase because it depends heavily on disposable income:

$$C = C(Y - T)$$

Logically, reducing taxes increases disposable income and boosts consumption. For example, if taxes are reduced and your monthly take-home pay increases, you probably spend more money, right?

Firms also care about taxes because lower taxes make investment opportunities look more attractive – the firm keeps more of the profit. So lowering taxes by increasing investment makes sense.

These effects – the increasing of consumption and investment – act to increase aggregate demand (AD). As we describe in Chapter 9, in the short run this causes real output and the price level to increase. As time passes and prices become flexible, output returns to its natural level, whereas the price level is permanently higher.

You see a similar story when considering an increase in government purchases (G), except that this time the effect is directly through G in the AD equation (AD = $C + I + G + NX$).

Reading about the Ricardian view

The *Ricardian view* of fiscal policy says something quite radical: not only is fiscal policy ineffective in the long run, but also it's not very effective in the short run. Here's why.

Imagine that the government increases government purchases (*G*) but leaves everything else unchanged. In the standard view of the preceding section, *G* increases but all other components of AD are unchanged, leading to an overall increase in AD. But is this really reasonable?

The Ricardian view says 'no'; a smart individual should realise that an increase in *G* is also an increase in future taxes (remember the intertemporal budget constraint from the earlier section 'Acknowledging that governments face budget constraints'). So it makes sense for individuals to reduce consumption (*C*) today in order to cover the future taxes they'll be made to pay! Thus AD may not increase very much in response to an increase in *G*. Firms may also reduce investment (*I*) today in the expectation of higher taxes in the future.

Similarly, if the government decides to decrease taxes (*T*) and leave everything else unchanged, this action may not have much impact on the economy. A smart individual should realise that a fall in taxes today (with no accompanying fall in government spending) is simply a change in the timing of taxes. After all, if present and future government purchases are unchanged, those same tax revenues will have to be collected at some point. So a fall in *T* today will be accompanied by an increase in taxes in the future. Thus individuals and firms should leave their consumption (*C*) and investment (*I*) unchanged, because taxes haven't really fallen – only the timing of the taxes has changed!

This idea that people don't care about the timing of taxes and act to offset the impact of fiscal policy changes is called *Ricardian equivalence*.

Debating who's right

Although Ricardian equivalence is elegant, it requires a very high level of sophistication on the part of individuals and firms. If people are given a tax cut, do they really save all the extra disposable income to pay for the future tax increase?

Economists suggest a number of reasons why the answer is 'probably not':

- **Myopia:** The idea that people don't look far into the future when making decisions today. They're short-sighted and so aren't really interested in future taxes – they only care about taxes now and in the immediate future.

- **Finite lives:** Ricardian equivalence requires people to believe that they'll be around to pay the future taxes. But if individuals think that the burden will be left for future generations, increasing consumption today is a rational response to a tax cut.

   Some economists think that you can get around this objection by saying that people care about their children and so an increased tax liability placed on their children is equivalent to increased taxes today. Furthermore, if you care about your children, and your children care about their children, and their children care about their children and so on, you may behave as though you'll live forever.

   This kind of *dynastic argument* is used quite a lot in macroeconomics research to justify why people behave as though they will live forever, even though their lives are finite. (Yes, we know, economists are a crazy bunch.)

- **Credit constraints:** Quite likely, many people who'd like to consume more today can't because they don't have access to credit. They're unable to borrow money and thereby increase their consumption today at the cost of reducing future consumption.

   The problem isn't that they can't afford to (the present value of their income is sufficient to cover the present value of their consumption), it's that no one is willing to lend to them. In this case, reducing taxes today leads to an increase in consumption today, as if the government is lending them money – 'here's some extra money today, but you'll have to pay it back in the form of higher taxes tomorrow.' But that's exactly what they want!

For these reasons, few economists believe that Ricardian equivalence literally holds true in the real world (including David Ricardo himself!). At the same time, it probably contains some truth, and it's a useful warning to those policy makers who'd try to stimulate the economy by making unfunded tax cuts or increases in government expenditure!

Chapter 12

Seeking Low Unemployment *and* Low Inflation: The Phillips Curve

....

In This Chapter

▶ Understanding the short-run trade-off between inflation and unemployment

▶ Looking at why this trade-off disappears in the long run

▶ Taking action to reduce inflation

....

*W*hether you have children, want to have children in the future, have no interest in children or are a child, you know one fact: small children cry. Even the most placid and happy baby cries – and sometimes screams. You may be wondering what on earth crying babies have to do with macroeconomics; well, the answer is – quite a lot.

Picture this: after a long day you've finally managed to put the little nipper to bed. You and your partner are relaxing on the sofa watching the latest episode of your favourite soap. Suddenly the baby monitor flashes red and you hear the unmistakable sound of little Jimmy crying. What should you do? You've noticed from past experience that when you go to comfort him, he tends to stop crying, and yet when you've left him alone, he continues to cry.

You don't like your baby crying, so you go and comfort him: as expected, he stops crying. Smugly you get back to your soap, thinking: 'I've cracked this – all I need to do when he cries is to comfort him'. The thing is, Jimmy has other plans. He learns quickly that whenever he cries, you come a-running and so he responds by crying more frequently. Now, not only are you comforting your baby throughout the night, but also he's crying as much as he did before! Only, now you are too – with frustration!

One way of thinking about what happened is that you notice a statistical relationship between how much you comfort him and how much he cries: more comfort equals less crying. But when you try to take advantage of this statistical relationship, it breaks down. Your baby is smart, and he now expects you to comfort him whenever he cries. He rationally responds by crying more frequently.

A very similar relationship exists in macroeconomics between unemployment and inflation, called the *Phillips curve*:

✔ Certain periods of history seem to show a statistical relationship between unemployment and inflation: low unemployment is associated with high inflation.

✔ When policy makers try to exploit this relationship by consistently having high inflation (in order to have low unemployment), the relationship breaks down because people now expect high inflation.

In the long run, therefore, by stoking up inflation, policy makers can only succeed in creating high inflation, not reducing unemployment.

In this chapter we discuss the relationship between unemployment and inflation in the short and long runs and why it breaks down over time. We also describe how policy makers can successfully reduce inflation in an economy when inflation is high – hopefully without increasing unemployment. The trick is to try to *shift* the Phillips curve by altering people's inflation expectations.

Boosting the Economy: A Good Strategy for Low Unemployment?

Imagine that you're a policy maker thinking about how to reduce unemployment. The economy is currently at its long-run equilibrium – and so output is at its natural level and unemployment is at its natural rate. You know that reducing unemployment by using expansionary fiscal or monetary policy is possible (as we describe in Chapter 9). But is this course of action likely to be a good idea?

In this section we answer this question by deriving the Phillips curve from the aggregate demand–aggregate supply (AD–AS) model (see Chapters, 7, 8 and 9). We also consider why the relationship between unemployment and inflation breaks down and look at a famous critique – the *Lucas critique* – that shook macroeconomics to its core.

Meeting the original Phillips curve

In 1958, the economist William Phillips looked at the historical relationship between unemployment and inflation. He noticed a strong negative correlation between the two in the UK from 1861 to 1957. Robert Solow and Paul

Samuelson carried out the same exercise for the US and found the same negative relationship between unemployment and inflation from 1900 to 1960.

In other words, when inflation was high, unemployment tended to be low; and when inflation was low, unemployment tended to be high. The good news is that this relationship is entirely consistent with the AD–AS model (from Chapter 9).

Check out Figure 12-1, as we talk you through it:

✔ **Point A:** The economy starts off here, with no inflation and unemployment equal to its natural rate (because output is equal to its natural level $\bar{Y}$). In Figure 12-1a you can see that the price level is unchanged at P_0 and output is at its natural level. In Figure 12-1b you can see that there is no inflation and unemployment is at its natural rate.

Figure 12-1:
Deriving
the Phillips
curve (PC):
LRAS =
long-run
aggregate
supply;
SRAS =
short-run
aggregate
supply.

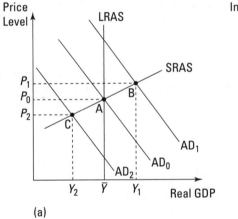
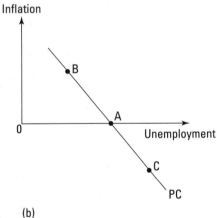

© John Wiley & Sons

✔ **Point B:** Represents a combination of falling unemployment and rising prices (inflation). In Figure 12-1a you can see that a positive aggregate demand shock shifts AD from AD_0 to AD_1, increasing output from $\bar{Y}$ to Y_1 and causing unemployment to fall. The price level also increases from P_0 to P_1. In Figure 12-1b you can see that unemployment has fallen and there is now positive inflation.

✔ **Point C:** Represents a combination of increasing unemployment and falling prices (deflation). In Figure 12-1a a negative aggregate demand shock shifts AD from AD_0 to AD_2: output decreases from $\bar{Y}$ to Y_2 causing unemployment to rise. The price level also falls from P_0 to P_2. In Figure 12-1b you see that unemployment has increased but there is now deflation.

The Phillips curve seems to imply that policy makers face a choice: they can either have low unemployment or low inflation, but not both. Therefore, their job is to pick their preferred point on the Phillips curve.

Watching the Phillips curve break down

In the 1960s the Phillips curve relationship was at the heart of policy making. It was so simple: if you want low inflation, you have to pay for it with high unemployment, and vice versa. The Phillips curve appeared to be a reliable guide to the unemployment–inflation trade-off.

But (you knew a 'but' was coming, didn't you?) in the 1970s the Phillips curve relationship started to break down: countries including the US and the UK experienced high inflation *and* high unemployment – sometimes called *stagflation*. Of course, this was contrary to the prediction of the Phillips curve. Economists have pointed to two main reasons why this happened: aggregate supply shocks and people's changing expectations.

Experiencing aggregate supply shocks

The Phillips curve makes sense when considering shocks to aggregate demand (AD). An increase in AD leads to more inflation but at the same time lowers unemployment. You can see this relationship in the earlier Figure 12-1. But when the shocks are to aggregate supply (AS), high inflation coincides with high unemployment (see Figure 12-2):

- **Point A:** The economy starts off in its long-run equilibrium, with no inflation and output and unemployment at their natural levels.

- **Point B:** Represents higher inflation *and* higher unemployment. A negative shock to aggregate supply (for example, an increase in the price of raw materials) caused aggregate supply – in the short run – to decrease from $SRAS_0$ to $SRAS_1$. This move to higher inflation *and* higher unemployment is the opposite of what the Phillips curve predicts!

- **Point C:** Represents deflation *and* lower unemployment. A positive shock to aggregate supply moved the economy – in the short run – to an increase in output (and a fall in unemployment), as well as a fall in the price level – again, contrary to the Phillips curve.

The 1970s saw some massive negative AS shocks due to large increases in the price of oil. These shocks shifted AS up and to the left and meant higher inflation and unemployment. (The oil price increased for a number of reasons, including the 1973 Yom Kippur War and the formation of the Organisation of Oil Exporting Countries (OPEC), which acted to restrict oil supply and drive up price.)

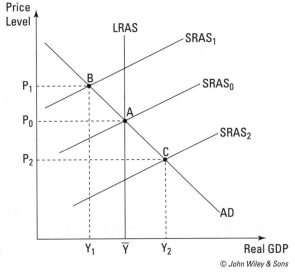

Figure 12-2:
Aggregate
supply
shocks
disrupt the
Phillips
curve.

© John Wiley & Sons

Changing expectations

Before the discovery of the Phillips curve relationship, inflation was sometimes positive and sometimes negative, and on average it was around zero.
When inflation was high today, people had no reason to believe that it would
be high tomorrow; when inflation was low or negative today, nobody had
cause to think that it would be tomorrow.

This situation was probably because policy makers weren't aware of the
Phillips curve and were therefore unable to take advantage of it. Thus, inflation (or deflation) was completely random and due to unpredictable future
events. As a result, at that time a reasonable prediction for inflation in the
coming year would be zero: that is, prices would remain unchanged on average, because that's what they'd always done.

Of course, actual inflation was rarely exactly equal to zero, but if it was positive this would be a surprise. This surprise inflation (assuming it's due to a
positive AD shock) would act to boost the economy and reduce unemployment. On the flip side, a surprise fall in AD caused surprise deflation and
acted to suppress the economy and increase unemployment (you can see
this effect in the earlier Figure 12-1).

By the 1960s and 1970s, however, policy makers knew about the Phillips
curve. They knew that they could achieve low unemployment so long as they
were willing to accept high inflation. They duly took advantage of this knowledge by creating persistently positive inflation.

This strategy worked for a while, as the public maintained their expectations of zero inflation and so each year were 'surprised' by positive inflation. But, people aren't stupid – you can only fool people for so many years; eventually they realised that positive inflation has some persistence. High inflation today probably means high inflation tomorrow!

Therefore, people changed their expectations so that they now expected positive inflation. Policy makers could no longer surprise them by creating inflation – they knew it was coming anyway! By the 1970s people understood this fact well, which explains why this period experienced high inflation but with no accompanying decrease in unemployment. Think about it this way: when negotiating wage increases, workers understood that a 10 per cent nominal wage rise was no wage rise at all if inflation was also going to be 10 per cent. So they would not work anymore than before. However, previously, when they expected no inflation, they incorrectly believed that they received a real wage increase and decided to work more.

Taking aim with the Lucas critique

The 1970s were a time of great tumult in macroeconomics, not only because of the breakdown of the Phillips curve (which at the time economists struggled to explain), but also resulting from a devastating critique of macroeconomics due to Robert E. Lucas, Jr (what a cool name).

In 1976, Lucas wrote a paper arguing that trying to predict the effects of a change in economic policy based on past historical data is a serious mistake because past historical data reflected the economic policy of *those* times. If a government changes economic policy today, it has no guarantee that those relationships between variables will continue to hold.

Lucas argued that the key to understanding the impact of policy changes was explicitly to take into account how people's expectations would change when a new policy was announced.

The Phillips curve is an excellent example of the Lucas critique in action. Before policy makers understood the relationship between unemployment and inflation and were therefore unable to exploit this relationship, rational individuals expected inflation to be zero (see the preceding section). This situation meant that, when inflation was unusually high (that is, positive), the economy experienced a boost that reduced unemployment; when it was unusually low (negative), the economy experienced a knock that increased unemployment.

But when policy makers understood the relationship and tried to exploit it by creating persistently positive inflation, rational individuals started to expect positive inflation (that is, their expectations changed). Thus they were no longer 'surprised' when inflation was high and so no reason existed for unemployment to fall.

As in the crying baby analogy with which we begin this chapter, if the baby doesn't expect his parents to arrive when he cries and someone does, he stops crying. But when he learns that someone comes when he cries, his expectations change, which causes his behaviour to change: he now cries more regularly even though he's being comforted more regularly!

The lesson of this story isn't that you shouldn't comfort babies when they cry (economists aren't that mean!), but that when considering a change of tack – in any walk of life – you need to consider how other people's expectations are likely to change. You can't just trust a statistical relationship that held in the past under some other policy.

The Lucas critique was so devastating because it meant that much of macroeconomics had to be rethought because it didn't explicitly take into account expectations. A lot of the collective wisdom of macroeconomics was, at best, potentially misleading, and at worst just plain wrong. Macroeconomists spent much of the next few decades taking expectations into account explicitly.

Zeroing in on the Short- and Long-Run Phillips Curve

In this section we take a closer look at the Phillips curve in the short and long runs, paying proper attention to the effect of changes in people's expectations that we describe in the preceding section.

'You can fool the people once': Short-run Phillips curve (SRPC)

Figure 12-3 shows the negative relationship between inflation and unemployment in the short run. You can see that if inflation is equal to expected inflation, unemployment must also equal its natural rate.

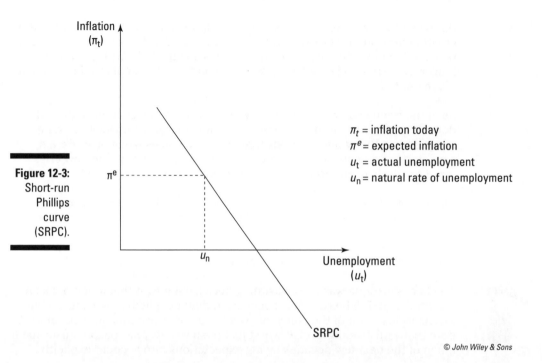

© John Wiley & Sons

Figure 12-3: Short-run Phillips curve (SRPC).

You can express this relationship mathematically as follows:

$$\pi_t = \pi^e - \gamma\left(u_t - u_n\right)$$

This equation says that inflation today (π_t) is equal to expected inflation (π^e) minus a term that depends on how far away actual unemployment (u_t) is from its natural rate (u_n). The symbol γ represents how responsive inflation is to deviations in unemployment from its natural rate.

If actual unemployment is equal to the natural rate ($u_t = u_n$), inflation must equal expected inflation ($\pi_t = \pi^e$).

The fact that the SRPC must always go through (u_n, π^e) has an important implication: changes in inflation expectations shift the Phillips curve. If people's inflation expectations increase, the SRPC shifts up; equally, if their inflation expectations fall, the SRPC shifts down.

In Figure 12-4, initially people expected inflation to be π_0^e, which means that the short-run trade-off between inflation and unemployment is represented by $SRPC_0$. If for some reason, however, people expect inflation to be higher, at π_1^e, the Phillips curve shifts up to $SRPC_1$.

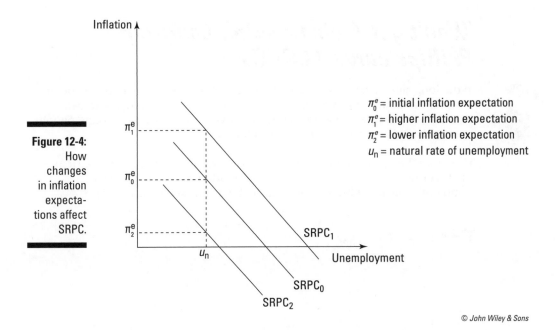

© John Wiley & Sons

Figure 12-4:
How changes in inflation expectations affect SRPC.

This relationship ensures that if actual inflation is equal to expected inflation, unemployment is at its natural rate. Conversely, if for some reason people expect inflation to be lower, at π_2^e, the Phillips curve shifts down to $SRPC_2$.

Notice that any policy makers who try to keep unemployment below the natural rate for a sustained period of time are in for a nasty shock. Sure, it may work the first time, stimulating the economy so inflation is higher than expected inflation and unemployment is lower than the natural rate. But doing so increases inflation expectations, causing the SRPC to shift up.

Now if the policy makers want to keep unemployment low, they must create even more inflation than they created last time. If this situation continues, quite soon inflation becomes explosive and uncontrollably high.

Thus building expectations into the Phillips curve makes clear that having low unemployment at the cost of high inflation in the long run is impossible.

'Won't get fooled again': Long-run Phillips curve (LRPC)

In the long run (when prices are flexible), no trade-off exists between unemployment and inflation. You can't persistently have unemployment away from its natural rate, because that would involve consistently fooling people by surprising them with ever higher inflation.

Therefore, basically, unemployment is going to be at its natural rate (u_n) whatever policy makers decide to do with inflation, which yields a completely vertical Phillips curve in the long run (see Figure 12-5).

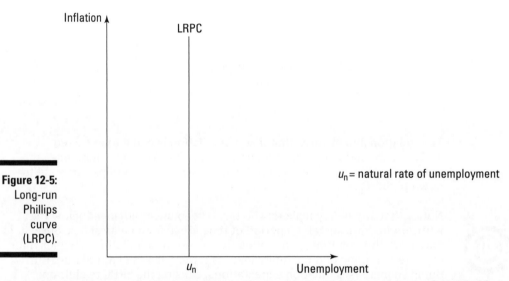

Figure 12-5: Long-run Phillips curve (LRPC).

The LRPC suggests that policy makers shouldn't get into the business of reducing unemployment by creating high inflation, because they just end up with high inflation *and* unemployment at its natural rate. Instead, they ought to decide on the level of inflation that they want (the consensus being that low, stable and positive balances the costs and benefits of inflation best) and target that figure. But they *shouldn't* use expansionary monetary and fiscal policy to reduce unemployment in the long run.

If policy makers really want to reduce unemployment, they must focus on reducing the natural rate of unemployment itself. They can achieve this by using supply-side policies, such as having a more flexible labour market (as we discuss in Chapter 6). Figure 12-6 shows that a government successfully undertakes supply-side policies to reduce the natural rate of unemployment (u_n^0), causing the LRPC to shift to the left (u_n^1), which is the only way of reducing unemployment in the long run. Trying to reduce unemployment by increasing aggregate demand only leads to higher inflation without any fall in unemployment in the long run!

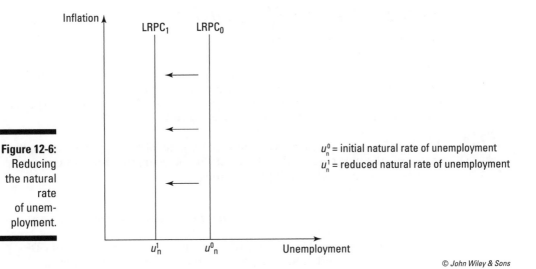

Figure 12-6:
Reducing the natural rate of unemployment.

u_n^0 = initial natural rate of unemployment
u_n^1 = reduced natural rate of unemployment

© John Wiley & Sons

Taking Action with Disinflation Policy

Disinflation policy refers to a policy intended to reduce inflation. Policy makers usually undertake it when the economy is experiencing persistently high inflation. As we describe in Chapter 5, high inflation is very socially costly. Furthermore, high inflation brings few, if any, benefits; certainly, it doesn't help to reduce unemployment (as the long-run Phillips curve makes clear – see the preceding section). The big question is: is it possible to reduce inflation and inflation expectations without increasing unemployment as the Phillips curve would suggest?

Here's how policy makers carry out disinflation policy:

1. **They make an announcement along these lines: 'inflation has been far too high for far too long, so we've decided to reduce it'.**

2. **They undertake contractionary monetary policy (see Chapter 9) by reducing the money supply (or reducing the growth rate of the money supply).**

In this section you discover that disinflation policy can be very painful and result in a period of high unemployment and low output. But you also find out how people forming expectations about the future is crucial in determining how painful disinflation is.

Seeing the sacrifice ratio: No pain, no gain

Quite simply, disinflation is painful, because it usually involves contractionary monetary policy and so reduces aggregate demand (as we discuss in Chapter 9). The result is a recession in the short run and reduced output and increased unemployment (as the earlier Figure 12-1 shows).

The *sacrifice ratio* is a measure of how painful disinflation is likely to be. It measures the percentage of real output (in one year) that has to be given up in order to reduce inflation by 1 percentage point:

$$Sacrifice\,ratio = \frac{\%\,fall\,in\,real\,GDP}{fall\,in\,inflation\,(in\,percentage\,points)}$$

For example, if you had to give up 10 per cent of one year's worth of GDP in order to reduce inflation by 2 per cent, the sacrifice ratio equals 5. Traditionally, economists thought that policy makers could choose how to spread the pain. So, for example, they could get it over and done with quickly by reducing GDP by 10 per cent this year, or spread it over a period of time by reducing GDP by 1 per cent each year for ten years, or even 2 per cent each year for five years and so on.

Given this understanding, many policy makers preferred the idea of spreading the pain over a longer period and gradually reducing inflation. We walk you through an example of that approach now, beginning with an economy as shown in Figure 12-7. Inflation (and inflation expectations) start off very high, at π_0^e, and the Phillips curve is represented by $SRPC_0$:

1. **Policy makers choose to aim for point B in order to reduce inflation.**

   Therefore, they increase unemployment.

2. **People see that inflation is equal to π_1^e and revise their expectations down about future inflation to π_1^e.**

   This shifts the Phillips curve to $SRPC_1$ – unemployment falls back to its natural rate and the economy is now at point C.

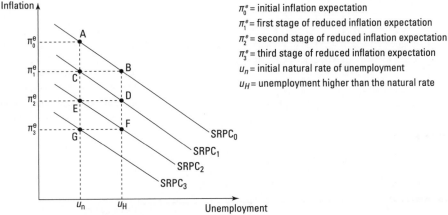

© John Wiley & Sons

Figure 12-7:
Gradual
disinflation.

3. Inflation is still high, so policy makers choose to aim for point D.

Again, they increase unemployment to lower inflation (and inflation expectations) to π_2^e.

4. People see that inflation is even lower and update their expectations again and the Phillips curve shifts again.

You get the idea. Finally, after repeating this process a number of times, the economy is at point G – inflation is relatively low and unemployment is at its natural rate.

The alternative to the gradual process is trying to disinflate the economy fully in one year – sometimes called *shock therapy* (see Figure 12-8).

Inflation again starts off very high at π_0^e, but this time policy makers decide to try to get inflation down quickly. The economy starts off at point A and policy makers increase unemployment by a huge amount by choosing point B. They do so to reduce inflation to π_1^e in one fell swoop – when people see that inflation has indeed fallen, they revise their expectations and this shifts the Phillips curve down to SRPC$_1$ in one go.

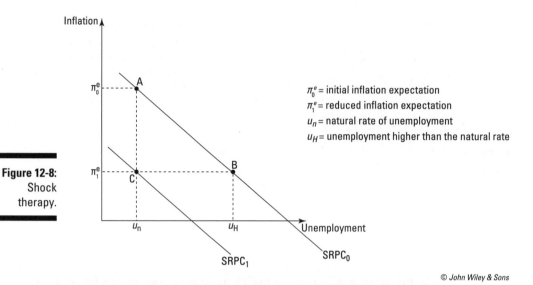

Figure 12-8:
Shock
therapy.

π_0^e = initial inflation expectation
π_1^e = reduced inflation expectation
u_n = natural rate of unemployment
u_H = unemployment higher than the natural rate

© John Wiley & Sons

Adjusting expectations for socially costless disinflation

One way of thinking about why disinflation is socially costly is that people's expectations about inflation take time to adjust. People don't necessarily believe the initial announcement that inflation will fall. A recession is necessary (and the accompanying lower inflation and higher unemployment) in order to get people to adjust their expectations downward.

These kinds of simple expectation – such as 'I think inflation this coming year (π_t^e) will be equal to inflation last year (π_{t-1})' – are called *adaptive expectations*:

$$\pi_t^e = \pi_{t-1}$$

But what if you could get people to adjust their expectations of inflation downwards without sending the economy into a recession? In theory, it should be possible. If policy makers are absolutely committed to bringing inflation down to, say, π_1^e as shown earlier in Figure 12-8, and so long as the announcement is credible, people should adjust their expectations of future inflation to π_1^e immediately. This would cause the Phillips curve to shift downwards and bring inflation down without the need to engineer a recession!

In order for this plan to work, you need two things:

- ✔ **Complete credibility:** Policy makers must be able to convince people that they're serious about achieving low inflation and that no matter what happens – no matter how painful it becomes – they *will* disinflate the economy.

- ✔ **Rational expectations:** Individuals in the economy need a quite sophisticated way of forming expectations. No longer can they have simple adaptive expectations and just look at inflation in the recent past in order to work out future inflation. They need to have *rational expectations*: that is, they use optimally all available information to make their forecasts, including announcements about future policy.

With adaptive expectations, it doesn't matter how you spread the pain – the total pain is unchanged. But with rational expectations, disinflating the economy quickly makes sense, because a short, sharp shock of disinflation is much more likely to be credible than committing to disinflate the economy over ten years.

Macroeconomists who strongly advocate rational expectations – such as Lucas (check out the earlier section 'Taking aim with the Lucas critique') – also believe that traditional estimates of the sacrifice ratio are far too high. They believe that reducing inflation in an economy without much pain is possible, so long as policy makers are credible when they make their announcement.

Inflation in the UK in 1980 was running at about 20 per cent. The prime minister at the time, Margaret Thatcher, decided to disinflate the economy, that is, reduce inflation. As the Phillips curve would suggest, this increased unemployment substantially – unemployment actually doubled. However, inflation was brought under control to a manageable 5 per cent in 1983.

Now, this was by no means a 'costless disinflation' – if it had been, unemployment wouldn't have increased at all. Nevertheless the costs (higher unemployment) were much less than some at the time had expected (that is, the sacrifice ratio was relatively low). So perhaps the Iron Lady's credibility forced people to change their inflation expectations and thereby reduced the negative impact of disinflation on employment.

Chapter 13

Following Rules or Using Discretion: Two Approaches to Economic Policy

*I*magine that you're on a diet – or perhaps just think about the one you're already on. To lose weight you need to follow the rules: a maximum number of calories each day; no carbs or all carbs; watch the fat and don't feed the gremlins after midnight. These rules – you can see them as comprising a policy – are crucial to your dieting success. But you also face other pressures: your own darned appetite, your spouse who likes you 'plump and friendly, not thin and grumpy' and the upcoming office Christmas dinner at which colleagues are sure to push you into letting go. These pressures tempt you to throw those pesky rules out the window! Or in other words, you're tempted to use your discretion.

Now relate these competing approaches of following rules or exercising discretion to macroeconomics, and you have the crux of this chapter: whether policy makers should carry out economic policy by following a fixed set of rules or whether they should be free to use their discretion.

In this chapter we describe a number of areas of macroeconomic policy that feature a tension between policy rules and discretion. We discuss the two options in detail, including some types of each, and lay out some problems with discretion that lead us to advocate rules over discretion in most situations. We describe the advantages that policy makers gain by following rules, notably increasing their credibility.

Introducing the Rules versus Discretion Debate

In the 20th century, macroeconomists realized that policy makers might be better off having to follow rules rather than having the ability to change their decisions whenever they want – that is, to have discretion.

This is quite a profound and counterintuitive realization. On the face of it, discretion looks superior to rules because by having discretion you can always make the same choices as those dictated by the rules. At the same time, discretion gives you many more options. So you might think that at the very worst, discretion would give you the same outcome as rules, and in most cases, discretion should give you a better outcome.

However, in this chapter you see that this intuition is wrong. Having discretion changes others' *expectations* about what you are likely to do. This leads to what economists call the *time inconsistency* of discretionary policy – basically, where it's no longer in your interest to follow through on what you said you were going to do. Don't worry if that sounds confusing. All will become clear shortly!

Here's an in-a-nutshell comparison of the two approaches:

- **Rules-based policy:** When conducting economic policy via rules, policy makers announce in advance how policy will respond to any given scenario in the future. As time unfolds, they stick to their announcements – in essence doing what they said they would.

- **Discretionary policy:** Here, policy makers aren't tied to preset rules and can exercise their own discretion at any point in time. They aren't committed to anything, including any past announcements they may have made.

For a description of a dilemma that we hope you never face but that illustrates the two approaches in a life-at-stake scenario, see the nearby sidebar 'Considering a terrible dilemma'.

We now spend a bit of time making clearer the distinction between policy rules and discretionary policy, illustrating some different types of each approach.

Considering a terrible dilemma

Here's an illustration of the rules-or-discretion dilemma at work.

Imagine that (God forbid) your parents are kidnapped by terrorists while on holiday. The kidnappers demand £10 million in order to release them. You love your parents but you don't have that kind of cash. You're a British citizen, so you ask the UK government to help you negotiate the release. The friendly people at the Foreign Ministry agree to send their top hostage negotiator. Unfortunately, no amount of sweet-talking is going to convince the kidnappers – they want to see the money, as it were.

Tired of waiting, you decide to go straight to the top. You petition the Prime Minister directly and explain that in the big scheme of things, ten-mil is a small sum to pay for the safe release of your parents. The PM listens sympathetically (the situation even brings a tear to her eye) and explains that if it were up to her *discretion* she'd pay the ransom. But she explains that she's bound to the policy *rule* of not negotiating with terrorists in the hope of deterring future hostage-takers.

Clearly this is devastating news, seems harsh and you'd never agree, but from the wider viewpoint it can be seen as the least bad course of action.

Allowing the rules to rule

When policy makers follow rules, they are attempting to tie their hands so they have to follow through on their promises; they establish these rules so people will believe that the policy makers will do what they've promised. This is the main benefit of following rules: it gives policy makers *credibility*. A downside of following rules is that policy makers may face situations where they need flexibility to respond effectively to some unforeseen economic problem. Ultimately, whether to follow a rule or have discretion is a matter of judgement.

Here we discuss three examples of policy rules: balanced budget rule, inflation targeting and always repaying your debts.

Balanced budget rule

A *balanced budget rule* simply says that, over a period of time, the amount of government spending should be exactly equal to the amount raised in taxes.

Every year the government has to decide how much money to spend. At the same time, it has to fund this expenditure somehow. The standard way of doing so is by raising tax revenue, be it from income tax, VAT, corporation tax and so on. Of course, the rule needs to specify the time period over which it must be met, perhaps yearly, or over the course of a Parliament or the course of a *business cycle* (a period of time that includes a boom and a recession). This final period is a bit tricky, because economists don't have an agreed way to measure the start and end of a business cycle.

The rule has some flexibility built in. That is, sometimes the government can run a *deficit* (it spends more than it receives in taxes) so long as it runs sufficient surpluses to balance the budget over the chosen period of time. Despite this, balanced budget rules aren't in widespread use (for reasons we discuss in Chapter 11). In the US, a number of state governments (but not the Federal government) follow a balanced budget rule.

Keep an eye out, though. In June 2015 UK Chancellor George Osborne announced his intention to pass a law requiring future governments to run a budget surplus so long as the economy is growing, which is essentially a balanced budget rule.

Inflation target

You may have heard this policy rule mentioned in the news. In the UK, the Bank of England (BoE) is responsible for monetary policy. In normal times this mainly involves setting the interest rate; in more recent times it has also involved deciding how much quantitative easing (QE) to carry out. (Check out Chapter 10 for all your monetary policy and quantitative easing needs.)

The BoE can't decide on its policy willy-nilly, though. The government gives it an explicit inflation target, which it's expected to attempt to achieve. In 2014, for example, the inflation target was 2 per cent annual inflation according to the consumer price index (CPI) measure. Although it has some discretion about how it achieves this target, the focus of monetary policy must be the inflation target and not any other measure of economic performance. In this sense you can see inflation targeting as a form of policy rule.

Always repay your debts

This rule may sound obvious, but it's important. Governments often borrow money by issuing bonds. Eventually the holders of these bonds turn up expecting to be repaid for the money they lent. The government can always refuse to pay – called *defaulting*. Bondholders can't do much to force governments to repay their debts. Despite this ability to default, most governments attempt to commit to a rule of always repaying their debts even if defaulting looks immediately attractive.

Exercising your discretion

With discretionary policy, policy makers can exercise their own judgement as and when they consider it necessary. This includes the freedom to change their minds and take an action they said previously they wouldn't.

Now, if you promise yourself to help your diet by ordering a skinny latte for lunch and then you change your mind and eat biscotti with your frappacino, nothing suffers except your waistline. But when policy makers choose to use their discretion when making macroeconomic decisions, the stakes can be huge.

In this section we explain different examples of discretionary policy. Even though there are certainly problems with discretion, discretionary policy is still widely used throughout the world – especially discretionary fiscal policy.

We cover three examples of discretionary policy, comparing and contrasting them to the three policy rules in the preceding section.

Discretionary fiscal policy

When politicians are free to decide how much the government should spend and raise in taxes, economists say that fiscal policy is conducted by discretion (in contrast to the balanced budget rule we discuss in the preceding section, which is a type of fiscal policy rule).

The government may decide to spend more every year than it raises in taxes – that is, run a deficit. Or it may decide to spend less every year than it raises in taxes – that is, run a surplus. (With politicians, the former is much more likely than the latter!) Or it can decide anything in-between. Contrast this with the balanced budget rule, which says that the government must balance its books.

In most places in the world, fiscal policy is conducted by discretion.

Discretionary monetary policy

If the central bank is able to decide on the interest rate it sets without having any well-defined objective, that monetary policy is said to be conducted by discretion (in contrast to inflation targeting in the preceding section, which is a type of monetary policy rule).

Before 1992, monetary policy in the UK was by discretion; after that, the country moved toward inflation targeting. 1992 was a tough year for the UK economy because it was forced out of the Exchange Rate Mechanism (ERM), which was the precursor to the euro. The ERM tried to ensure that the exchange rates between different European countries didn't fluctuate too much.

Discretionary monetary policy was somewhat of a disaster in the UK – if you're old enough, you may remember inflation of over 25 per cent in 1975 (ouch!).

The trend over the past few decades has been away from discretionary monetary policy towards some kind of monetary rule, typically inflation targeting. Interestingly, the Federal Reserve in the US only formally announced an inflation target of 2 per cent in 2012 – much later than most other developed economies – although it was understood that they were informally targeting inflation for some time.

Sometimes repay your debts

Governments can often rack up mind-bogglingly large amounts of debt. To give you some idea, as of 2014, US government debt was more than $17 trillion (that is, 17 followed by 12 zeros!). UK government debt was over £1 trillion, and Japanese government debt was around $10 trillion. These debts must be paid from taxes raised from current residents or taxes on future generations.

Not paying its debts can appear tempting for a highly indebted country, because that huge liability disappears and presumably the citizens can now enjoy life debt free. If policy makers are free to decide whether to repay debts at their discretion, they may pay them back sometimes and not at other times. Your intuition is probably telling you that this doesn't sound like the best plan – and your intuition is spot-on.

Discerning the Problems with Discretion

Imagine a politician making the case to you for discretionary policy. She tells you that discretion must be better than following rules because discretion gives her flexibility to respond to changes in the economic environment by tweaking policy in the best possible way. Discretion allows her to pursue the same policy as if she was constrained by rules while also giving her many other options.

In short, she doesn't see why she should tie her hands unnecessarily. In this section we give a couple of compelling reasons – and they have nothing to do with keeping her hand out of the parliamentary expenses trough (or, perhaps more appropriately, moat!).

The fact is that, although discretionary policy may sound like a good deal, most economists are sceptical about it for a number of reasons. Not least, that policy makers have discretion regarding whether they follow through on previously announced policies.

Allowing politicians off the leash

The ideal politician is a benevolent figure. When looking at any problem, she collects all relevant information about the issues, considers everyone's preferences and finally chooses the option that best serves society as a whole. This is an important function because no one else has the time to find out about all the different functions of government and then sit down and think about what would be best.

You're probably thinking something like 'Yeah right, if that's what a politician is, then I've yet to meet one'.

Economists share your scepticism – they know that politicians are only human and face particular incentives that affect the way they make decisions. In fact, a whole branch of economics exists called *public choice theory*, which looks at how self-seeking politicians and policy makers behave.

Here are two examples to show that economic policy is just too important to be left to the whim of whoever happens to be in political power today.

Creating artificial booms: Political business cycles

Policy makers have powerful tools at their disposal: using fiscal and monetary policy they can temporarily create an economic boom where wages are rising, unemployment is falling and so on. Unfortunately, if politicians were to do this, eventually they'd have to reign in the economy using policies that have the opposite effect. (See Chapters 9–11 to understand why this is true).

But what if, before an election, the ruling party decides to create a temporary boom so that when people come to vote, the economy looks rosy. People could easily misinterpret this as a sign of sound economic policy and vote for the current government. Of course after the election is won, the government has to rein in the economy, causing a recession. The incumbent party hopes that the voters have forgotten about this by the time of the next election, especially if another artificial boom is engineered at that time too!

Clearly this behaviour isn't the hallmark of good economic policy: it creates unnecessary uncertainty for people and gives rise to what economists call *political business cycles* – in other words, stimulating the economy before an election, only to reign it back in after the election.

Borrowing against future generations

Another way politicians can act strategically if policy is at their discretion is by borrowing too much money. Everyone likes government spending: it means better public services, better infrastructure and more generous benefits. What people are more reticent about is paying for them in the form of taxes.

Is it possible to have large amounts of government spending and low taxes simultaneously? Well, sort of: the government can run a budget deficit and fund it by borrowing. This borrowing has to be repaid at some point, however – which means higher taxes for future generations. The thing is that only the current generation votes in elections – people who aren't yet born can't vote (great idea for a sci-fi movie though)!

The worry is that politicians have incentives to borrow large amounts of money now to provide inflated living standards for today's electorate at the expense of tomorrow's electorate. Economists quite rightly are concerned about this because it goes against what they call *intergenerational equity* – which is the idea that policies should be fair across generations.

Encountering time inconsistency

Discretionary policy may also not be a good idea in that it can lead to what economists call *time inconsistency*. This is the idea that you make a plan today about what you're going to do in the future; however, when the future arrives, you want to change your plan and do something else.

Here's a good way of thinking about it. Imagine that your house is in need of a tidy. You don't want to do it now, but you make a plan that you'll do it tomorrow. However, tomorrow arrives, and if you have discretion, you face the same choice as you faced yesterday: should I tidy now or delay it another day? Since you chose to delay yesterday, what makes you think that you won't delay again today?!

To build or not to build

Some parts of the country experience regular floods. Policy makers, wishing to discourage people from building homes on floodplains, announce, 'If you build a house here, the next time it floods you're on your own.'

The problem is, when a flood occurs, the media descend and show the difficulties people are facing. Then politicians face irresistible pressure to renege on their earlier announcement and help rebuild. Knowing this, people discount the announcement and build anyway.

It's clearly not optimal to build a house on a floodplain and then for the taxpayer to regularly pay for the damage. What would be much better is if policymakers were able to tie their hands and bind themselves to not help rebuild. Households, understanding that they really will be on their own when a flood occurs, decide to build elsewhere. Now no homes are flooded, there's no media furore and no taxpayer money is wasted – everyone wins!

Inflation bias

We now apply the time-inconsistency problem to some economic policy problems. Policy makers face a short-run trade-off between unemployment and inflation (as we discuss in Chapter 12 and show in the Phillips curve). That is, they can reduce unemployment temporarily by creating 'surprise' inflation (see Figure 13-1).

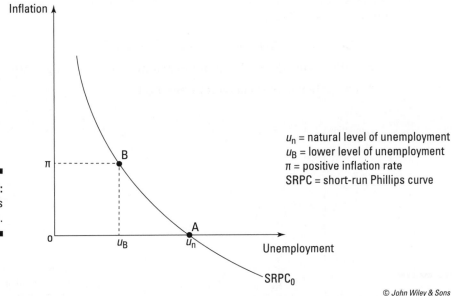

Figure 13-1:
The Phillips
curve.

u_n = natural level of unemployment
u_B = lower level of unemployment
π = positive inflation rate
SRPC = short-run Phillips curve

© John Wiley & Sons

Assume that a policy maker who dislikes inflation and unemployment carries out policy according to the following three stages:

1. **The policy maker announces the desired rate of inflation.**

2. **The individuals in the economy hear the announcement and form expectations about what inflation is likely to be.**

3. **The policy maker chooses the actual rate of inflation.**

Given that the policy maker dislikes inflation, the sensible approach is for her to announce that the desired rate of inflation in Stage 1 is zero. She hopes that in Stage 2, individuals in the economy believe her announcement and set their inflation expectations equal to zero. So far so good. However, the problem comes in Stage 3: when individuals have formed their inflation expectations, the policy maker notices that she can reduce unemployment by choosing to increase inflation. You can see this in the earlier Figure 13-1: the policy maker prefers situation B to situation A.

As usual, economists assume that people are smart and that they realise in Stage 2 that the announced policy (zero inflation) is just not credible. Given this, it no longer makes sense for them to expect zero inflation. Instead, they form their expectations based on the rate of inflation the policy maker actually chooses in Stage 3. (Remember that higher inflation expectations shift the short-run Phillips curve up.) So here's what ends up happening under discretion (see Figure 13-2):

1. The policy maker announces zero inflation.

2. Individuals ignore the announcement and expect high inflation.

3. The policy maker chooses high inflation.

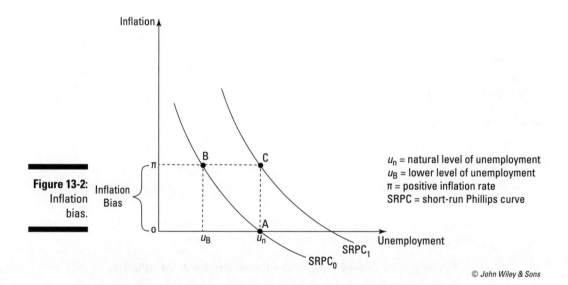

Figure 13-2:
Inflation bias.

u_n = natural level of unemployment
u_B = lower level of unemployment
π = positive inflation rate
SRPC = short-run Phillips curve

© John Wiley & Sons

Actual inflation and expected inflation are equal, so the policy maker has failed to 'surprise' the individuals in the economy and the result is situation C in Figure 13-2. Comparing A with C, you notice that in both cases unemployment is equal to the natural rate; however, C is associated with higher inflation.

This difference in inflation between the two is called the *inflation bias*. It's caused by the fact that individuals don't believe the announcement of the policy maker in Stage 1, because they know she has discretion in Stage 3 to choose whatever inflation rate she likes.

But if the policy maker has to follow policy rules, she can convince people that she really is telling the truth and then follow through on her announcement. She can then eliminate the inflation bias and end up at situation A.

Risk premium

You can apply similar reasoning to analyse a government trying to borrow money from financial markets. As you know, governments often spend more than they receive in taxes and typically need to borrow the money needed to make up the difference. Investors may be willing to lend the government the money, but only at a price: that is, they expect some return on the money they're lending out. The return that they demand depends largely on how likely they think they are to be repaid.

For example, the UK government is able to borrow at very low interest rates because investors think it's highly unlikely to default. The Greek government, in contrast, has to pay substantially higher interest rates because it's seen as a riskier bet.

Investors demand a *risk premium*: a higher expected return to compensate them for the additional risk. The more risky an investment, the higher the premium they demand.

To see how discretion can lead to investors demanding a higher risk premium, consider a timeline with different stages:

1. **The policy maker announces what priority the government will give to debt repayments.**

2. **Investors hear the announcement and form expectations about how likely the government is to repay them, which determines the interest rate at which they're willing to lend.**

3. **The government decides whether to repay the debt or not.**

In Stage 1 the policy maker announcing that the government will give the highest possible priority to repaying its debts makes sense. The policy maker hopes that investors believe the announcement and only demand a small risk premium in order to lend to the government. But a problem occurs in Stage 3: if the policy maker has discretion and finds herself in tough economic times, she may prefer to take the easy option and default.

Investors aren't stupid; they realise that the *announced* policy isn't what counts: it's what the policy maker is going to do in the case of tough economic times. If the policy maker has discretion as to whether or not to repay the investors, when times are hard she may face irresistible pressure to default. This is true even if the investors have lent to the government at a low interest rate. Knowing this, investors demand a much higher risk premium in order to lend to the government (which paradoxically increases the probability that it's going to default!).

But if the policy maker has to abide by some preset rules, she can convince the investors that even if times are hard they'll be repaid, so she really can follow through on her promise. As a result, her government can borrow at low interest rates and investors are more likely to be repaid.

Solving the Problem: Tying Your Hands Voluntarily

In this section, we show that tying your hands by committing to the rules can be better than having full discretion, because it can change individuals' expectations in an advantageous way. Removing the discretion solves the troublesome time inconsistency problem (that we describe in the preceding section).

Creating a credible commitment

Central to understanding why you'd tie your own hands, seemingly restricting your room for manoeuvre, is the concept of *credible commitment*: committing to something in a way that is believed by others.

The advantage is that when politicians have their discretion taken away from them, they can't break the rules and submit to other, perhaps short-term or self-interested, imperatives, even if they want to.

The question is: how does a policy maker go about making a commitment credible? A number of ways have been proposed, but here we consider the case of monetary policy. The problem with discretionary monetary policy is that policy makers have an incentive to take advantage of the Phillips curve relationship in order to reduce unemployment below the natural rate. Private sector agents understand this, which ultimately leads to inflation bias (higher inflation without any reduction in unemployment) (see the preceding section and earlier Figure 13-1).

In order to commit credibly to low inflation, the central bank can try the following:

- ✔ **Write it into the law/constitution:** The law specifies a precise rule that the central bank must follow. An example is increasing the money supply by 2 per cent every year, or even not at all. In this way the central bank loses its ability to deviate from the announced policy of low inflation.

- ✔ **Become independent:** Politicians then no longer have control or influence over monetary policy. The idea is that politicians may want to reduce unemployment in the short run in order to improve their election prospects. When monetary policy is conducted independent of political considerations, the hope is that the central bank sees no need to reduce unemployment artificially. We discuss this concept further in the following section.

- ✔ **Appoint a 'conservative' central banker:** This is an interesting one: it implies appointing policy makers who are known to really dislike inflation. Sometimes these types of people are called 'inflation hawks' – they hate inflation and everyone knows it. The reason for appointing them is clear: people trust them to keep inflation low.

- ✔ **Pay for performance:** Make the salary of policy makers depend entirely on how well they perform in keeping inflation low; this really makes them 'put their money where their mouth is'. If they don't follow through on their announcement, they simply don't get paid!

The intention behind all of these approaches is to make the central bank's commitment to low inflation credible and to thereby reduce people's inflation expectations, which in turn reduces actual inflation. Out of these different strategies, the one that has been taken up most widely and that is seen as the most successful is central bank independence. We look at that concept in more detail in the following section.

Making central banks independent

Many experts believe that central bank independence leads to lower inflation because it should reduce or eliminate the inflation bias (see the earlier section 'Encountering time inconsistency'). Does the empirical evidence support this proposition? The answer is a qualified yes.

The historical data from the second half of the 20th century show that the degree of central bank independence varies across countries. In some countries, central banks were very independent, in others less so. A good example of a strongly independent central bank is the US, where governors of the Federal Reserve are appointed by the president for 14 years at a time. Furthermore, the president can't get rid of them if he doesn't like the way they're doing their job! Cushy number, eh?

The length of the term combined with the difficulty of removing Federal Reserve governors means that they have a high degree of independence and limited interference from politicians. You'd therefore expect that the US and similarly independent countries (for example, Switzerland, Germany before the euro) would have low levels of inflation compared to countries where (over the time period in question) central bank independence was very limited (for example, New Zealand, Spain). Indeed, looking at Figure 13-3, this is exactly what you find.

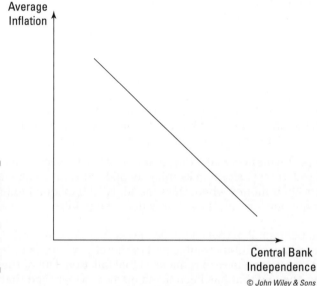

© John Wiley & Sons

Figure 13-3:
Central
bank inde-
pendence
versus infla-
tion rate.

The answer is only a qualified yes, however, because although central bank independence is associated with lower average inflation, this doesn't prove that central bank independence *causes* low inflation. Perhaps, for example, countries with low levels of inflation choose to have more independent central banks. Nevertheless, the data combined with the theoretical argument provide a compelling case that central bank independence is good for lowering rates of inflation in an economy.

You may be wondering what impact central bank independence has on economic performance. The answer is no discernable impact on levels of unemployment or economic growth.

So despite the fact that economists are always shouting about how 'there's no such thing as a free lunch', central bank independence may well be one. Independent central banks are able to have low inflation without having to sacrifice on growth or unemployment. Success!

Part V
Understanding the Financial Crisis

ALL OTHER BANKS

	Moderate Risk	Excessive Risk
Moderate Risk	Bank A's Profit : £10m Financial System : Stable	Bank A's Profit : £0 Financial System : Unstable
Excessive Risk	Bank A's Profit : £20m Financial System : Stable	Bank A's Profit : £5m Financial System : Unstable

Bank A

© *John Wiley & Sons*

To better understand why the 2008 financial crisis happened, it helps to have a basic understanding of macroeconomics. For a quick rundown of key economic information, check out the Cheat Sheet at www.dummies.com/cheatsheet/macroeconomicsuk.

In this part . . .

- Banks would like you to think they're all powerful, but in reality, they're just as susceptible to financial troubles as firms and individuals. Get the lowdown on the financial system's weaknesses.

- Bankers sometimes try to get away with excessive risk-taking in order to boost their profits, and then the government must decide whether to bail them out if things don't turn out well. Find out the details on this Catch-22.

- Few people were immune to the 2008 financial crisis. Discover what caused the crisis, why economists didn't predict it and how future crises can be prevented.

Chapter 14

Considering Fundamental Weaknesses of the Financial System

In This Chapter

▶ Understanding that the financial system isn't perfect

▶ Realising why banks aren't 100 per cent safe for your money

▶ Seeing how financial institutions rely on each other

*T*he global financial crisis of 2008 was a huge event, which arguably touched the lives of almost everyone on the planet: businesses went bankrupt; assets such as property and shares lost large chunks of their value; people lost their jobs; and policy makers ran around like headless chickens trying to make sense of it all. Mostly, you may remember the real fear and uncertainty that people felt about the future.

If economists are to get their heads around financial crises, they need to understand the underlying weaknesses in the financial system as it stands today. In this chapter we look at two main weaknesses – fractional reserve banking and systemic risk – and analyse the implications of each one.

These two weaknesses aren't necessarily problems that have to be fixed; instead, they present risks that need to be managed in order to have a well-functioning financial system.

Understanding Weaknesses in the Financial System

No structure, method, organisation or indeed person is perfect, and the financial system is no exception. If anything positive is to be gained from the terrible events of 2008, economists need to analyse what happened and ensure – as much as possible – that history does not repeat itself. Identifying specific weaknesses is the start so systemic vulnerabilities can be addressed.

The financial system is an extremely large and complex system with many actors all interacting with one another: banks, insurance companies, households, regulators, traders and more. Unsurprisingly the system has weaknesses, including: the propensity for problems to spread quickly from one part of the system to another; the fact that a loss of confidence in a bank can cause it to fail; the incentives individuals and organisations sometimes face to behave badly; and constant innovation that makes it tough for regulators to monitor financial institutions.

We choose to focus in this chapter on two main weaknesses, as follows:

- ✔ **Fractional reserve banking:** Where banks keep only a small fraction of the money deposited with them in reserve.
- ✔ **Systemic risk:** The risk that – due to the interconnectedness of financial institutions – problems in one bank can quickly spread to others.

These two weaknesses make clear two of the scariest lessons about our financial system as it currently stands:

- ✔ Any bank, no matter how well run, can fail if it suffers a loss of confidence.
- ✔ The failure of one financial institution can lead to the failure of many more financial institutions.

Finding Out about Fractional Reserve Banking

Fractional reserve banking is the method of banking practised throughout the world. As the name suggests, it involves banks keeping a fraction of deposits in reserve. Here we discuss what fractional reserve banking means in practice, including how it works and potential problems. You discover what happens to your money when you put it in the bank, how banks can quite literally create money out of thin air and how an otherwise healthy bank can fail.

Discovering what happens when you put your money in the bank

The best way to understand fractional reserve banking is with an example of what you might reasonably think happens to your bank deposits as opposed to what actually happens. What really happens is a lot scarier than you might think!

Imagine that today is your birthday, and you receive a clean, crisp £50 note as a present from an old friend. You consider all the exciting things you can possibly buy with your note (such as some tasty chocolates for sweet-toothed authors, perhaps?). But in the end you come to the conclusion that saving it for a rainy day would be more prudent (shame!). You take the note to your local bank branch and deposit it in your account. The cashier kindly takes your money downstairs to the bank vault for safe-keeping.

At some point in the future you need the money back (perhaps you have a date you want to impress); you return to your bank to withdraw the £50. Again the cashier goes downstairs, this time to retrieve your note, which has been faithfully waiting for you all along.

If this story doesn't quite sound right to you, that's because it isn't right! What we've just described is known as *100 per cent reserve banking*: for every pound deposited, the bank keeps exactly a pound in reserve. In fact, no modern banks use this system.

In reality, banks retain only a fraction of deposits in reserve. So when anyone deposits £50, the bank keeps only a small part (say, £5) in reserve. With the remaining £45 the bank aims to get a return on it by lending it out. The percentage kept in reserve is called the *reserve ratio*. In this example the reserve ratio is 5/50 = 0.1 = 10 per cent.

But if the bank has lent out most of your money, how can it possibly hope to repay you when you come to withdraw your cash? The answer lies in the fact that many different people hold accounts at the bank. At any one time, only a few of the account holders are likely to make withdrawals. So long as the bank has sufficient reserves to cover these withdrawals, everything is fine. Problems arise when the bank's reserves aren't sufficient to cover the withdrawals, as you see later in the 'Experiencing bank runs: Why any bank can fail' section.

Creating money out of thin air

A somewhat scary implication of fractional reserve banking is that banks can create money out of thin air. To discover how, consider your birthday example in the preceding section. So far, you've deposited £50 at your bank, Bank X (yes, that's how imaginative economists are). Bank X has kept £5 in reserve and lent out the remaining £45 to Mickey, who deposits the money in Bank Y (even if Mickey decides to spend the money instead, eventually someone else will deposit the money in Bank Y).

You may think that the total is still only £50. But not only cash is considered to be money; bank deposits are also seen as a form of money. So actually the total amount of money is £50 (your deposit at Bank X) + £45 (Mickey's deposit at Bank Y) = £95.

Another way of seeing this is to consider that you're asked how much money you have in Bank X. What's your reply? You're unlikely to say, 'I deposited £50 but £45 of it was lent out, so I only have £5 in my account.' You're more likely to say, 'I have £50 in my account, and I can show you my bank statement to prove it!' Similarly, if you ask Mickey how much money he has deposited in Bank Y, he's sure to say £45.

But as a terrible old comedian used to say, 'wait, there's more, there's more!'. As you know, Bank Y doesn't keep all of Mickey's £45 in reserve; instead, it retains a small fraction and lends out the rest. Eventually the money lent out will be deposited in Bank Z and so on. At this stage you may be thinking, 'this is madness, when does it end?' The answer is – it doesn't. The process continues *ad infinitum*, but with each successive round becoming less and less significant, until eventually it peters out (see Figure 14-1).

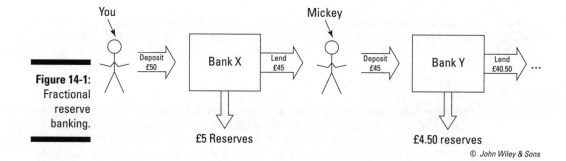

Figure 14-1:
Fractional
reserve
banking.

© John Wiley & Sons

For every £1 initially deposited, the financial system multiplies it so it becomes £$(1/r)$ of money (where r is the reserve ratio). For this reason $(1/r)$ is called the *money multiplier*. Notice that when the reserve ratio is small, that is, when banks lend out a large proportion of deposits, the money multiplier is large and vice versa. In the earlier birthday example, the money multiplier is equal to $1/0.1 = 10$.

Experiencing bank runs: Why any bank can fail

As the preceding sections show, banks keep only a fraction of deposits in reserve. This observation has a startling implication: any bank can fail if depositors lose confidence in its ability to pay them back. To see how, in this section we consider a well-run, very conservative bank called Cautious Bank.

The rumours begin

Cautious Bank has a large reserve ratio and is careful about to whom it lends money. You'd have thought that such a bank would be the last candidate to fail.

But suppose that some mischievous fellow starts a (false) rumour that Cautious Bank is unable to honour its obligations. As a depositor you may be unsure whether the rumour is true, but to be on the safe side you decide to withdraw your funds. After all, you can easily transfer money to another one of your accounts and who knows, doing so may save you from losing your shirt.

Other depositors reason similarly to you and also decide to pull their funds. Now the executives at Cautious Bank are getting nervous, because they see the bank's reserves depleting quickly. Depositors who initially didn't believe the rumour see on the evening news that large queues of anxious customers are waiting outside bank branches. They decide that they too need to withdraw their funds. As you can see, things can quickly spiral out of control until Cautious Bank doesn't have sufficient reserves to meet all the withdrawal requests.

The bank fails

At this stage without outside (usually government) support the game is up – Cautious Bank will fail. Notice that all the fundamentals at the bank were sound: it was well managed and didn't engage in risky lending. Nevertheless, the mere rumour that it was in trouble led to a bank run, which meant that it was unable to meet its obligations.

Think of it as a kind of self-fulfilling prophecy: if people believe a bank is going to fail, in all likelihood it will fail. This shows just how important people's beliefs and expectations are in determining macroeconomic events.

Types of bank failure

Economists draw a distinction between those businesses that are in trouble due to being *insolvent* and those that have *liquidity* problems:

- ✔ **Insolvent:** A business is insolvent when all its assets combined aren't sufficient to cover its liabilities. For example, suppose you own a bakery that owes £1 million to Jessica. If you're unable to pay her even after selling all the bakery's assets (the building, the oven, unpaid invoices and so on), we're sorry to tell you that your business is insolvent.

- ✔ **Liquidity:** A business has liquidity problems when it has short-term cash flow problems. Cautious Bank seems to have more of a liquidity problem than a solvency problem.

Cautious Bank's problem

To understand why Cautious Bank's issue is liquidity, imagine that its total deposits stand at £10 million and its reserve ratio is 0.5 (see the earlier 'Discovering what happens when you put your money in the bank' section for more on the reserve ratio). In other words, the bank has £5 million in reserves and has loaned out £5 million. Before moving on, just spend a minute thinking about Cautious Bank's assets and liabilities.

Are Cautious Bank's £10 million of deposits an asset or a liability? They're a liability, because at any time depositors can turn up and ask for their money back. What assets does the bank have in order to meet this liability? Well, it has reserves of £5 million and £5 million of loans. If Cautious Bank has done a good job in allocating the loans, they should be worth more than £5 million, because they're likely to be repaid and earn the bank a healthy return. Suppose that the bank considers them to be worth £6 million.

Table 14-1 outlines Cautious Bank's assets and liabilities.

Table 14-1	**Cautious Bank's Balance Sheet**
Assets	*Liabilities*
£5 million reserves	£10 million deposits
£6 million loans	

Inspecting the table shows clearly that Cautious Bank's assets are worth more than its liabilities. This is good news – Cautious Bank certainly isn't insolvent. Why, then, is it suffering financial difficulties?

Looking at its assets, you notice that they differ in their liquidity:

- ✔ A *liquid* asset is one that's easy to turn into cash.

- ✔ An *illiquid* asset is one that's difficult to turn into cash.

Cautious Bank's reserves are liquid by definition – they're cash! But what about the loans it's made? These are certainly valuable assets; however, the loans won't be paid back until perhaps many years into the future. Moreover, the bank can't use them to pay a depositor who wants to make a withdrawal. Just imagine going to your bank to make a withdrawal and being told 'Sorry, we've run out of cash, but take this loan that will pay you back in a year's time'!

One possible solution is that Cautious Bank sells the loans to someone else. The problem is, in these circumstances, it's unlikely to get a good price. In this distressed state, potential buyers of the loans know that Cautious Bank is desperate for cash, which substantially weakens its bargaining position. Furthermore, potential buyers may not know the quality of the loans and assume that because Cautious Bank is in trouble, the loans are of low quality – that is, less likely to be repaid.

Catching a Cold! Systemic Risk

In this section we show that financial institutions are connected to one another in a complex web of transactions. As a result, problems in one financial company can quickly spread to others – like a financial virus.

The transmission of problems from one financial institution to another is called *financial contagion*, because, just like a cold, financial problems are contagious!

We describe the nature of this systemic risk and the dangerous phenomenon of a cascade of business failures. We also include the story of one famous company failure as illustration.

Struggling with a complex web of transactions

Financial institutions are highly interlinked and engage in huge, complex transactions with each other. No doubt you can see how many potential things can go so terribly wrong in such an environment.

The sheer magnitude of financial transactions is hard to get your head around. For some kind of idea of the enormous numbers involved, check out the nearby sidebar 'Trading in the trillions'.

Trading in the trillions

We estimate that around $5 trillion worth of transactions are made every *day* in the foreign exchange market (the market for currencies, for example, dollars, pounds, euros). Around $2 trillion of this trade takes place in London alone.

Another astonishing statistic is that the notional value of all outstanding over-the-counter (OTC) derivative contracts is around $700 trillion. Putting things into perspective, the value of everything produced in the world in a year is well short of $100 trillion (not that that's a small number!).

As well as transactions between financial institutions being massive in size, they also vary in their complexity. Some transactions between financial institutions are very simple. For example, Bank X may sell £100 million to Bank Y in exchange for $150 million. This straightforward trade is easy to understand and not that different to when you go on holiday and purchase holiday money from the bureau de change.

Other transactions are more complex – *derivative contracts* (which are financial products that *derive* their value from some underlying asset) are a good example. Their complexity and widespread use mean that understanding them is key to understanding how and why our financial system is so complex and also how deeply interconnected financial institutions are due to their dealings with each other (in derivatives as well as in other ways). Finally, understanding how a derivative works will give you a good idea of what *leverage* is: the multiplying up of rewards and losses. Leverage means that even small changes in the prices of things can have a large impact in financial markets.

Derivatives themselves vary in complexity; relatively simple derivatives are described as *vanilla* (like vanilla ice cream, the standard version). In contrast, complex derivatives are described as *exotic*. People can trade derivatives on an *exchange* (an organised market where buyers and sellers meet to trade a standardised product) or *over-the-counter* (where the two parties meet and write their own contract without going through a third party).

We go through an example to help you see why a derivative is more complex than a standard financial product (like a stock or commodity). The example also demonstrates how trading in derivatives can quickly involve large losses (or gains) being incurred by different parties. Because financial institutions engage in huge amounts of derivate contracts with one another, derivatives clearly show the interconnectedness of the financial system.

A *call-option* is a particular kind of derivative. It gives the holder the *right but not the obligation* to purchase some asset in the future at some agreed-upon price (called the *strike price*). Imagine that you think that the price of BP shares is going to go up. You could buy BP shares now – if BP shares cost £5 each and you have £50 to spend, then you can buy 10 BP shares. For every £1 that BP shares increase in price, you'll make £10 in profit.

But if you're feeling more ambitious, instead of buying BP shares outright, you can buy call-options today, which give you the right but not the obligation to buy BP shares in a year's time for £5. Obviously, if BP shares are less than £5 in a year's time you don't exercise your options – after all, why would you buy something for £5 that you can buy cheaper on the open market? Conversely, if the shares rise to more than £5, you'd certainly exercise your options – even if you no longer wanted to hold BP shares, you'd still exercise your options to purchase them for £5 and then immediately sell them in the market. You can see how this may be a risky option (no pun intended!) – if BP shares are below £5 in a year's time you lose your entire stake.

Why may you prefer to buy the call-options rather than the shares directly? Because the options only give you the *right* to buy the shares, they're considerably cheaper than the shares themselves. The call-option may only cost 50 pence, and so with your £50 you can buy 100 call-options instead of only 10 shares. This changes things dramatically: now for every £1 that BP shares increase in price, your profits increase by £100 instead of £10. This potential multiplication of returns is called *leverage*.

Does this mean that everyone should go out and start buying call-options? Probably not. First, owning the shares means that you own a part of the company and are entitled to a share of the profits. Owning the call-options gives you no such right. Second, although call-options do well when the price of the underlying asset increases above the strike price (the price at which you have the option to buy), they do *terribly* if, at the time of expiry, the price of the asset is less than the strike price. This is because they're now completely worthless – no rational person would exercise a call-option in these circumstances (so only Homer Simpson, then).

In this example, if BP shares fall in price to £4.50 (or even stay unchanged at £5) the option to purchase them at £5 isn't worth the paper it's written on! You'll have completely lost the £50 you spent on them. Table 14-2 shows how the profit (or loss) from the two strategies compares as the stock price varies.

As you can see, buying the options does particularly well if the stock price increases substantially. If the stock doubles to £10 you surely exercise the buy options to buy them for £5. You make £5 profit for every option that you own (£5 × 100 = £500), but don't forget the £50 to purchase the options in the first place, leaving you with £450.

Table 14-2	Buying Call-Options versus Buying Shares	
Stock Price in 1 Year (£)	Profit from Spending £50 to Buy 10 Shares at £5 Each (£)	Profit from Spending £50 to Buy 100 Call-Options at 50 Pence Each (£)
3	−20	−50
4	−10	−50
5	0	−50
6	10	50
7	20	150
10	50	450
20	150	1450

In contrast if you buy the shares, you make £5 profit per share, but because you only own 10 shares in total, you make £50. Notice, however, how the options perform terribly if the stock price fails to rise – you lose the whole stake. By owning the shares, your losses are more limited.

In general, although leverage increases the potential reward, it also increases the risk. Call-options are only considered a vanilla (simple) derivative. Derivative contracts can be as complex as you like, and many derivatives are substantially more complicated. Furthermore, financial institutions take on leverage in many ways other than derivatives. We don't go into them here, but the principle remains: leverage amplifies gains and losses. Leverage adds to the complexity and the interconnectedness of the financial system. It means losses (and gains) can be huge but also small changes in financial markets can have big effects on financial institutions.

Fearing contagion: When one gets sick, they all follow

Problems at one financial institution, which mean that it can't meet its obligations to others, can lead to substantial losses and ultimately the failure of other financial businesses. Furthermore, these problems can be easily transmitted to the *real economy* (by which we mean things that you notice on a day-to-day basis about the economy, for example, increased unemployment or lower real wages).

This domino effect, in which the failure of one financial institution leads to failures at others and in businesses more generally, is known as a *cascading failure*. A nice name for a not so nice phenomenon.

Somewhat like hanging out with someone with the flu is likely to make you ill, having dealings with a financial institution with problems is likely to give you financial problems of your own. This financial contagion can happen in many ways, but we look at just one simply illustrative example.

Imagine that you own an airline – sure, jetting around the world for a while is fun, but at some point you have to sit down and make some important decisions. For example, you have to think carefully about fuel. Airlines purchase large amounts of fuel, so say that (at current prices) your airline spends £100 million a year on fuel.

Although fuel is a big chunk of your costs, you're confident that it's affordable. What worries you is that the price of fuel may rise in the future. In particular, you estimate that if the price of fuel rises by 20 per cent in the next year, you'll make a loss and may have to exit the industry (no more free flights for you!). The question is: can you do anything today in order to protect yourself from the risk of fuel prices rising substantially in the future?

One thing you can do is approach a bank to see whether it would be willing to *hedge* (offset) your risk. How might this work? Well, wouldn't it be great if the bank reimbursed you for the additional cost if fuel prices did increase? For example, if fuel prices increase by 30 per cent you'd have to spend an additional £30 million on fuel. This wouldn't be a problem because the bank would pay you £30 million to offset the additional cost.

Here are the two (inevitable) catches:

- ✔ If the price of fuel falls, you have to pay the bank any gains due to the price fall. For example, if fuel prices fall by 40 per cent – potentially saving you £40 million – you have to pay the bank £40 million. Thus the bank is offering you a service that looks a lot like insurance: whatever happens to the price of fuel, the effective amount that you pay for fuel remains unchanged.

- ✔ The bank is unlikely to offer this insurance for free. It demands to be compensated for taking the risk off your hands. Say that the bank charges £5 million for this service, which you have to pay regardless of what happens to the oil price. If you enter into this agreement, you will (in theory) pay £105 million (£100 million + £5 million) regardless of what happens to the price of fuel. This ensures that you don't go out of business if fuel prices skyrocket. This type of contract is called a *swap* (see Figure 14-2).

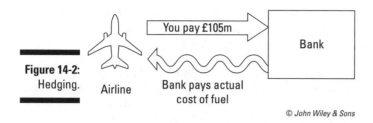

© John Wiley & Sons

Figure 14-2:
Hedging.

So far everything looks hunky-dory: your airline is hedged (insured) against changes in the price of fuel, and the bank is happy because it's getting paid for its services.

But your bank is now holding quite a lot of risk – if the price of fuel rises a lot, it will have to make large payments to you. Can it do anything about this? Well, yes, with a little bit of financial magic, it can. You see, although airlines dislike high fuel prices, airline fuel producers like them. Say that FuelCorp produces airline fuel – what really worries it is that fuel prices will collapse and leave the firm bankrupt. Therefore it can enter into a similar contract to yours with some other bank, except that this time the bank makes payments to FuelCorp if fuel prices fall and FuelCorp makes payments to the bank if fuel prices rise. This hedges FuelCorp's risk, because it's now guaranteed a certain price for its fuel (see Figure 14-3).

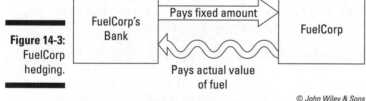

© John Wiley & Sons

Figure 14-3:
FuelCorp
hedging.

Both your airline and FuelCorp are now protected from changes in the price of fuel. You've guaranteed the price that you pay for fuel, and FuelCorp has guaranteed the price it receives for fuel. But what about the banks? Well, your bank has taken on your risk – so it loses money if fuel prices rise and makes money if fuel prices fall. And FuelCorp's bank has taken on its risk – so it loses money if fuel prices fall and makes money if they rise. Because your bank does well when FuelCorp's bank does badly (and vice versa), they can hedge each other by entering into the following swap: if fuel prices rise, FuelCorp's bank makes a payment to your bank, and if fuel prices fall, your bank makes a payment to FuelCorp's bank.

Looking at Figure 14-4, you can see that not only are your airline and FuelCorp hedged, but the two banks aren't holding any of the risks associated with changes in the price of fuel. The financial system appears to have done its job well: it has acted as an intermediary between your airline (which wanted to fix the price it paid for fuel) and FuelCorp (which wanted to fix the price it received for fuel). Economists get quite excited when markets work the way they're supposed to by allowing parties to enter into contracts that make them all better off. But this isn't the end of the story. Contagion hasn't yet reared its ugly head.

Figure 14-4:
Taking away
all the risk?

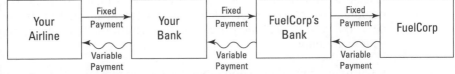

© John Wiley & Sons

Economists say that the *market risk* has been eliminated due to these transactions, that is, the risks associated with the uncertain future price of fuel. But another risk applies here – called *counterparty risk* – that one of the institutions you've dealt with won't honour its side of the bargain. Counterparty risk can be a huge problem and can lead to the wholesale unravelling of all these contracts.

Imagine that FuelCorp's bank gets into some kind of trouble (possibly due to a bank run – see the earlier section 'Experiencing bank runs: Why any bank can fail'), which means it can't honour its liabilities. This situation is likely to cause substantial difficulties for anyone who does business with FuelCorp. Suppose that fuel prices rise substantially: ordinarily this would trigger a payment from FuelCorp's bank to your bank. But FuelCorp's bank is in trouble and can no longer make this payment. You're also due a payment from your bank to compensate you for the higher fuel price. As you can see, the waters are getting murkier as the 'virus' threatens to spread.

Your payment should've been straightforward, with any money your bank owed to you being covered by the payment made to your bank from FuelCorp's bank. Your bank still has to honour its obligation to you regardless of the failure of FuelCorp's bank. However, your bank may have been relying heavily on the offsetting payment, which will now no longer be paid. This has the potential to cause substantial difficulties for your bank. So much so, that it may be unable to make its payment to you, which in turn may cause your airline to fail.

The contagion we mention at the start of this section has finally reached you after different companies have sneezed on each other – and now your firm has caught a nasty cold.

The problem isn't just the large amounts of complex transactions taking place between financial institutions – it's the fact that these transactions are often opaque.

Seeing systemic risk in practice: The case of Lehman Brothers

We now present an example that illustrates the sheer scale of the devastation caused when a huge business fails: the bank Lehman Brothers. The highly complex and interconnected financial system meant that Lehman's collapse quickly transmitted problems throughout the financial system and the wider economy.

What happened in mid-September 2008 set in motion a quite extraordinary cascade of events. People still discuss and debate the decisions made and are likely to do so for decades to come. The story begins late-afternoon on Friday 12 September; the heads of all the major US banks (except Lehman Brothers) are summoned to the Federal Reserve (the central bank of the US) at short notice. As John Thain, the head of Merrill Lynch at the time, commented, 'Those types of phone calls are always bad.'

He was right. At the Fed, they were met by Hank Paulson (then secretary of the Treasury) and Timothy Geithner (then president of the New York Fed). Paulson and Geithner informed the bank heads that Lehman Brothers (a seriously large US investment bank) was on the verge of bankruptcy. This announcement probably wasn't a huge surprise – people knew that Lehman was in serious financial difficulty due to its exposure to the US housing market.

What probably did surprise the bankers was that the US government wasn't willing to bail out (give financial assistance to) Lehman in order to save it. Only recently, Bear Stearns (another investment bank) and Fannie Mae and Freddie Mac (two large financial institutions at the heart of the US mortgage market) had found themselves in similar trouble and were bailed out. The size and interconnectedness of Lehman meant that people assumed that something similar would be arranged for it. Paulson and Geithner were smart guys and knew about the dangers of systemic risk and cascading failures (see the two preceding sections): surely they wouldn't allow Lehman to fail?

Nevertheless, they told the bank heads that if they were unable, between themselves, to come to the aid of Lehman, by the time that financial markets opened on Monday morning, Lehman Brothers would be no more. Everyone present knew that such an outcome would be enormously destructive to the other banks present and to the wider economy. One idea was that the banks would lend Lehman large sums of money in the hope that this would stave off bankruptcy.

This idea didn't get very far for a number of reasons:

- **Lehman's problems weren't primarily due to a lack of liquidity (a shortage of short-term cash).** Instead, Lehman had serious solvency problems (its liabilities substantially exceeded its assets). You may wonder how on earth such a major investment bank can find itself in such a desperate position.

  A crucial explanation is that Lehman took leverage to the extreme – by some estimates its leverage ratio at its peak was 44, which means that Lehman borrowed £44 for every £1 of its own capital! If true, this would mean that a fall in the value of Lehman's assets of only 3 per cent would be sufficient to bankrupt it: because Lehman was insolvent, the other banks were quite rightly worried that any loans made would never be repaid.

- **The other banks had financial problems of their own.** They were all exposed to the US housing market and incurred substantial losses as a result. They had little appetite to lend money to anyone, let alone Lehman.

- **Each bank hoped that someone else would come to Lehman's rescue so it wouldn't have to.** Never mind that the outcome where no one came to Lehman's rescue would be much worse than everyone contributing a little bit.

  This is known as the *free-rider problem*, because each bank has an incentive to free-ride on the contributions of the other banks.

- **Lehman's failure would be so catastrophic that many of the bank heads must have thought that Paulson and Geithner were bluffing when they said that a public bailout wouldn't happen.** The bank heads soon found that the two men meant what they said.

With no one willing to lend to Lehman, the next possibility was that one of the banks take over Lehman outright. Lehman had lots of very valuable assets; unfortunately they also had substantial liabilities. Potential buyers were interested in the assets, of course, but they wanted the government to take at least some responsibility for the liabilities.

At the time Lehman was effectively insolvent: its liabilities outweighed its assets (see the earlier section 'Types of bank failure'). Without some kind of government support, taking over Lehman just wasn't an attractive proposition. Ultimately, the two initially interested banks, Bank of America and Barclays, walked away. In fact, Bank of America did a deal with Merrill Lynch in the hope that the combined company would be able to better weather the financial storm that was to come.

So even though each bank knew that Lehman's failure would be potentially devastating for them (due to systemic risk and contagion), no one bank was willing to take on the responsibility of saving Lehman. Each bank hoped that someone else (either another bank or the government) would come to the rescue.

On Monday 15 September 2008, with nowhere else to go, Lehman Brothers – one of the oldest and most prestigious banks on Wall Street – filed for bankruptcy. It was the largest bankruptcy in history by some distance: ten times bigger than the collapse of energy giant Enron. The fallout was felt immediately as global stock markets tanked; by the end of the day $700 billion had been wiped from their value. Chaos ensued and global credit markets effectively shut down – companies found that borrowing money was almost impossible.

Many well-run businesses rely on being able to borrow money on a short-term basis: as a result even large blue-chip companies were struggling with their cash flow. The potential collapse of insurance giant AIG was the final straw and forced the US government to intervene on a massive scale: AIG was bailed out with $85 billion and Hank Paulson went before the US Congress to ask for a $700 billion bailout package (yes, you read that right, Hank Paulson, the man who only a few days earlier said that no public money was available for a bailout!).

The interconnected web of financial transactions meant that the problems wouldn't be restricted to the US. The UK was always going to be hit hard by these events: London vies with New York as the world's pre-eminent financial centre. Just two days after Lehman's failure, HBOS, the UK's largest mortgage lender, had to be rescued (read: taken over) by Lloyds TSB. By the end of the month two further US banks had failed: Washington Mutual and Wachovia. Things didn't improve: in October, HBOS and Lloyds TSB found themselves in trouble again; as if things weren't bad enough, Royal Bank of Scotland (RBS, one of the world's largest banks) was on the edge of failure – to avoid the collapse of the entire UK banking sector, the UK government had to bail out all three banks. All this chaos was the result of systemic risk and the contagion that resulted from the failure of Lehman.

The jury is still out on whether US policy makers were correct to allow Lehman to fail. Critics point to the ensuing devastation and argue that the $20–30 billion it would have cost the government to save Lehman was small fry in comparison. Others point out that policy makers were in an impossible situation and that eventually they had to let someone fail in order to show the world that taxpayers can't always be expected to bail out failing banks.

Chapter 15

Getting Away with Excessive Risk-Taking: Moral Hazard

The media has been filled with stories about bankers' bad behaviour over the last few years: Libor fixing, subprime lending and foreign exchange manipulation – sometimes the list seems endless. In good economic times, policy makers and perhaps even the public may be willing to 'let some things slide'. But the part that this behaviour played in the 2008 financial crisis means that any hint of a 'free pass' has been abruptly cancelled.

The problem is one of *moral hazard* – where people are more likely to behave badly in a situation in which they think they can keep their actions hidden from others. In essence, if the likelihood of them being caught or punished is low or nonexistent, some people will take the chance, ignoring any wider risks that may be involved.

As a result of bankers' excessive risk-taking and the subsequent financial collapse, governments have had to use public funds to bail out some enormous and previously highly profitable companies.

In this chapter, we discuss why bankers sometimes end up behaving badly and why financial institutions take excessive risks, as well as the difficulties policy makers have in tackling the problem.

Banks Behaving Badly: Watching Out for Moral Hazard

Moral hazard matters (who says economists beat around the bush). Not only does an understanding of it help you to grasp one of the underlying causes of financial instability, but it also allows you to see more generally when markets (not just financial markets) work well and when they don't.

Moral hazard refers to a situation in which people are able to hide their actions. For this reason, it's sometimes called the problem of *hidden action*. Unsurprisingly, when people's actions are hidden from others, they may have incentives to behave badly.

Just imagine what would happen at your local supermarket if the owners couldn't tell whether people had paid for their groceries or not. Unless you live in an unusually honest area, large amounts of food would 'go missing' in such a supermarket!

Moral hazard has become increasingly linked to the financial system following the 2008 crisis and a series of damaging scandals. For example, a widely held view is that banks knowingly took on excessive risk in the prelude to the crisis because they understood that, in the event of a crisis, they would be bailed out by taxpayers.

Avoiding Financial Armageddon: Bailouts

Unsurprisingly given the results, policy makers take a great interest in moral hazard as regards the financial sector: governments hate bailing it out. Bailouts are typically very expensive, very risky and very unpopular with the electorate – after all, cancelling pensioners' free bus passes and winter fuel payments to help wealthy bankers is never going to go down well.

So if the financial sector gets into trouble, why bail it out at all? Surely, the whole point of a market economy is that badly run businesses fail and good ones succeed? When applied to the financial system, this argument seems quite attractive for about 30 seconds, until you realise that allowing a large financial institution to fail is likely to send massive shockwaves of destruction pulsating throughout the economy. This problem is called *systemic risk* (for a detailed look, turn to Chapter 14).

Even in the rare cases where a large financial institution is allowed to go under (Lehman Brothers being the most well-known example – again, see Chapter 14), governments invariably attempt to bail out the rest of the financial sector in order to stop the problems from spreading and causing a cascade of failures.

Policy makers can come to the aid of a fragile financial system in a number of ways:

- **Lending money directly to struggling financial institutions:** Central banks regularly lend money to financial institutions, even in normal times. To do so, they usually demand that high-quality collateral is posted with them (for example, AAA-rated government bonds).

  As in any loan, the point of the collateral is to ensure that the borrower pays back the loan – if not, the lender keeps the collateral. But during times of crisis, banks are often short of high-quality collateral. In this case, central banks may relax the quality requirement of the collateral that they're willing to accept in order to make loans. But doing so increases the risk of taxpayers having to incur losses.

- **Guaranteeing deposits:** Fractional reserve banking means that if depositors lose confidence in a bank (whether the bank is actually in trouble or not), that bank is likely to experience substantial difficulties (check out Chapter 14 for more details).

  In order to increase confidence in the financial system, governments can guarantee deposits. In the UK, the Financial Services Compensation Scheme (FSCS) guarantees the first £85,000 held in accounts of authorised banks, building societies and credit unions. In the US, the Federal Deposit Insurance Corporation (FDIC) similarly guarantees the first $250,000. (Trust the Americans to do things bigger and better!) In times of crisis, governments often go even further: when Northern Rock suffered a bank run in 2007, Chancellor Alistair Darling guaranteed all deposits held at Northern Rock regardless of the size.

- **Injecting capital directly into financial institutions:** In this way, instead of being a lender, the government takes ownership of a portion of the company. These financial institutions often find themselves in trouble in the first place because they're *undercapitalised* (they don't hold enough capital in order to safely cover any potential losses), so the idea is that if you're going to intervene, why not intervene directly and inject fresh capital into the bank?

  For example, when Royal Bank of Scotland (RBS) found itself in trouble in 2008, the UK government injected capital and thereby took a majority stake in the firm. Similarly in the US, a scheme called the Troubled Asset Relief Program (TARP) saw the government take large stakes in a number of banks.

You can see these interventions as being 'direct', in that they're clearly designed to help the banking sector. But other interventions are considered to be indirect bailouts, the most prominent being the aggressive use of monetary policy. When the financial system is in a state of distress, many financial institutions and firms that rely on financial institutions suffer from liquidity problems: that is, they find borrowing money difficult. By increasing the money supply, the central bank can reduce the interest rate (see Chapter 10 for how this works) and, it hopes, make it easier for those who need to borrow money to do so.

This scenario occurred in 2008–09, when the US Federal Reserve and the Bank of England reduced official interest rates to close to zero. But even these ultra-low interest rates were seen as insufficient, and both central banks went on to pursue a policy of *quantitative easing* (printing money on an enormous scale) to flood financial markets with liquidity (again, take a look at Chapter 10 for an in-depth look at quantitative easing).

If all these different options are making your head spin, don't worry. The bottom line is that if you work at, manage or are a shareholder of a large financial institution, you can be quietly confident that if you find yourself in big trouble, someone is going to come to your rescue. Or in other words, you're just 'too big to fail'.

Providing Incentives for Excessive Risk-Taking

Bankers aren't fools. They understand that the dangers of systemic risk (see Chapter 14 for a description) mean that governments are unlikely to let them fail. This implicit government guarantee acts a lot like a form of insurance – which unfortunately has an unintended effect.

In this section we take a closer look at the incentives that banks and bankers face, which encourage them to take excessive risks. We also discuss the government guarantee to bail out financial institutions as a form of insurance.

Rigging the game: Heads we win, tails you lose

Here we introduce a simple example that shows why financial institutions may want to take excessive risks.

Imagine that we're sitting down with you to play the following game: a coin is tossed. If it comes up heads, £1 falls from the sky into our pockets; if, however, it comes up tails, £1 disappears from your pocket. How would you feel about this game? Probably not very good, because it's impossible for you to win any money; the best possible outcome is that you break even. We, however, love this game: we can only win (or at worst break even), and in fact we'd play it over and over again!

Draw an analogy between this game and the financial sector. If banks take on large amounts of risk, they may do very well and make a lot of money – this is a case of 'heads we (the bank) win'. But of course things can also go pear-shaped and the bank makes large losses. The thing is, no matter how large the bank's losses, as we describe in the preceding section, the government is unlikely to let it fail. This corresponds to 'tails you (the government) lose'.

Furthermore, the worst that can happen to you as a bank is that you make a loss and the government bails you out – despite their name, toxic assets don't kill you and you don't even go to jail (although policy makers are trying to change this). Therefore, arguably it makes sense for banks to take on as much risk as possible – if they win, they win big – and if they lose, well, they don't really lose because the government takes most of the losses!

Obviously this analogy is a massive simplification, but it contains more than a grain of truth.

Investigating insurance and moral hazard

The implicit government guarantee to save failing banks looks a lot like insurance. This is an important observation, because insurance almost always gives rise to moral hazard problems. Here we explore the connection between insurance and moral hazard to help you gain a deeper understanding of what exactly is going on.

Insurance is great. Typically, in return for a premium (money that you pay to the insurance company upfront), you can insure yourself against some kind of loss. You encounter all kinds of insurance: car insurance, travel insurance, health insurance and even against bad weather! Insurance works by pooling the risks of a large number of individuals. So, for example, most people don't make a claim on their travel insurance, but their premiums are sufficient to cover the emergency medical treatment and evacuation for someone who becomes very ill while abroad.

Insurance companies offer insurance because they expect that the total premiums that they receive will be more than they have to pay out to cover any claims.

Things get more complicated, however, when you realise that being insured changes people's behaviour (the moral hazard phenomenon). When people have health insurance (or even a publicly funded NHS), they can take less care of their health in the knowledge that if they get sick, someone else will foot the bill. Similarly, someone with mobile phone insurance is more likely to leave her phone lying around.

Perhaps more interesting is the underlying cause of moral hazard: the fact that one person can hide her actions from the other. Why does this matter? Well, your insurance company (or your NHS doctor) doesn't know if you're having a huge fried breakfast every morning or you start each day with a grapefruit, porridge and a 3-mile run. It doesn't know if you spend your leisure time taking long walks or are a couch potato who watches endless DVD box sets. Similarly, your mobile phone insurer can't observe whether you're taking good care of your latest smartphone or if you regularly let a toddler play with it. The level of monitoring that would be required to avoid moral hazard on the part of the insured just isn't practical or feasible.

In principle, if it were able to observe your actions, the insurance company could write into the contract that it would only pay out if you took sufficient care. This would solve the moral hazard problem. But it can't, so instead insurance companies try to give people incentives to take care. Some prominent ways to encourage people to take care include no-claims bonuses (your premium falls the longer you go without making a claim) and an excess on every claim (for example, you're responsible for the first £100).

No doubt you can see that governments are effectively providing insurance to financial institutions by standing behind the financial system in times of crisis. The institutions have strong incentives to take excessive risk: if things work out, they win big; if things don't, it's the taxpayers' problem. In a nutshell, that's the moral hazard problem in the financial sector.

The underlying cause of this moral hazard is the hidden action, because a government can't easily observe how much risk banks are taking on. Otherwise, it could legislate to make taking excessive risk illegal and intervene immediately when rules were broken, before any trouble started. We look further at the problem of making excessive risk illegal in the later section 'Tackling moral hazard to avoid bailouts'.

A major difference exists between traditional types of insurance such as car insurance and the implicit insurance that governments provide to financial institutions:

✔ **Traditional (explicit) insurance:** The insured party (for example, the car owner) pays a premium to the insurance company, which pays out in the case of a claim.

✔ **Government (implicit) insurance to financial institutions:** The insured parties (financial institutions) pay no premium to the government providing the insurance.

You can argue that banks pay the government in the form of taxes, but that misses the point: banks, like all businesses, pay taxes due on the profits they make. However, unlike other businesses, banks receive a massive implicit subsidy in the form of insurance that they don't have to pay for.

Estimating the value of this free insurance to banks is difficult, and the amounts vary substantially: the Bank of England estimates that the value of too-big-to-fail insurance for the UK's largest banks alone is around £100 billion a year. For economists (and we hope non-economists), this situation is worrying: it means that effectively every year large transfers are being made from taxpayers to the owners and employees of financial institutions.

Factoring in the problem of compensation

Here's something you don't need telling if you read the tabloids: bankers get paid a lot. Unlike the redtops, however, this fact doesn't necessarily bother economists. In a well-functioning market economy, people get paid according to the personal contribution they make (in economist speak, they're paid according to their *marginal product*). Nonetheless, some issues are of concern as regards bankers' remuneration.

Overall compensation

This issue is fundamental: if bankers are extremely productive and add large amounts of value for their clients, economists typically have no problem with stratospheric bonuses. If, however, large amounts of bankers' pay can be attributed to the large public subsidy that banks receive due to their systemic importance, they do have reason to be concerned, for two reasons:

- ✔ **Inequality:** The subsidy is effectively a transfer of money from the general taxpayer to bankers. Because bankers are on average much better paid than the average taxpayer, this transfer is from the relatively poorer to the relatively richer. You may be surprised, but economists care quite a lot about *equity*: all other things equal, economists prefer more equal outcomes and therefore dislike inequality. Thus seeing money flow from poor people to rich people annoys economists (to varying degrees).

- ✔ **Rent-seeking:** The bankers aren't creating much value but *are* competing for a share of the subsidy. In effect, they're competing for already existing resources rather than creating a valuable service. Economists call this *rent-seeking* behaviour. When people rent-seek, instead of putting their efforts towards creating a good or service valued by the marketplace, they spend their time and effort competing with each other for some existing surplus. For why the term is a bit of a misnomer, see the nearby sidebar 'Don't be DUPed, dope'.

Don't be DUPed, dope

Economists aren't *per se* against people seeking out rents. For example, a person may build a house in order to rent it out, or a pharmaceutical giant may spend large sums in order to create a new drug that it knows it can sell for a premium. These activities are carried out to 'seek rent', but they can't be considered 'rent-seeking', because something of value is being created.

This is a bit confusing, which is partly why the prominent economist Jagdish Bhagwati coined an alternative phrase to describe rent-seeking behaviour: he calls it a kind of *directly unproductive profit-seeking* or DUP (pronounced, quite appropriately, 'dupe') for short.

A good example of DUP is lobbying activity: lobbyists typically spend a lot of time and resources influencing policy makers to carry out policies that favour their special interest. Often lobbying takes place in an attempt to divert public spending in a way that makes the special interest the beneficiary (for example, defence companies lobbying for greater military expenditure). Another favourite for lobbyists is trying to protect their industry from competition (for example, farmers trying to restrict imports of food). Although these activities are potentially very profitable for those undertaking them, their contribution to output is zero. Moreover, real resources have to be expended in order to carry out these activities.

Rent-seeking in the financial sector matters partly because, due to the large implied subsidies the financial sector receives, it's able to pay substantially more than most other types of work. If a large portion of the activities of banks can be considered a form of rent-seeking, by attracting the lion's share of the brightest graduates, the financial sector is depriving other industries of their talents. These bright young things could have made substantial contributions to society, whether in the fields of teaching, scientific research, medicine, politics and so on (not that these fields are free of rent-seeking!).

Structure of the compensation

People also raise serious concerns about the structure of bankers' compensation. In financial services, employees are commonly paid a base salary (which on its own would be considered generous to most people) supplemented by a bonus, which for high-performing staff can be many multiples of the base salary.

This structure has been blamed for creating a whole new level of moral hazard inside a financial institution. Even if a bank's senior managers do want to do the right thing and not take excessive risk (that is, not take advantage of the fact that they're too-big-to-fail and that the government can't fully see their actions), those senior managers can monitor only imperfectly the actions of the bankers under them. This arrangement gives bankers almost irresistible incentives to take on risk.

Here's a simple example. Imagine that you're responsible for trading currencies for a bank and that you haven't the foggiest about what's going to happen to the value of the pound in the future: it might go up, it might go down, who knows. Nevertheless you reason that if you take a big bet that the value of the pound will go up and it does indeed go up, you're in for a nice fat bonus. If you're wrong, and the pound falls, probably, the worst that happens to you is that you lose your job.

The moral hazard problem here is clear: taking on lots of risk has huge upside potential but limited downside. Banks are aware of this issue and have risk-management departments meant to ensure that no one is taking on too much risk on behalf of the bank. However, because monitoring people's actions is difficult, they have a tough job on their hands. Furthermore, seeing the true impact of a complex deal for a bank can take years, by which time the employees responsible may no longer even work there.

Jérôme Kerviel and SocGen

Jérôme Kerviel was a trader at French bank Société Générale (SocGen) who took on massive risks and ended up losing the bank €4.9 billion(!). This enormous loss almost brought SocGen, one of France's largest banks, to its knees.

Kerviel joined SocGen's compliance department in 2000. The role of a bank's compliance department is to attempt to ensure that the bank and its employees operate within the law and follow all the relevant rules and regulations. The assumption is that Kerviel gained a good understanding of the internal working of the bank, which later helped him cover up his risk-taking activities.

In 2005 Kerviel was promoted to the role of a junior trader, where his job was supposed to be taking advantage of the mispricing of shares in companies (a supposedly low-risk activity). But Kerviel actually placed very large bets on the stock market (estimated at around €50 billion, more than the value of the entire bank!). You'd have thought someone would've spotted such a large amount of money being played with, but the bank claims to have noticed his activities only in 2008, by which time he'd accrued billions in losses.

In 2010 Kerviel went on trial and was found guilty of 'forgery and breach of trust'. Initially, he was sentenced to five years in prison (with two years suspended) and ordered personally to repay the full €4.9 billion (not likely!). In 2012, on appeal, Kerviel's sentence was reduced by two years (so that he'd serve only one year in prison), and ultimately in 2014 a French court ruled he wouldn't have to repay the €4.9 billion.

The Kerviel case is an extreme example of a general principle: the way people are paid in financial services can incentivise them to take excessive risks, because the potential rewards if things go right seem relatively large and the potential costs (to them) if things go wrong seem relatively small. Kerviel's bets went sour, of course, but had they gone his way, most likely the media would've taken no interest and he'd have been rewarded with a substantial bonus.

Modelling risk-taking as a Prisoner's Dilemma

When a bank decides to take on excessive risk, it not only increases the chances of getting into financial difficulties, but also increases the chances that other banks will too. This is because of the highly interconnected nature of the financial system (see Chapter 14).

Here we show how the incentives that banks face can be thought of as a 'Prisoner's Dilemma' – where each bank finds it in its interest to take excessive risk even though this leads to a highly unstable financial system and increases the probability that it will fail.

Affecting others negatively

Economists say that one bank deciding to take on excessive risk has a *negative externality* on all the other banks, because it makes the entire financial system less stable. An *externality* is a positive or negative effect on a third party. For example, if someone lights up a cigarette and smokes it standing right next to you, as well as being very rude that person is also causing a negative externality. In contrast, if you choose to get your child immunised from all sorts of nasty illnesses, you're reducing the chances of other children getting ill as well – this is an example of a positive externality.

Economists are interested in activities that create externalities, because if left to their own devices, people undertake too much of an activity that creates negative externalities and too little of an activity that creates positive externalities.

Seeing the Prisoner's Dilemma

Left to their own devices, banks don't take into account that their risk-taking activities have a negative impact on other financial institutions. For this reason they all tend to want to take on too much risk. The resulting outcome (all banks taking on excessive risk) leads to an exceptionally unstable financial system. Ironically, all the banks would be better off if they all took only moderate risks, because this would ensure the stability of the financial system. Economists call these types of scenario the *Prisoner's Dilemma*.

Imagine that you and a friend carry out a robbery (not that *For Dummies* readers ever would, but just play along). You're not particularly skilled robbers and the police quickly catch you. They know that you're the culprits, but they lack enough evidence to charge you. They do, however, have sufficient evidence to charge you for a less serious crime (say, trespass).

The only way they can put you away for robbery is if one of you confesses to it. Clearly, confessing to your crime doesn't seem like a wise move: you'll both go to jail for many more years than if you just keep quiet.

Here's the twist. A particularly cunning police officer separates you and your friend so you can't communicate and offers you the following deal: if you confess to the crime and your friend doesn't, you get off scot-free but your friend does 15 years. If you both confess, you both go to jail for ten years, and if you both deny, you both go to jail for one year for trespassing. The same offer is made to your friend. Assuming that your only objective is to minimise the amount of time that you spend in jail, what should you do?

To try to answer these kinds of questions – where you have to think strategically – economists model them as *games* (in the sense of any situation where the outcome depends not only on your own actions but also on the actions of others). Figure 15-1 models the Prisoner's Dilemma as a *normal form game*.

A normal form game has to specify three things:

- **Players:** The Prisoner's Dilemma has two players, you and your friend.

- **Possible actions each player can take:** Here each player has to decide whether to 'Confess' or 'Deny'.

- **Payoffs:** How good (or bad) each outcome is for the different players.

Looking at Figure 15-1 you can see the four possible outcomes. Associated with each outcome are the payoffs, in this case how long you and your friend go to jail (the minus signs show that you dislike going to jail): the first number is your payoff and the second number is your friend's. For example, if you deny and your friend confesses, you get a payoff of –15 and she gets a payoff of 0.

		FRIEND	
		Deny	Confess
You	Deny	−1, −1	−15, 0
	Confess	0, −15	−10, −10

Figure 15-1: The Prisoner's Dilemma.

© John Wiley & Sons

The important thing to notice is that regardless of what your friend does, you're better off confessing. You can check this for yourself:

- ✔ **Your friend denies:** You can either deny (in which case you go to jail for a year) or you can confess (in which case you don't go to jail).

- ✔ **Your friend confesses:** You can either deny (in which case you go to jail for 15 years) or you can confess (in which case you go to jail for 10 years).

Therefore, confessing is your *dominant strategy*, because it's better than any other course of action available to you, regardless of what your friend does. Notice that confessing is also a dominant strategy for your friend (spend a moment looking at Figure 15-1 to convince yourself). Even though you've both done what's best for yourself, the resulting outcome where you both confess looks quite bad – you both go to jail for ten years. Had you both kept quiet you'd only have spent a year in prison each. You have a dilemma; more precisely, you have a Prisoner's Dilemma!

Applying the Prisoner's Dilemma to bank risk-taking

Now consider the case of a number of banks each choosing between taking on a moderate amount of risk or an excessive amount of risk. Of course, things are a bit different compared to the original Prisoner's Dilemma, with more (potentially many more) than just two decision-makers. Therefore, we look at the world from the perspective of a particular bank (Bank A) and consider how (a) its profits and (b) the overall stability of the financial system depend upon its actions and the actions of all the other banks.

Taking a look at Figure 15-2, you can see that, regardless of the risk-taking behaviour of the other banks, Bank A is better off taking excessive risk. As in the original Prisoner's Dilemma, taking excessive risk is a dominant strategy.

Any one bank taking excessive risk has little effect on the overall stability of the financial system. Sure, it certainly increases the chances that the financial system will find itself in trouble, but this negative impact is more than offset by the increase in profits that the bank earns from taking on more risk.

The problem is that all the banks notice the same thing: the marginal increase in financial instability is small if they engage in excessive risk-taking and the benefits to the bank are potentially large. This leads to the undesirable outcome where all banks take on excessive risk leading to an exceptionally unstable financial system.

As in the original Prisoner's Dilemma, they'd have all preferred the outcome where none of them take on excessive risk, because this would guarantee the stability of the financial system. However, each of them pursuing their own private interests leads them all to take on too much risk!

ALL OTHER BANKS

		Moderate Risk	Excessive Risk
	Moderate Risk	Bank A's Profit : £10m Financial System : Stable	Bank A's Profit : £0 Financial System : Unstable
Bank A			
	Excessive Risk	Bank A's Profit : £20m Financial System : Stable	Bank A's Profit : £5m Financial System : Unstable

Figure 15-2: Bank risk-taking as a Prisoner's Dilemma.

© John Wiley & Sons

The underlying problem is that when a bank is deciding whether to take on excessive risk, it considers only the cost of doing so for itself. It doesn't consider the fact that taking excessive risk has a negative externality on all the other banks by making the financial system less stable.

Committing to No Bailouts (Dream On!)

Governments really dislike bailing out the financial sector when it gets into trouble: it's expensive and deeply unpopular politically. Then why do it? The short answer is because they feel forced to. The alternative of widespread bank failures would be so catastrophic that it doesn't bear thinking about. In principle, if the government could somehow convince the financial sector that it wouldn't bail it out in times of crisis, this approach would reduce banks' excessive risk-taking and substantially reduce the risk of a financial crisis and therefore the need for a government bailout.

In this section we look at these issues in more detail, including the effectiveness of policy makers' threats not to bail out and whether they can 'solve' the moral hazard problem.

Making (and ignoring) incredible threats

Imagine that Barack Obama and David Cameron (perhaps their celebrity couple name would be 'Obameron') appear side by side at a press conference and both declare that the US and UK governments will never again bail out the financial sector and that therefore banks and other financial institutions need to take much more care in the future about the amount of risk that they take. Would this strategy successfully prevent excessive risk-taking? Probably not.

Banks would understand that even though now, in calm times, the two leaders are saying that they'll never bail them out, they know that if banks did get into trouble, the governments would have little choice but to do so. Basically, the banks would think: they're bluffing.

Economists formalise this idea by saying that when people bluff they're making an *incredible threat*. That is, although they're saying that they'd take one course of action in the future, if it ever came to it, they never would.

Starting the extensive form game

A useful way to model incredible threats is to use an *extensive form game* – a simple way of representing a strategic interaction where decision-makers take actions sequentially. Don't worry, it's much less complicated than it sounds! Consider the following scenario:

- Banks collectively decide whether to take a moderate amount of risk or an excessive amount of risk.

- If banks decide to take a moderate amount of risk, no financial crisis occurs and the game ends.

- If banks decide to take an excessive amount of risk, a financial crisis occurs and the government has to decide whether to bail out the banks.

We represent this scenario as an extensive form game (see Figure 15-3).

At the top of the extensive form, we start with the 'player' who 'moves' first. In this case, the banks have to decide whether to take moderate or excessive risk. If they choose moderate risk, the game progresses down the left branch and no financial crisis results. No one else then has to move (no need for a government bailout) and the game ends. If, however, the banks choose excessive risk, the game progresses down the right branch. This triggers a financial crisis and the government has to decide whether to bail out or not.

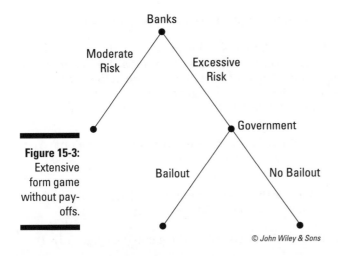

© John Wiley & Sons

Figure 15-3:
Extensive form game without pay-offs.

Adding payoffs

But we're missing an important ingredient: the payoffs. Without them, we can't possibly say how the players in the game will act. Payoffs reveal how good or bad a player thinks an outcome is.

In this game, we have three possible outcomes:

- **Outcome A:** Banks take on a moderate amount of risk. Everything in the financial system is hunky-dory. Policy makers can relax.

- **Outcome B:** Banks take on excessive risk. The government comes to the rescue with a bailout but at great cost to the taxpayer.

- **Outcome C:** Banks take on excessive risk. The government refuses to bail out the financial sector, and the result is widespread bank failures. In short, all hell breaks loose.

We look first at these outcomes from the perspective of the banks:

- **Outcome C is clearly by far the worst.** Most if not all banks fail. We assign the payoff of –£100 billion.

- **Outcome A is a decent outcome for the banks.** They go about their activities and make a reasonable profit, say £10 billion.

- **Outcome B is particularly enticing for the banks.** If the risk-taking works out in their favour, they get to keep their large profits, and if it doesn't, the government absorbs their losses ('heads we win, tails you lose'). On average, we say that this outcome makes the banks £50 billion.

Now look at the outcomes from the perspective of the government:

- **Outcome C is clearly by far the worst.** The banks fail, companies can't borrow money and thus go bust, people lose their jobs and savings, salaries aren't paid, the country comes to a halt, widespread looting takes place, armed gangs roam the streets, you get the idea. . . . Quantifying just how bad things get is difficult, but a conservative number may be –£1,000 billion.

- **Outcome A is certainly the best for the government.** It doesn't have to do anything and probably even raises some taxes from the banks: £5 billion would be a reasonable guess.

- **Outcome B is pretty bad for the government.** It has to use substantial taxpayer funds to bail out the banks: –£50 billion may be enough.

We add these payoffs to Figure 15-3 to complete the game (see Figure 15-4).

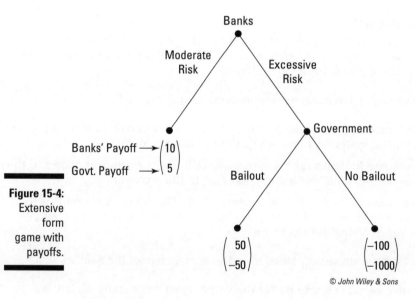

Figure 15-4:
Extensive form game with payoffs.

© John Wiley & Sons

Finishing the game

To 'solve' (work out the likely outcome of) the game, you need to use a procedure called *backward induction*. This process involves going to the end of the game, working out what players will do if they're called upon to act and then working backward until you reach the start of the game.

Here, the government acts last: it has to decide what to do if the banks take on excessive risk. Looking at the payoffs to the government, it has to choose between –1,000 and –50. Clearly –50 isn't great, but it's a lot better than –1,000. Thus, you can be quite confident that if the government is faced with a choice between bailing out and not bailing out, it will choose to bail out.

Moving back to the start of the game, the banks have to decide between moderate and excessive risk. They already know (because they understand backward induction) that if they take excessive risk, the government will choose to bail them out. Thus, the banks face a choice between a payoff of 10 (if they take moderate risk) and 50 (if they take excessive risk, safe in the knowledge that a bailout will be forthcoming).

Therefore the outcome of the game is that banks take on excessive risk and the government bails them out. Economists call this the *subgame perfect equilibrium* of the game, because it was derived using backward induction: that is, when deciding how to act, the banks looked into the future and thought about how the government was likely to act if they took on excessive risk (see Figure 15-5).

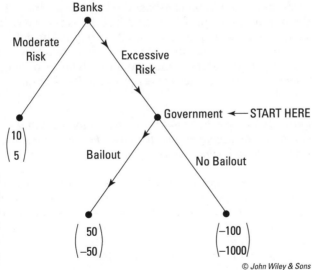

Figure 15-5:
Subgame
perfect
equilibrium.

© John Wiley & Sons

Notice that if the government had announced at the start of the game that it wouldn't bail out banks if they took excessive risk, and banks believed the threat, the banks would prefer to take moderate risk (a payoff of 10) rather than excessive risk (a payoff of –100). Economists call these kinds of threats *incredible threats*, because when push comes to shove they won't be carried out. For this reason, rational decision-makers should rule out incredible threats, which is precisely what performing backward induction does.

In the example, the banks should consider Obama and Cameron's statement that they won't bail out banks to be an incredible threat, because in a time of crisis they'll have no incentive to stick to their statement and every incentive to bail out the banks!

Tackling moral hazard to avoid bailouts

Economists worry deeply about the moral hazard problem. A well-functioning financial system is crucial to any market economy in order to match those who have savings to those who have profitable investment projects and need to borrow money.

Be in no doubt, without banks and other financial institutions, everyone would be a lot poorer. But at the same time, the way that the financial system currently operates too often incentivises people in the wrong way.

Economists aren't interested in banker-bashing for the sake of it. They're interested in the moral hazard problems that lead to excessive risk-taking, which then leads to financial instability and ultimately to the suffering of ordinary people. Equally, economists worry that the implicit subsidy that banks receive effectively transfers money from relatively poor people to relatively rich people. As the former governor of the Bank of England, Mervyn King, put it:

> In good times, banks took the benefits for their employees and shareholders, while in bad times the taxpayer bore the costs. For the banks, it was a case of heads I win, tails you – the taxpayer – lose.

One of the key insights of economics is that people respond to incentives. To fix the financial system, people need to be given the right incentives. One potential solution is to make excessive risk-taking by banks illegal – in terms of the earlier Figure 15-5, simply to shut down the possibility of banks choosing to take the path of 'excessive risk', in effect leaving them with no option except to take on moderate amounts of risk.

At least two problems exist with this idea:

✔ **How do you decide when a bank is taking on excessive risk?** Risk isn't easy to measure; it's not like measuring your weight (something we avoid wherever possible!) or how many pints of milk you consume in a month. No agreed-upon way of measuring risk exists.

Therefore the government would have to define somehow what kind of behaviour is acceptable and what kind of behaviour is unacceptable and therefore illegal – no small task. Moreover, no matter how carefully policy makers write the rules, inevitably some loopholes will exist that people will try to exploit. To convince you, think how difficult designing a tax system is in which people can't avoid paying tax.

✔ **Making something illegal isn't enough.** The government needs to be able to detect when excessive risk-taking is occurring. Given that the underlying problem behind moral hazard is that people's actions are often hidden, detecting when they've broken the rules isn't going to be easy (even more so when they're purposely trying to obfuscate their actions). Furthermore, even if the government did detect transgressions, the punishments would need to be sufficiently severe such that people would think twice before breaking the rules. This aspect is particularly important given the huge potential financial rewards from breaking the rules.

Instead of trying to shut down the very possibility of taking on excessive risk in financial markets, another method is to make bankers believe that they'll personally have to pay for any resulting losses – that they won't be bailed out if they find themselves in trouble. Again, this isn't straightforward: the problem of systemic risk and the possibility of cascading bank failures (see Chapter 14) mean that any threat not to bail out financial institutions is likely to be seen as incredible.

How can the government make its threat credible? One idea is to break up banks into smaller pieces so that none of them is 'too big to fail'. Allowing a small bank to fail is unlikely to have systemic consequences; thus, the government can credibly threaten not to bail out financial institutions. For a more detailed look at potential ways to stop future financial crises, turn to Chapter 16.

Chapter 16

Considering the Lessons of the 2008 Financial Crisis

The 2008 global financial crisis was painful for people all over the world: many countries went into recession, living standards fell, assets such as houses and shares experienced large falls in value, businesses went bankrupt and people lost their jobs. Given the enormous negative impact of financial crises, the question is: is it likely to happen again, and if so can policy makers and/or economists do anything to reduce its frequency and impact?

The fact that such a major crisis occurred with few – if any – economists predicting it led to a wave of criticism of economics and economists. After all, they're constantly reminded, what's the point of having economists if they can't even predict when crises will occur?

We argue that a lot of this criticism is misplaced and that economists have never claimed to be able to predict financial crises. On the contrary, economic theory suggests that financial crises are inherently *unpredictable*! In this chapter we explain why and take a closer look at the causes of the 2008 crisis to see what lessons can be learned.

Delving into the Global Financial Crisis

We're going to let you in on a little secret, but please don't tell anyone: economists don't really understand why financial crises occur. They can point to general factors that contribute to financial fragility, such as those we cover in Chapters 14 and 15, but they're very far from having a general theory to explain, let alone predict, financial crises.

This situation isn't really surprising, because modelling the economy is a tricky business: at any moment in time large numbers of individuals and firms are all making their own decisions. These individual choices need to be aggregated in some way in order to reveal how the economy as a whole is going to behave. During times of crisis, doing so is even more difficult, because people become uncertain and fearful, which affects their ability to make rational decisions.

Despite these problems, whenever a crisis hits you find no shortage of commentators who are confident that they 'know' exactly the cause. Always be sceptical of such claims, because the cause of financial crises is very much an open question and one about which macroeconomists disagree the most.

Nevertheless, a popular narrative does exist about why the 2008 crisis occurred. In this section we go through this account and describe the roles of subprime lending, securitisation and leverage. Read and understand it, but also take it with a pinch of salt, because – for the reasons above – it's unlikely to be the full story.

Overinflating the housing bubble: Subprime lending

Houses are expensive. Even if you have a good job and you scrimp and save every month, by the time you've saved up enough to buy a house outright, retirement is likely to be knocking at your door! Most people don't want to wait until their fifties or sixties in order to buy a property, so they commonly take out a large loan called a mortgage when they're relatively young and pay it back over the course of their working life.

The traditional 'prime' mortgage

Enter the banks: they act as an intermediary between those who want to save money and those who want to borrow money. So if John inherits a large sum of money that he wants to save, and he deposits it at his local bank branch, his bank can lend out some of that money to Jane who wants to buy a house.

This procedure is profitable for the bank, because it typically pays a low rate of interest (or none at all) on deposits and charges a relatively high rate when making loans. Part of the reason for this difference in interest rates is that John probably views the bank as a relatively safe place to keep his money. He's confident that it'll give his money back when he comes to withdraw it (whether he should be so confident is another matter – check out Chapter 14!).

Jane, however, seems a riskier prospect to the bank: sure, she has a good job *now*, but who knows whether she'll still have it in 20 or 30 years' time. The bank may even worry about whether Jane will still be alive at the end of the repayment period (sorry to be morbid, but banks have to take into account such real risks). To compensate it for the risk that Jane may not repay the mortgage, the bank charges a *risk premium*: that is, it charges her a higher interest rate. If a bank makes a large number of loans, some of which aren't repaid, this risk premium is supposed to ensure that it still makes a healthy profit.

In 'times of old, when knights were bold' (well, a number of decades ago), banks were relatively *risk averse* – they were very careful about who they lent money to. In order to get a mortgage, you typically needed a longstanding relationship with your bank and your bank manager. The idea was that the bank knew you very well before giving you a mortgage and therefore could tell whether you were likely to repay it.

Subprime loans

In many ways the traditional approach was a good model, except that it excluded large numbers of people – basically everyone with a less-than-perfect credit record. This group was a huge and potentially very profitable untapped market. Soon banks thought to themselves: 'you know what, maybe we can lend to these guys. They're riskier than our usual customers, but that's okay because we'll charge a higher interest rate to compensate us for the additional risk.'

These higher risk loans came to be known as *subprime* loans, because they were riskier than the old 'prime' loans. Subprime loans led to a large increase in the pool of potential borrowers. Whereas in the past perhaps only two interested buyers for a property could raise the required funds, now maybe ten interested buyers could, all with access to credit. In response to this massive increase in demand, the inevitable happened: property prices skyrocketed (for example, in Miami between 2002-06 the price of an average house doubled!).

As prices continued to rise year-on-year people started to believe that property was a one-way bet – that it would always increase in value and never decrease. Speculators with no intention of ever living in (or even renting out) their houses bought property in the hope that prices would continue to rise.

Banks weren't immune from this optimism either, which led many to relax their lending rules so even more people became eligible for home loans. To understand why, consider that in order to limit a bank's losses in case of a borrower defaulting, the loan contract says that if the borrower is unable to keep up with his repayments, the bank can repossess the property. In other words, if you don't repay the loan, the bank can take the property and sell it in order to cover its losses.

Now, usually before a bank gives you a mortgage, it demands a substantial deposit (say 20 per cent of the value of the property). Then if house prices fall by 20 per cent and at the same time you default on the loan, the bank is able to recover most of the money it lent out. But if banks become very optimistic and think that house prices won't fall, they don't need to ask for a deposit! They began asking for smaller and smaller deposits: 15 per cent, 10 per cent and then 5 per cent.

Eventually, many banks were willing to lend without the need for any deposit at all; some banks were so optimistic they were even willing to lend *more* money than the total value of the property! Loans of 110 or even 120 per cent of the value of the property weren't unheard of. Unsurprisingly, consumers lapped up these loans.

Banks that had made large loans without requiring decent deposits were now heavily exposed to the property market. If house prices fell substantially and people stopped paying their mortgages, these banks would suffer substantial losses. They weren't worried, though: banks, like almost everyone else, thought houses were, well, as safe as houses.

They were wrong – 2006 saw the start of a massive slump in property prices in the US. Over the next few years, prices fell by almost one-third.

Becoming unbalanced: Securitisation and asymmetric information

You may wonder after reading the preceding section why banks and other financial institutions were falling over themselves to make these subprime loans. After all, lending large amounts of money to people on low incomes with unstable jobs and a history of not paying back their loans seems like a very risky business! To comprehend why they did so, you need to understand a big innovation that was occurring in the world of finance at the time called securitisation.

Explaining the role of securitisation

Securitisation refers to the packaging of a number of *illiquid assets* (ones that are difficult to turn into cash) into a *liquid asset* (that's easy to turn into cash). (Chapter 14 describes in more detail liquid and illiquid assets.)

Here's a concrete example to clarify. In the past when you took out a mortgage with a bank, it lent you money and you paid it back over a number of years. Your mortgage was a valuable asset for the bank – giving the right to a stream of monthly payments from you. However, the bank couldn't easily sell on this right to someone else – in economist speak, no well-functioning *secondary market* existed for your mortgage.

Selling on the mortgage meant that instead of making repayments to the original bank that made you the loan, you repaid the current holder of your mortgage. A secondary market didn't develop because a single mortgage isn't really an attractive proposition for an investor. A potential buyer would have to do quite a lot of research into you and your family circumstances to try to work out whether you were likely to repay or not. Of course, *For Dummies* readers would never renege on their loans, but the potential buyers don't know that! The hassle of finding out just wasn't worthwhile.

Moreover, the bank that originally made the loan had much better information about the credit-worthiness of the borrower than the potential buyer. It therefore had a strong incentive to sell on only those mortgages that were least likely to be repaid. Economists call this situation an *information asymmetry*.

So the clever people in the City had an idea that took off in the 2000s (later on you can decide just how clever, or not!). Here are the main attributes of this brainwave:

- ✔ Instead of trying to sell one mortgage at a time, let's package together a whole bunch of mortgages.

- ✔ With, say, 100 mortgages packaged together, most of them will repay, even though some will be duds (say 10 per cent).

- ✔ Someone who buys one of these packages can be confident that 90 per cent of the mortgages will be repaid.

- ✔ Clearly, a potential buyer wants a discount on the package of loans to take into account that some of them won't repay, but other than that, they don't need to research each family's individual circumstances.

- ✔ What matters to the potential buyer is that 90 per cent of the mortgages are repaid; it doesn't matter *which* 90 per cent.

That was how it was supposed to work in theory. In practice, however, banks and other financial institutions quickly realised that they could easily sell on any loans they made. This meant that the risk of default (the risk that the borrower doesn't repay) was no longer the bank's problem. Now, when a mortgage application was received, the bank wasn't too bothered about carefully assessing it to see how affordable it would be for the borrower. Instead it was eager to lend, safe in the knowledge that selling the mortgage on would be a piece of cake.

Banks started to outdo each other as to who had the most liberal lending policy. No deposit? No problem! Don't have a stable job? That's fine! No proof of income? Just *self-certify* (sign a piece of paper saying what your income is)! Things went from bad to worse; ultimately some banks were willing to make so-called NINJA loans – that is, loans to people with No Income, No Job or Assets! Crazy stuff indeed, but it happened.

Slicing and dicing loans

But surely people would quickly cotton-on that the 'safe' package of 100 mortgages wasn't so safe after all? Well, the financial whizz-kids had one last trick in their book:

- ✔ Instead of selling the entire package of 100 mortgages, including both 'good' loans (those that are repaid) and 'bad' loans (those that aren't), let's slice them into different levels called *tranches*; for example, say, five tranches, each one containing 20 mortgages.

- ✔ If you own the 'top tranche', you get paid first – so long as at least 20 people out of the 100 repay their loans, you get paid. After the top tranche owners are paid, the second tranche would be next and so on.

Figure 16-1 shows the 100 mortgages being sliced into five tranches. The tranche owners get paid in order of seniority, making the top tranche the safest, the second tranche less so, the third tranche even less safe and so on. The bottom tranche holders are least likely to get repaid.

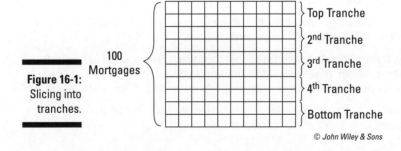

Figure 16-1:
Slicing into
tranches.

100
Mortgages

Top Tranche
2nd Tranche
3rd Tranche
4th Tranche
Bottom Tranche

© John Wiley & Sons

Why would anyone want to hold the lower tranches? Well, they were offered a risk premium to compensate them for the additional risk. In this case, purchasing the loans in the lower tranches costs substantially less than those in the higher tranches. For example, £1 million worth of top tranche loans may cost near enough to £1 million to buy, whereas the same amount of bottom tranche loans may only cost £200,000, the trade-off being that you're less likely to ever see your money again!

The idea behind the different tranches was that even if, on average, the loans being made were of low quality, it was so unlikely that more than 80 people out of the 100 would fail to repay their mortgages that the top tranche was safe. Like modern-day alchemists, the 'clever' people in finance thought that they'd found a way of turning junk (low-quality loans) into pure gold. Before they could start selling this stuff as gold, though, they had to convince everyone else that it was gold.

Meeting the credit rating agencies

Debt instruments (financial products issued in order to borrow money) can be complicated. Moreover, so many exist that no single person can be reasonably expected to understand the ins and outs of the products on offer in order to compare them – plus, all the different groups trying to borrow money: governments, large corporations, banks, households and so on. You can see how easily things get messy, quickly.

To help potential lenders work out how likely they are to be repaid, companies called *credit rating agencies* assess how risky a product is. In doing so, they take into account a number of things, including

- ✔ **Financial 'health' of the borrower:** How much debt does it already hold? Is it likely to make a profit or a loss in the future? If it's a government, is it running a budget deficit or a surplus?

- ✔ **Reputation of the borrower:** Is the borrower a rich government with a history of making repayments or a company that defaulted in the recent past?

- ✔ **Terms of the contract:** In what circumstances will the lender get repaid? If the borrower finds itself in financial difficulty and can't cover all its liabilities, in what order do lenders get repaid? This aspect is called the *seniority* of the debt.

Three main credit rating agencies exist: S&P, Moody's and Fitch. They all have slightly different ways of making ratings, but here's roughly how they go, from best to worst:

- ✔ **AAA:** Typically corresponds to the safest products – the borrower defaulting is almost inconceivable.

- ✔ **AA:** Slightly more risky, but still very safe.

- ✔ **A:** Still pretty safe, but not as safe as AA.

- ✔ **BBB:** Getting into riskier territory.
- ✔ **BB, B, CCC, CC, C:** Progressively riskier loans.
- ✔ **D:** The borrower has defaulted.

Now, the credit rating agencies were asked to give ratings on different *mortgage-backed securities* (financial products that rely on people repaying their mortgages in order for the holders to get paid), such as the tranches of loans shown in Figure 16-1. They gave a number of these products very high ratings – they even accorded some of them an AAA rating, meaning in theory that they were as safe as the government bonds of the world's richest countries!

In fact, of course, these mortgage-backed securities were anything but safe. When US house prices started to fall in the mid-2000s, many subprime mortgages went into default. As house prices continued to fall, many people found that the current value of their property was less than their outstanding mortgage. In other words, they had *negative equity*. Instead of struggling to repay their hefty mortgages, many people defaulted, reducing house prices even further and leading to more defaults – a vicious cycle ensued.

Those 'top tranche' mortgages that were supposedly as good as gold were finally revealed as fool's gold! Sadly, by the time people realised that these 'AAA' securities were about as safe as being owed money by Del Boy, it was already too late.

Facing the failure of financial institutions

The big question on everyone's mind in 2007 was 'who owned all these super risky mortgage-backed securities?'. Any financial institution that did would suffer potentially huge losses. The thing is, putting your hands up and admitting to owning this junk would be suicide: people would immediately doubt whether your company could weather the storm and stop doing business with you. Predictably, everyone kept schtum.

The result was much anxiety and uncertainty. The bank or financial institution that you were dealing with could be on the brink of collapse and you wouldn't know! This situation stopped banks lending to one another and made their problems even worse. To add insult to injury, most banks were highly leveraged, which meant that any losses would be multiplied many times over. The highly interconnected nature of the global financial system meant that problems at one bank were quickly transmitted to others. Economists call this situation *contagion* (see Chapter 14 for a detailed look at leverage, systemic risk and contagion).

Many banks and financial institutions did collapse or had to be bailed out during, or in the aftermath of, the 2008 crisis, including: in the US, Lehman Brothers, AIG, Bear Stearns, Fannie Mae and Freddie Mac; and in the UK, RBS, Lloyds TSB and Northern Rock. It was one big mess that caused much suffering for people throughout the world: the effects are still around today.

Asking Why Economists Didn't Predict the Crisis

The events that we describe in the preceding section raise an intriguing question: were economists partly to blame for the 2008 crisis? Gasp!

Being an economist at a dinner party used to be a fun experience. People readily asked for our opinions on the state of the economy, inflation, house prices, you name it, and usually listened with respect to the answers. Since the financial crisis, people are noticeably more sceptical about economists and economics generally. A standard question is: 'How can we trust you guys and your models if you couldn't even predict the financial crisis?'

In this section we look at whether this criticism is fair. We discuss why averages don't work for financial investments and introduce one of the most important results in financial economics: the Efficient Market Hypothesis (EMH).

Appreciating the limitations of the 'average': Asset returns have fat tails!

Investing your money can be a risky business. If you play your cards right, you can make substantial returns; on the flip side, if things don't go to plan, you can lose everything! The reason is that different assets have different risk profiles. For example, *equities* (shares in companies) tend to be seen as relatively risky – prices can fluctuate wildly from day to day. Buying *bonds* (lending money to governments or companies) tends to be a bit less risky (but not always!).

Cash tends to be seen as one of the safest assets, but even this isn't certain: the bank where you hold your cash can go out of business, and if the government doesn't bail it (and you) out, things can end badly. At the less extreme end of things, the value of cash is eroded by inflation: if inflation turns out to be very high, the real value of your cash can fall substantially.

But even though asset prices can fluctuate wildly, most of the time they don't. Usually, assets yield a return of a few percentage points every year. Now and again, their value may fall by a few percentage points and similarly, at certain times, they provide double-digit returns. Extreme returns – very high and very low – are relatively uncommon.

Think of this situation as being a bit like most people having near average birth weight, IQ test scores, blood pressure, height and so on. For example, you don't see many very tall or very short people, but once in a while you may see someone over 6 and a half feet tall (rarely a good idea to challenge such a person to a game of basketball!).

All sorts of things follow this kind of pattern. In fact, it's so ubiquitous that it has a name: the *normal distribution*. In Figure 16-2, the population is normally distributed (according to some variable of interest), which means that most of the population is concentrated near the average. As you move away from the average, observations become less and less frequent.

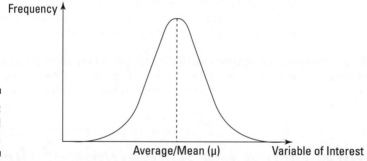

Figure 16-2:
The normal distribution.

© John Wiley & Sons

Observations that are far from average are very rare according to the normal distribution. Sometimes asset returns are approximated using a normal distribution, and so, for example, most of the time if you buy equities you may expect a return of close to 7 per cent per year; however, sometimes you get higher returns and sometimes lower returns.

But financial economists point out that actually a normal distribution isn't a good fit for asset returns, because as you move away from the mean of a normal distribution, the likelihood of observing an outcome falls dramatically. In technical speak, over two-thirds of observations are within one *standard deviation of the mean* (the standard deviation tells you how dispersed the data is); over 95 per cent of observations are within two standard deviations, and over 99 per cent are within three standard deviations. You can see this in Figure 16-3.

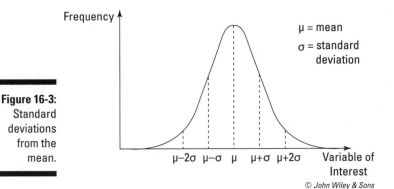

Figure 16-3:
Standard
deviations
from the
mean.

Frequency

μ = mean

σ = standard
    deviation

μ–2σ μ–σ μ μ+σ μ+2σ   Variable of
                            Interest

© John Wiley & Sons

If asset returns *did* follow a normal distribution, you'd expect asset prices to fall sometimes. When they did fall, you'd expect them only to fall by a few percentage points. Maybe once in your lifetime you'd see a substantial fall in asset prices (say, 20 per cent). In reality, however, large asset price falls happen relatively frequently. For example, large stock market falls occurred around the world during the 2008 financial crisis, after the 9/11 attacks, after the dot-com boom of the late 1990s, during the East Asia crisis of 1997 – the list goes on. Clearly, instead of being a once-in-a-lifetime event, large falls in asset prices happen every few years.

For this reason, economists say that asset returns have *fat tails* – which basically means that extreme (usually bad) outcomes happen relatively frequently. Fat tails sounds quite funny, at least to us, but the idea is that the normal distribution has 'thin tails' because extreme events are so unlikely.

Take a look at Figure 16-3: the tails of the distribution cover those events to the far left and right of the mean. As you can see, those events are so unlikely that the tails are very 'thin'. To make the distribution of asset returns more representative of reality, we need to fatten up those tails and in particular the left tail. Figure 16-4 shows a distribution that's closer to the actual distribution of asset returns.

So here's the economists' first line of defence when challenged about their knowledge of financial crises, or rather lack of: 'Look, we've been telling you guys for years, asset returns have fat tails! Some major crisis is always on the horizon!'

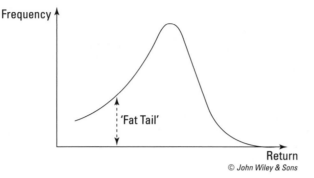

© John Wiley & Sons

Figure 16-4:
Asset
returns with
fat tails.

Understanding why no one can predict crises

Knowing about economics is unlikely to make you rich – at least it certainly hasn't for us! But (we hope) it can stop you from being conned.

Be highly sceptical when people tell you that they know what's going to happen to the price of an asset. As we describe in this section, if what they're telling you is true and based on public information, it would have already happened today. If you can make money out of this information, a good chance exists that the person has insider information, which is illegal to trade on!

The Efficient Market Hypothesis

Economists (to varying degrees) think that financial markets are *informationally efficient*, that is, today's price already contains all publicly available information. Therefore, asset prices jump instantly in response to new public information: it's called the *Efficient Market Hypothesis* (EMH). So if no one can truly predict (with 100 per cent certainty) price movements, no one can predict financial crises.

Imagine that a friend tells you that he's certain that shares in FlowerCorp are going to double by this time next year. We hope that before selling your house and buying as many shares as possible in FlowerCorp, you'd ask him some questions.

A good first one is, 'How do you know?'. Suppose that he replies that he read in the news that the firm was going to have a stellar set of sales next year that will push up the share price. Now you may be thinking: this sounds a bit fishy! After all, if he read it in the news, presumably many other people also read the same story: economists call this *public information*.

If true that the shares would double in a year's time, people wouldn't hang around and wait a year to buy them: they'd buy them right now! This would increase the price today. By how much? Well, by double. Thus if prices were definitely going to double next year and your friend is making this claim on the basis of public information, they'd have already doubled today!

In Figure 16-5, notice that the stock price today is relatively low (at A). If the stock price is going to double in the next year (to B) and this is public information – so that everyone knows it – the price jumps today (to C).

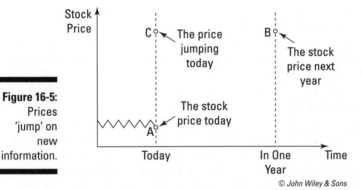

© John Wiley & Sons

Figure 16-5: Prices 'jump' on new information.

Another possibility is that your friend has some *private information*, for example he works as a lawyer or banker for the company and has access to some sensitive information not known to the general public. In this case, your friend may be telling the truth: the stock price could double but the general public just doesn't know it yet.

Before you go out and make a pretty penny, however, remember that in most countries trading on private information of this sort is illegal and called *insider dealing*.

The EMH confirms that people can't possibly make 'free money' by buying things below their 'true price' and selling overpriced things. Just as you don't expect £20 notes to be lying in the middle of the street, don't expect to be able to make free money in financial markets.

EMH and forecasting

EMH is a simple idea with some powerful implications. Despite newspapers being full of people's opinions on what's likely to happen to house prices in London, or the price of oil, or the stock price of some company, EMH means that economists are sceptical of the forecasting abilities of any individual.

After all, if markets are informationally efficient, the price of an asset already contains all publicly known information. Sure, as time passes new information will be revealed, but this is as likely to be 'good' news that makes the price go up as 'bad' news that makes the price go down.

Therefore, the best (most likely to be correct) forecast of the price of a *dividend-paying asset* (one that pays you an income for as long as you own it) tomorrow or next year is just today's price (plus inflation).

For example, most shares pay dividends (a fraction of the profit earned) every year; owning a house gives you a dividend, in the form of rental income or the fact that you can live in it. This means that even if, on average, the price doesn't rise in real terms over a year, you're still getting a return. Some shares don't pay substantial dividends (or even any at all), because the managers prefer to reinvest the profits. In this case, you'd expect the share price to rise on average in real terms.

EMH and financial crises

We now apply the same logic to financial crises. Suppose that someone could predict that a financial crisis would occur next month. What would you do today? Most probably you'd sell all your shares (and maybe even your house), take all your money out of the bank and stuff it under the mattress. If everyone did the same, it would cause a financial crisis all right, not next month, but today!

Thus the very act of correctly being able to predict a financial crisis would cause it to happen immediately. Man, that's deep! Therefore, no responsible economist would ever claim to be able to predict when a financial crisis will occur, even though they know that they can happen anytime and probably more often than you'd think (check out the earlier section on those dreaded fat tails, 'Appreciating the limitations of the 'average': Asset returns have fat tails!').

So please don't judge economists by their ability to predict financial crises. Economic theory says that it's impossible!

Trying to Stop the Next Crisis

Financial crises are so devastating and their social costs so huge that anyone who could come up with a way of stopping them from happening (or reducing their frequency and impact) would deserve a Nobel Prize (in Peace as well as Economics!).

This area is another one where economists' knowledge is far from perfect. Nevertheless, join us as we go through three possible, potential solutions.

Suggesting smarter regulation

For a long time, regulation was a dirty word in the financial sector. After all, the argument went, why would a nation want to restrict people trading with each other by introducing red tape? The crisis changed everything: policy makers quickly realised that rather than having too much regulation, countries had far too little! Here we take a look at some of the major changes to the regulatory framework in the UK, but other advanced economies (including the US) have taken similar measures.

As you know, during the crisis a number of banks failed. These failures were bad news because people began to lose confidence in the financial system as a whole. To make matters worse, policy makers were taken by surprise and found that they didn't have the tools to deal with bank failures in a calm and orderly fashion. Instead, they made policy on a rather chaotic ad-hoc basis.

Also no single body had overall responsibility for ensuring the nation's financial stability. One of the first changes occurred in 2009, when the Bank of England ('the Bank') was formally given responsibility for safeguarding the financial system. Alongside this change, a Special Resolution Unit was set up inside the Bank whose job was to manage the failure of banks that found themselves in trouble. The idea was that future bank failures should be carried out in an orderly fashion that minimised the systemic impact of the failure on other parts of the financial system.

In 2013 a number of major changes were introduced that built on the earlier reforms: an independent Financial Policy Committee (FPC) was created at the Bank that had substantial new powers it could deploy in order to maintain financial stability. At the same time two new financial regulators were created:

- ✔ **Prudential Regulation Authority (PRA):** Part of the Bank, it focuses on the approximately 1,700 most systemically important financial institutions, including banks, building societies, credit unions, insurers and investment firms. It monitors and sets how much capital these firms need to hold to ensure that they have sufficient liquidity. Despite their best efforts, financial institutions may still fail. In this case, the PRA works with the Special Resolution Unit to try to limit the fallout.

- ✔ **Financial Conduct Authority (FCA):** An independent body and not part of the Bank. Its remit is to prevent financial firms from using dishonest practices as well as ensuring that consumers don't get ripped off. The FCA is quite different from the FPC and PRA, because it doesn't focus on issues of systemic risk directly – although arguably, protecting consumers' interests hopefully means that people have more faith in the financial system as a whole.

The hope is that these reforms will reduce excessive risk taking on the part of financial institutions and thereby reduce the probability of bank bankruptcy (see what we did there?!) and a subsequent financial crisis. Whether the new regulations are indeed 'smarter' than the old ones remains to be seen.

Breaking up the 'too-big-to-fail' banks

Banks suffer from substantial moral hazard problems: they have incentives to take excessive risk, safe in the knowledge that if things get sticky Mr and Ms taxpayer will save the day (check out Chapter 15 for all about moral hazard). Governments feel obliged to come to the aid of a failing bank, because allowing it to fail will have a bad impact on all other financial institutions, possibly leading to a cascade of failures (as we discuss in Chapter 14).

Generally, the larger the bank, the worse the impact of its failure is on everyone else. One idea is that any bank that's 'too big to fail' (so big and the impact of its failure so catastrophic that governments will always bail it out if it gets into difficult) is really just too big to exist.

Advocates suggest breaking up large banks into small parts so that none of them is too big to fail. They present two, linked, advantages that will result from doing so:

- ✔ Taxpayers are no longer on the hook for the bad decisions of bankers.
- ✔ Banks take less risk, because they know that they really will be allowed to fail if they mess up.

Thus if a government announces that it will no longer bail out a failing financial institution, people take the threat seriously. In other words, it's now a *credible threat* as opposed to an incredible one (that banks treat as a bluff, see Chapter 15).

In reality no jurisdictions have seriously tried to break banks up into small pieces. Instead they've attempted to 'ring fence' a bank's high-street operations from its more risky investment banking operations. The idea is that if the investment banking arm of a bank makes a bad call, the ordinary depositor is protected.

The reality is, in today's globalised world it is difficult to regulate large financial institutions because they can relocate to somewhere else if the regulation is seen as too tough. In that context, ring fencing might not be a bad compromise.

Playing safe with 100 per cent reserve banking

The term *100 per cent reserve banking* refers to a situation in which banks keep all the money that people deposit with them safely in reserve. Therefore, it's the opposite of fractional reserve banking, where banks only keep some fraction of deposits in reserve (we take a detailed look at fractional reserve banking in Chapter 14). People who argue for 100 per cent reserve banking used to be seen as crazies, but now some serious economic thinkers have started to talk about it as a possibility.

Here are the pros and cons of 100 per cent reserve banking:

- ✔ **Advantages:** No more bank runs and no need for government bailouts. For every £1 deposited at the bank, the bank would hold exactly £1 in reserve, so that whenever you wanted to withdraw your money, it would be waiting for you.

- ✔ **Disadvantages:** Banks would be little more than safe places to keep your money. Having a bank account would probably cost quite a bit of money – how else would the bank make any money from depositors? Banks would also not be able to act as an intermediary between savers and borrowers.

A halfway house would be that banks offer two types of account:

- ✔ **A 100 per cent reserve account that people pay to use:** This option is a bit like paying to use a bank's safety deposit box. The advantage is that (in theory) you'd never lose your money.

- ✔ **A risky account where only a fraction is held in reserve:** People get 'free' banking services and maybe even some return on their savings. The bank can then use some of their money to lend to people who want to borrow. The downside is that if the bank goes under, customers may lose everything!

In reality, 100 per cent reserve banking is nowhere on the horizon at the moment; although it is no longer seen as just the preserve of crazies. Who knows? If another major financial crisis hits, the calls for some kind of 100 per cent reserve banking will only get louder.

Part VI
The Part of Tens

the part of tens

You don't have to do a lot of mathematics in microeconomics, but the field does have some equations that explain certain concepts. Check out ten of the most important equations in the free article at www.dummies.com/extras/macroeconomicsuk.

In this part . . .

- ✔ Meet ten influential macroeconomists who have made contributions that make macroeconomics what it is today.

- ✔ See which of the many macroeconomic concepts are the ten most important.

Chapter 17

Getting to Know Ten Great Macroeconomists

*L*ike any academic discipline, macroeconomics relies on the incremental progress of researchers, each building upon and improving previous work – like bricks building a wall or, more tastily, adding toppings to a pizza!

Here are ten famous economists who had a huge impact on macroeconomics. Ladies and gentlemen, it gives us great pleasure to introduce. . .

Adam Smith (1723–1790)

Here he is . . . the big daddy, not just of macroeconomics but economics as a whole. Adam Smith was the first person to think seriously about modern economic problems.

Smith wrote his most influential work in 1776: *An Inquiry into the Nature and Causes of the Wealth of Nations*. He argued that people acting in their own self-interest may serve the common good better than if they try to 'do good' intentionally. Smith writes:

> *It is not from the benevolence of the butcher, the brewer, or the baker, that we expect our dinner, but from their regard to their own interest. We address ourselves, not to their humanity but to their self-love, and never talk to them of our own necessities but of their advantages.*

This idea was – and still is – extremely radical. Smith thought that individuals and firms acting according to their own interests can lead to a socially desirable allocation of goods and services, as though people were being guided by an *invisible hand* to do what was right for them and for society simultaneously!

John Maynard Keynes (1883–1946)

If Adam Smith is the father of economics, John Maynard Keynes is the father of modern-day macroeconomics.

In 1936, he wrote *The General Theory of Employment, Interest and Money*. He was writing during the *Great Depression*, a prolonged period from 1929 until the late 1930s that saw large and persistent falls in output and high unemployment. The economists of the day had a hard time explaining the causes of the Great Depression.

Keynes argued that in the short run, aggregate demand determined output and that it might take a very long time for output to adjust to its natural level. Thus, a clear case existed for governments to intervene with expansionary policies (see Chapter 3) in order to get economies out of recession.

Keynes famously quipped that 'in the long run, we are all dead'. He meant that policy makers shouldn't be concerned only about what happens to an economy in the long run – the short run matters a lot too.

Importantly, the short run determines economic conditions such as unemployment, living standards and inflation *today*.

Milton Friedman (1912–2006)

The ideas in Keynes's *General Theory* (see the preceding section) dominated macroeconomics for several decades. So much so that many macroeconomists identified themselves as *Keynesian*.

Enter Milton Friedman, who led a small group of influential economists known as the *monetarists*. The monetarists were very concerned that economists still only understood very little about how the economy works. They argued that trying to *fine tune* the economy by constant government intervention was likely to lead to even more instability. They believed that just following simple rules was better – such as a steady rate of growth in the money supply.

Friedman was an early critic of the Phillips curve – the seeming trade-off between unemployment and inflation (which we discuss in Chapter 12). Friedman argued that such a trade-off can't exist in the long run: it goes against basic economic theory that money (something nominal) can affect unemployment (something real). Ultimately Friedman was proved correct, because the Phillips curve relationship broke down when policy makers tried to exploit it.

Paul Samuelson (1915–2009)

Paul Samuelson was one of the great economists of the twentieth century. He stressed the importance of modelling economic phenomena mathematically and completely changed the way economists look at the world.

Samuelson introduced two key principles:

- ✔ **Constrained optimisation:** Individuals choose the best option they can from all the options available. Although sounding rather obvious, this idea means that economists can model consumers as individuals who try to maximise their _utility_ (their welfare) subject to their _budget constraint_ (the things they can afford). Similarly, firms can be modelled as maximising their profits subject to their technology constraint (how well they can turn inputs into output).

- ✔ **Equilibrium:** The idea that most of the time economic systems should be 'at rest'; that is, with no tendency for things to change. This simple but powerful idea is used throughout economics: for example, in the AD–AS model (see Chapter 9) economists assume that the price level and output adjust to ensure that aggregate demand equals aggregate supply.

Robert Solow (born 1924)

Bob Solow has done fundamental work on economic growth. In 1956, he wrote a paper that made clear the relationship between a country's living standards, its capital stock and its technology. This model became known as the _neoclassical growth model_, and it's still the most widely used model to explain why some countries are rich and others are poor.

Solow found that two things can explain average living standards in a country:

- ✔ **Capital stock per person:** Basically, the more capital each person has to work with, the higher her marginal product of labour: that is, the more stuff she can produce when working. Factors of production are paid their marginal product (see Chapter 18), so more capital per person means higher wages!

- ✔ **Technology:** How good the country is at converting labour and capital into output.

The Solow model has a number of important implications:

- ✔ **A country can grow by _capital accumulation_:** That is, accruing more capital over time through investment.

✔ **Growing using capital accumulation alone is difficult:** At some point the economy reaches a 'steady state' where the total amount of investment (new capital goods) is just enough to cover the depreciation of existing capital.

✔ **Technological progress is necessary to explain long-run economic growth:** Economies need to get better at turning inputs into goods and services that people want.

Robert Lucas (born 1937)

Bob Lucas led a massive sea change in macroeconomics called the *rational expectations revolution*. Essentially, Lucas and his colleagues argued that much of the earlier Keynesian macroeconomics (see the earlier 'John Maynard Keynes' section) was misleading, because it doesn't explicitly take into account how people form expectations. If people create their expectations in a forward-looking and rational way, policy makers shouldn't be able consistently to fool them.

For example, the original Phillips curve relationship (see Chapter 9) suggested that policy makers could 'buy' low unemployment at the cost of high inflation. But for this policy to work consistently, it would require people to be consistently fooled: they'd have always to believe that inflation would be low and always be surprised when it turned out to be high!

Edward Prescott (born 1940)

Ed Prescott (along with his colleague Finn Kydland) ran with the whole rational expectations revolution (see the preceding section) and built on it in two important ways:

✔ **In general, governments deciding on future policy have a *credibility problem*:** That is, rational individuals understand that the policy announced today may in fact not be implemented in the future if the government gets a chance to 'cheat' and change its plans. Thus they don't believe the announcement, and the failure of the government to change people's expectations leads to a worse outcome (for everyone) than if the government was able credibly to commit to a policy. In their 1977 article, 'Rules Rather than Discretion: The Inconsistency of Optimal Plans', Kydland and Prescott argue that if policy makers follow rules rather than discretion, they can overcome this commitment problem.

✔ **Fluctuations in output in an economy with fully flexible prices can be explained as the economy responding optimally to technology shocks:** In other words, output isn't deviating from its natural rate, the natural rate itself is constantly varying. Thus, government intervention to smooth the business cycle is misguided.

Kydland and Prescott's research agenda led to *real business cycle* (RBC) models. These models stress the importance of rational expectations and *microfoundations*: the agents (individuals and firms) in the model must be optimising.

Robert Barro (born 1944)

Robert Barro, like Robert Lucas, is one of the intellectual heavyweights behind the rational expectations revolution (see the earlier section on 'Robert Lucas').

Barro's most famous work is in two areas:

✔ His work with David Gordon built on Kydland and Prescott's work (see the preceding section) on time inconsistency, which showed that discretionary monetary policy may lead to higher inflation than if policy makers follow rules. That is, discretionary monetary policy leads to an *inflation bias*.

✔ Barro resurrected and built on much older work by David Ricardo to argue that rational individuals may act to offset completely changes in fiscal policy. For example, if the government increases spending by borrowing, rational individuals understand that this amount has to be paid back at some point by future taxes. Therefore, individuals save more today and consumption falls to offset the increase in government spending. This result is called *Barro–Ricardian equivalence* (or just Ricardian equivalence for short, sorry Robert!). We discuss this idea in more detail in Chapter 11.

Robert Hall (born 1943)

Consumption is the largest component of Gross Domestic Product (GDP; see Chapter 4), so it's an important macroeconomic variable that economists have spent a lot of time trying to understand.

Robert Hall (yes, another Robert, what's the deal?) had a revelation: rational expectations mean that trying to forecast what's going to happen to consumption in the future is a mug's game. Why? Well, when deciding how much to consume today, a far-sighted person with rational expectations should take into account all available information about her future income and circumstances. Only if she receives new information about the future should she change the amount that she consumes today.

But new information is by its very nature unpredictable – you can have good news (for example, you land a well-paid job) that should boost your consumption, or you can have bad news (you get skipped over for promotion) that should reduce your consumption.

Therefore, consumption should follow a *random walk*: it should be equally likely to go up or go down and the best prediction for people's consumption tomorrow is just their consumption today! Hall's argument about why consumption should be unpredictable is very similar to the explanation provided by the Efficient Market Hypothesis regarding why asset prices should be unpredictable (see Chapter 16).

Janet Yellen (born 1946)

Sadly, like many areas of business and academia, macroeconomics has a dearth of women at the top. With the new generation of talented female scholars coming through, we hope that this situation will change in the years to come. Janet Yellen, however, is a woman who managed to reach the very top of macroeconomic policy making – she's the current Chair of the Federal Reserve.

Having overall responsibility for monetary policy in the United States makes her one of the most powerful people in the world (certainly the most powerful economist): monetary policy (see Chapter 3) determines a nation's inflation rate in the long run, and in the short run has a strong influence on unemployment and output. The US is still the largest economy by far, so the Fed's decisions reverberate throughout the world economy.

Yellen has made fundamental contributions in explaining why firms may want to pay workers *efficiency wages* – wages higher than the going market rate – in order to motivate them and make them more productive. She's also a prominent figure in *New Keynesian macroeconomics*. New Keynesians take the critique of the rational expectations revolution seriously, but they attempt to explain why prices and wages may still be 'sticky' in the short run.

Chapter 18

Ten Top Tips to Take Away

In This Chapter

▶ Digesting the most important macroeconomic ideas

▶ Noting ten things you need to know about macroeconomics

Macroeconomics covers a massive range of subjects, but in this chapter we take on the huge task of narrowing it down to just ten core concepts.

So, if you remember nothing else from this book, ensure that you take away these important points.

Factoring in Factors of Production

A nation's output depends on two things: the available factors of production, and how good the country is at turning those factors of production into goods and services that people want to buy.

Factors of production are basic inputs such as land, labour and capital (the latter is things such as machines and offices, not money). Firms convert factors of production into goods and services that consumers want to purchase. How successfully they do so depends on how good their technology is. *Technology* is a broad term that just means the process of turning inputs into outputs.

You can see this process clearly using a production function:

$$Y = f(K, L)$$

In words, this equation says that a nation's output (Y) is a function (f) of its factors of production, in this case capital (K) and labour (L). The function $f(.)$ represents how good the technology is.

This simple observation has important implications. If an economy wants to grow it must do one of the following:

- ✔ Increase the quantity (or quality) of its factors of production, for example by having more and better machines or a more skilled workforce.
- ✔ Become better at using those factors of production through technological progress.

Paying Factors of Production Their Marginal Products

Factors of production (such as labour) have to be compensated. No one is going to work for free, and similarly the owners of capital stock want to be compensated for its use. But how much are factors of production paid?

In a competitive labour market the answer is their *marginal product*: that is, their additional contribution to the firm's output. Therefore, if someone works in a chocolate factory and the factory is able to produce 100 more chocolate bars because he's employed, that person can be paid an amount equal to 100 chocolate bars.

But hold your horses there: how is the firm supposed to make any profit if all workers are paid their marginal product? Think about it this way: suppose that the market wage for a chocolate factory worker is £10. At the moment the firm has no workers but is considering hiring one. It works out that the first worker hired would allow the firm to produce £100 worth of chocolate instead of no chocolate. Should the firm hire him? Yes, of course!

The managers now think about hiring a second worker: his addition would produce £90 of additional chocolate (compared to when the firm had just one guy). Should they hire him? Of course, that's an extra £80 of profit!

Notice that the second worker isn't as productive as the first one, not because he's less smart or anything but because of the *diminishing marginal product of labour*: as you add more workers – keeping everything else fixed – each additional worker adds less.

What about hiring a third person? He'll bring in an extra £80 worth of chocolate. Hired! You get the idea. . . . This process continues until the firm notices that, say, the tenth person brings in an extra £10, and even though it costs £10 to hire him the firm goes ahead (it makes no difference to the firm). Now, all ten workers have marginal product equal to £10 – that is, without any individual worker the firm would make £10 worth of chocolate less.

So even though each worker's marginal product is exactly equal to his wage, the firm makes money on each and every worker, except the last guy, where it breaks even.

Understanding that Excessive Growth in the Money Supply Causes High Inflation

In the long run, increasing the growth rate of the money supply has only one effect: higher inflation. Intuitively, the more money that's circulating in an economy, the less scarce it is. People are then only willing to swap goods and services for money if more money is offered to them in exchange for goods and services: that is, the price of things is higher.

Here's a simple way of thinking about this situation: imagine that the amount of money in an economy doubles suddenly, but the amount of goods and services produced remains unchanged. All that would happen is that the prices of everything (including wages) double – nothing changes in real terms.

This simple fact has an important implication: if a country wants to reduce its inflation rate, it needs to reduce the growth rate of the money supply.

Minimising Unemployment (Though Some Is Inevitable)

Eliminating unemployment completely is impossible, but you may be able to reduce it. In essence, unemployment has two main causes:

- ✔ **Labour market frictions:** Firms and workers have difficulty matching with each other. For example, you may want to work for Hawkin's Saxophones Ltd, and it may want to employ you, but you don't know that the firm is hiring and it doesn't know that you're looking for a job.

- ✔ **Structural problems stop the market clearing:** These problems are things that stop the real wage from adjusting to ensure that labour supply and labour demand are equal.

Any attempt to reduce unemployment has to deal with these two underlying causes. Doing anything about frictional unemployment is very difficult, except perhaps improving the sharing of information about available jobs and workers. But here are some ways of reducing structural unemployment:

- **Not having a minimum wage above the market-clearing wage:** A high minimum wage is particularly harmful for young and inexperienced workers, because they tend to be the least productive workers (so the equilibrium wage can be a lot lower than the minimum wage) and also because a large part of their 'salary' is on-the-job training.

- **Deregulating protected industries so new workers can enter more easily:** A good example is training to be a Black Cab driver in London. To be one in Central London, you need to pass a test called The Knowledge, which takes about four years of full-time study. Economists are highly sceptical of the idea that memorising an *A–Z* for four years is necessary to drive a taxi well and find, say, Cheyne Walk in Chelsea; they think that the test really exists to make it very difficult for aspiring drivers to enter the market.

- **Having a little bit of inflation:** Evidence suggests that a bit of inflation helps the labour market to clear, because sometimes the real wage needs to fall in a particular industry. Inflation allows the real wage to fall without requiring cuts to the nominal (cash) wage. For this reason, you hear economists speak of a bit of inflation 'greasing the wheels' of the labour market.

Stimulating Aggregate Demand Can Increase Output Only in the Short Run

Policy makers can stimulate aggregate demand, for example, by pursuing expansionary monetary and fiscal policies (see Chapters 10 and 11, respectively). An increase in aggregate demand typically leads to an increase in output in the short run, because prices haven't yet had a chance to adjust fully to the increase in demand.

In the long run, however, output is determined solely by the supply side of the economy (see the earlier section 'Factoring in Factors of Production'). Therefore, unless fiscal/monetary policy increases the quantity or quality of factors of production or leads to technological progress, it has no impact on output.

This fact means that governments should avoid trying to grow the economy by increasing aggregate demand – it only leads to inflation. Instead, they should direct their efforts towards the supply side of the economy.

Accepting that Financial Crises Are Certain and Impossible to Predict

Financial crises happen with surprising regularity (although the global crisis of 2007–08 was unusual in its severity, reach and persistence). Macroeconomists have known this for some time – asset prices have *fat tails*: that is, they suffer large falls relatively frequently.

Macroeconomists still don't fully understand the causes of financial crises (it's an active area of research), but they do know that the financial system is always vulnerable to a sudden loss of confidence for the following reasons:

- ✔ **Banks keep only a small fraction of deposits in reserve in case customers want to withdraw their funds.** In normal times this approach is fine, because only a small proportion of a bank's deposits are withdrawn on any given day. But a loss of confidence in a bank (for whatever reason) can lead to a bank-run, where large numbers of depositors want to withdraw. Therefore, any bank, no matter how healthy, can fail if people believe it may be in trouble.

- ✔ **Banks are so interconnected that trouble at one can easily spread to many others.** This problem is known as *contagion*.

Crises are also very difficult, if not impossible, to predict. The reason is the *Efficient Market Hypothesis*, which says that the current price of a financial asset already contains within it all publicly known information. Thus, if predicting a financial crisis occurring (say) next year were possible, it would cause a crisis *right now*, as people would rush to sell their financial assets.

Chapters 14 to 16 contain all you want (or fear you need) to know about financial crises.

Seeing that No Trade-Off Exists between Inflation and Unemployment in the Long Run

The Phillips curve relationship (which we describe in Chapter 9) tells economists that in the short run policy makers can reduce unemployment below its natural rate by creating surprise inflation. Therefore, they may be able to reduce it by pursuing expansionary fiscal/monetary policy (Chapters 10 and 11 have lots more).

But any reduction in unemployment is short-lived. In the long run, unemployment is always equal to its natural rate, so inflating the economy in this way leads only to one thing: higher inflation. Thus policy makers should resist the temptation to reduce unemployment below its natural rate.

To help people, policy makers need instead to reduce the natural rate of unemployment by making labour markets more flexible (see 'Minimising Unemployment (Though Some Is Inevitable)' earlier in this chapter).

Discovering Why Policy Makers Should Constrain Themselves

Economists think that people are pretty smart. As a result, they believe that policy makers can fool people now and again, but shouldn't be able to fool them persistently.

For example, policy makers can create some surprise inflation and reduce unemployment below the natural rate. But after they've done that once, people realise what the sneaky policy makers are up to and fooling them a second time is much more difficult – everyone now expects inflation to be high. So, not only is inflation high, but also unemployment isn't reduced.

Policy makers may be better off constraining themselves by following a fixed set of rules instead of using their discretion (check out Chapter 13 for more). Following rules gives their announcements credibility: they're bound to do what they say they're going to do. Therefore, when policy makers announce that inflation is going to be low, people believe that inflation is going to be low, which then leads to inflation being low in reality.

Fixing the Financial System without Solving Moral Hazard Is Impossible

The financial system has serious problems (but unless you've been living under a rock for the last eight years, you know that!). The problem of *systemic risk* (if one large bank fails, many banks may fail) means that financial institutions (especially large ones) face a *moral hazard* problem: they have incentives to take on excessive risk in the knowledge that governments are likely to bail them out if things go pear-shaped.

Without solving the moral hazard problem, fixing the financial system is impossible. Unfortunately, it's a very difficult problem. A number of solutions have been proposed, including these two:

- **Breaking up large banks:** The idea is to reduce systemic risk so that governments can commit credibly not to bail out a failing bank. If a bank goes under, so be it. The hope is that, with this knowledge, the bank itself doesn't want to take on excessive risk.

- **Forcing banks to take less risk:** Introducing regulations, such as requiring banks to hold a greater proportion of their deposits in reserve. The idea is that this will substantially reduce the probability of a bank failure.

Recognising that, Ultimately, Real Things Are What Count

This point is especially important. People shouldn't care about nominal things – they should care about real things. Here are some examples:

- **Real wage:** What really matters about your wage is how much stuff you can buy with it, not its numerical value. So if your boss offers you a 5-per cent pay rise when inflation is running at 10 per cent, you're getting a raw deal: your real pay will fall by 5 per cent.

- **Real interest rate:** When you're borrowing (or saving), the real interest rate is what matters, not the nominal interest rate, because the real interest rate tells you the cost of borrowing in terms of goods, not in terms of money. Money is useful only for buying goods, and so this is what counts.

- **Real Gross Domestic Product (GDP):** The value of goods and services produced in a country rises over time due to inflation, even if the total quantity and quality of those goods are unchanged. Saying that this situation represents an increase in a nation's productive capacity or its living standards would be silly. Therefore, macroeconomists focus on real GDP (that is, GDP adjusted for the effects of inflation). Chapter 4 has all the gen on GDP.

Index

• G •

About the Authors

Manzur Rashid read economics at Trinity College, Cambridge, where he graduated with a double first and was elected to junior, senior and research scholarships. He completed his doctoral studies in economic theory at University College London (UCL) under the supervision of Martin Cripps, where he specialised in game theory, bounded rationality and industrial organisation. Manzur has taught economics at UCL, Cambridge University, New College of the Humanities and Charterhouse.

Peter Antonioni is a senior teaching fellow in the Department of Management Science and Innovation at UCL, where he teaches strategy. His research interest focuses on the economic history of music production. When not working, he can usually be found crying over Tottenham Hotspur's most recent performance or channelling his angst into playing blues guitar.

Dedications

For Ilyas —Manzur Rashid

To Tanya, Mum, Dad, Paul and Jen, who suffered most from me writing this —Peter Antonioni

Authors' Acknowledgements

Manzur Rashid: I am grateful to all the people at Wiley who have helped us get this book into shape, including Mike Baker, Simon Bell, Steve Edwards, Andy Finch, Annie Knight, Kate O'Leary and Vicki Adang. I am also grateful to Ron Smith for his helpful suggestions and comments. Thanks to my friends and family for their endless support. Finally, thank you to my teachers: Martin Cripps, Hamish Low, Rupert Gatti, Steve Satchell, Gernot Doppelhofer and Kevin Sheedy.

Peter Antonioni: With many thanks to the support of my colleagues at UCL, and to the many economists who once had to explain patiently all this material to me.

Publisher's Acknowledgements

Commissioning Editor: Annie Knight

Project Managers: Simon Bell, Victoria M. Adang

Development Editor: Andrew Finch

Copy Editor: Kate O'Leary

Technical Editor: Ron Smith

Project Coordinator: Antony Sami

Cover Image: ©iStock.com/Jezperklauzen

Take Dummies with you everywhere you go!

Whether you're excited about e-books, want more from the web, must have your mobile apps, or swept up in social media, Dummies makes everything easier.

Visit Us

Like Us

Follow Us

Watch Us

Join Us

Pin Us

Circle Us

Shop Us

FOR DUMMIES®

A Wiley Brand

BUSINESS

978-1-118-73077-5

978-1-118-44349-1

978-1-119-97527-4

MUSIC

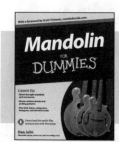

978-1-119-94276-4

978-0-470-97799-6

978-0-470-49644-2

DIGITAL PHOTOGRAPHY

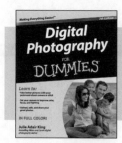

978-1-118-09203-3

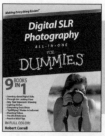

978-0-470-76878-5

978-1-118-00472-2

Algebra I For Dummies
978-0-470-55964-2

Anatomy & Physiology For Dummies, 2nd Edition
978-0-470-92326-9

Asperger's Syndrome For Dummies
978-0-470-66087-4

Basic Maths For Dummies
978-1-119-97452-9

Body Language For Dummies, 2nd Edition
978-1-119-95351-7

Bookkeeping For Dummies, 3rd Edition
978-1-118-34689-1

British Sign Language For Dummies
978-0-470-69477-0

Cricket for Dummies, 2nd Edition
978-1-118-48032-8

Currency Trading For Dummies, 2nd Edition
978-1-118-01851-4

Cycling For Dummies
978-1-118-36435-2

Diabetes For Dummies, 3rd Edition
978-0-470-97711-8

eBay For Dummies, 3rd Edition
978-1-119-94122-4

Electronics For Dummies All-in-One For Dummies
978-1-118-58973-1

English Grammar For Dummies
978-0-470-05752-0

French For Dummies, 2nd Edition
978-1-118-00464-7

Guitar For Dummies, 3rd Edition
978-1-118-11554-1

IBS For Dummies
978-0-470-51737-6

Keeping Chickens For Dummies
978-1-119-99417-6

Knitting For Dummies, 3rd Edition
978-1-118-66151-2

FOR DUMMIES

A Wiley Brand

SELF-HELP

978-0-470-66541-1

978-1-119-99264-6

978-0-470-66086-7

LANGUAGES

978-0-470-68815-1

978-1-119-97959-3

978-0-470-69477-0

HISTORY

978-0-470-68792-5

978-0-470-74783-4

978-0-470-97819-1

Laptops For Dummies 5th Edition
978-1-118-11533-6

Management For Dummies, 2nd Edition
978-0-470-97769-9

Nutrition For Dummies, 2nd Edition
978-0-470-97276-2

Office 2013 For Dummies
978-1-118-49715-9

Organic Gardening For Dummies
978-1-119-97706-3

Origami Kit For Dummies
978-0-470-75857-1

Overcoming Depression For Dummies
978-0-470-69430-5

Physics I For Dummies
978-0-470-90324-7

Project Management For Dummies
978-0-470-71119-4

Psychology Statistics For Dummies
978-1-119-95287-9

Renting Out Your Property For Dummies, 3rd Edition
978-1-119-97640-0

Rugby Union For Dummies, 3rd Edition
978-1-119-99092-5

Stargazing For Dummies
978-1-118-41156-8

Teaching English as a Foreign Language For Dummies
978-0-470-74576-2

Time Management For Dummies
978-0-470-77765-7

Training Your Brain For Dummies
978-0-470-97449-0

Voice and Speaking Skills For Dummies
978-1-119-94512-3

Wedding Planning For Dummies
978-1-118-69951-5

WordPress For Dummies, 5th Edition
978-1-118-38318-6

Think you can't learn it in a day? Think again!

The *In a Day* e-book series from *For Dummies* gives you quick and easy access to learn a new skill, brush up on a hobby, or enhance your personal or professional life — all in a day. Easy!

Available as PDF, eMobi and Kindle